Discovering Kanban

The Evolutionary Path to Enterprise Agility

David J Anderson

BLUE HOLE PRESS Chicago, Illinois   Kanban University PRESS Bilbao, Spain

Blue Hole Press
Chicago, Illinois
www.blueholepress.com

Kanban University Press
Bilbao, Spain
https://kanban.university

Book One in the Better with Kanban series
Discovering Kanban: The Evolutionary Path to Enterprise Agility

For any publishing enquiries please email contact@kanbanbooks.com for rights requests, customized editions, translation requests, licensing, bulk orders or other enquiries. Additional print copies of this and other Kanban publications can be purchased via https://kanbanbooks.com and regional distribution partners.

Access to this book will also be available online via kanban.plus where you will find additional learning resources.

For enquiries relating to Kanban University directly, please contact info@kanban.university.

ISBN 978-1-960442-08-6 color (a)
     978-1-960442-09-3 black and white(a)
     978-1-960442-06-2 color (l)
     978-1-960442-07-9 black and white (l)

Cover art copyright © Mauvius Group Inc, d.b.a. Blue Hole Press
Cover photo copyright © Mauvius Group Inc, d.b.a. Blue Hole Press
Cover design by Nastya Kondratova
Interior design by Vicki L. Rowland
Photos on page 2 used with permission, Thomas Blomseth

Contents

For Nicola, Natalie, & Nastya

In memory of Mikiko

Foreword to *Kanban*[1]

I always pay attention to David Anderson's work. My first contact with him was in October 2003, when he sent me a copy of his book, *Agile Management for Software Engineering: Applying Theory of Constraints for Business Results*. As its title implies, this book was heavily influenced by Eli Goldratt's Theory of Constraints (TOC). Later, in March 2005, I visited him at Microsoft; by this time he was doing impressive work with cumulative flow diagrams. Later still, in April 2007, I had a chance to observe the breakthrough kanban system that he had implemented at Corbis.

I trace this chronology to give you a sense of the relentless pace at which David's management thinking has advanced. He does not get stuck on a single idea and try to force the world to fit it. Instead, he pays careful attention to the overall problem he is trying to solve, stays open to different possible solutions, tests them in action, and reflects on why they work. You will see the results of this approach throughout this new book.

Of course, speed is most useful if it is in the correct direction; I am confident David is headed in the right direction. I am particularly excited by this latest work with kanban systems. I have always found the ideas of lean manufacturing more directly useful in product development than those of TOC. In fact, in October 2003 I wrote to David, saying, "One of the great weaknesses of TOC is its under-emphasis of the importance of batch size. If your first priority is to find and reduce the constraint, you are often solving the wrong problem." I still believe this is true.

In our 2005 meeting I again encouraged David to look beyond the bottleneck focus of TOC. I explained to him that the dramatic success of the Toyota Production System (TPS) had nothing to do with finding and eliminating bottlenecks. Toyota's performance gains came from using batch-size reduction and variability reduction to reduce work-in-process

---

1. Anderson, David J. *Kanban: Successful Evolutionary Change for Your Technology Business.* Seattle: Blue Hole Press, 2010 (widely known as the Blue Book).

inventory. It was the reduction in inventory that unlocked the economic benefits, and it was WIP-constraining systems like kanban that made this possible.

By the time I visited Corbis in 2007 I saw an impressive implementation of a kanban system. I pointed out to David that he had progressed far beyond the kanban approach used by Toyota. Why did I say this? The Toyota Production System is elegantly optimized to deal with repetitive and predictable tasks: tasks with homogeneous task durations and homogeneous delay costs. Under such conditions it is correct to use approaches like first-in-first-out (FIFO) prioritization. It is also correct to block the entry of work when the WIP limit is reached. However, these approaches are not optimal when we must deal with non-repetitive, unpredictable jobs; with different delay costs; and different task durations—exactly what we must deal with in product development. We need more advanced systems, and this book is the first to describe these systems in practical detail.

I'd like to offer a few brief warnings to readers. First, if you think you already understand how kanban systems work, you are probably thinking of the kanban systems used in lean manufacturing. The ideas in this book go far beyond such simple systems that use static WIP limits, FIFO scheduling, and a single class of service. Pay careful attention to these differences.

Second, don't just think of this approach as a visual control system. The way kanban boards make WIP visible is striking, but it is only one small aspect of this approach. If you read this book carefully you will find much more going on. The real insights lie in aspects like the design of arrival and departure processes, the management of non-fungible resources, and the use of classes of service. Don't be distracted by the visual part and miss the subtleties.

Third, don't discount these methods because they appear easy to use. This ease of use is a direct result of David's insight into what produces the maximum benefit with the minimum effort. He is keenly aware of the needs of practitioners and has paid careful attention to what actually works. Simple methods create the least disruption and almost always produce the largest sustained benefits.

This is an exciting and important book that deserves careful reading. What you will get from it will depend on how seriously you read it. No other book will give you a better exposure to these advanced ideas. I hope will you enjoy it as much as I have.

Don Reinertsen,
February 7, 2010
Redondo Beach, California
Author of *The Principles of Product Development*

Question:
How many psychologists does it take
to change a lightbulb?

☼

Answer:
Only one, but the lightbulb really
has to want to change!

Foreword

In the years since 1988, when John Krafcik coined the term, people have put a lot of effort into applying "lean manufacturing" to other activities. Of these, the Kanban Method is the only one that has achieved widespread success. Why? As Don Reinertsen noted in the Foreword to *Kanban: Successful Evolutionary Change for Your Technology Business* (2010), lean manufacturing is "elegantly optimized to deal with repetitive and predictable tasks." Knowledge work is quite different. Kanban succeeded because it did not try to force practices from manufacturing into areas where they do not apply. Rather, Kanban represents an evolution from the deeper, fundamental principles that underlie the Toyota production system—the same principles, it turns out, that one finds in much of Eastern philosophy, the martial arts, and modern "maneuver" warfare.

Hints of this foundation appear in the first chapter. David Anderson describes his epiphany, where he experienced a flash of enlightenment upon seeing an official collecting little plastic cards. Such events, "instant enlightenment," are a common phenomenon in Zen but not so much in today's management theory.

My own brush with *satori* was more mundane. It was 1987. As it did every year, Lockheed closed our facility for three weeks around Christmas. I was browsing our community library in suburban Atlanta, when the bright-red cover of *Thriving on Chaos* jumped out. It was my own awakening: Tom Peters had made a clean break with the prescriptions of *In Search of Excellence* and was preaching concepts of leadership that were still being hotly debated by military leaders and strategists.

I was familiar with some of these ideas because years earlier, as a junior staffer in the Office of the Secretary of Defense in the Pentagon, I had served as our office's point of contact for the F15 fighter aircraft and a technology demonstrator program then called the "Lightweight Fighter Prototype," which led to the F16 and F18. A philosophical godfather of these was an Air Force Colonel named John Boyd, who was also stationed at the Pentagon. In the late 1960s, Boyd had developed a mathematical framework for comparing the fighting abilities of jet fighters, a method which, incidentally, is still used to this day. This framework shaped the designs of all three aircraft.

A few years later, Boyd had retired and was beginning to turn his attention to conflict in general—war, in other words. He became fascinated by the phenomenon that, as often as not, the smaller or less technically advanced side won. Boyd spent the next decade studying why this happened, from the Sun Tzu text (around 400 BCE) to the present. He collected his findings in an 185-slide presentation that he gave hundreds of times to members of Congress, senior military and defense officials, and leaders of industry.

So what does count?

Boyd concluded that when a smaller force won, it had used a variety of means to mislead and confuse opponents and then exploit their clouded mental pictures before they figured out what was going on. The result was surprise, shock, late responses, falling into traps and ambushes, and destruction of internal cohesion. The larger force, in other words, was unable to benefit from its superior numbers and firepower.

What types of organizations could do this? The key to success was an organizational climate that produced units that could create and spot opportunities and then exploit them while they were still opportunities. Create and then thrive on chaos—very similar to Taleb's notion of antifragility. Boyd codified this climate as:

- Mutual trust and cohesion, particularly similar orientations shared among members
- Maintaining a more accurate orientation than an opponent
- The ability, based on experience, to make most decisions intuitively and communicate them implicitly
- "Mission command," where senior leaders specify what is to be done (their overall intent) but leave to their subordinates most of the how-to-do-it

It was easy to find the same principles in Sun Tzu's writing, in *Thriving on Chaos*, in the Toyota production and development systems and, as I discovered, in Kanban. They are also central to the US Marine Corps' doctrine of "maneuver warfare," which draws on Boyd's work and was published shortly after Peters's book. Because antifragility is the common thread, it shouldn't be surprising that Boyd's climate powers them all.

What you will find in this book is a new manifestation of these ancient ideas. Because of its wider application, however, Kanban will change the world more profoundly than any of its predecessors.

Chet Richards
March 9, 2023
Hilton Head, South Carolina
Author, *Certain to Win*

Editor's Note

Throughout this text, we've used a simple convention when referring to kanban and the Kanban Method: proper nouns are capitalized. For example, let's consider for a moment that we were running a different business, The Football Association, and that our product was defined by The Rules of Association Football. In these cases, the word "Football" is being used as part of a proper noun. It would be bizarre if the Football Association capitalized all uses of the word "football" in their literature. So, the Football Association is a proper noun and is capitalized, while a football, a football field, a football stadium, and so on are not proper nouns and are not capitalized.

Likewise, the Kanban Method is a proper noun and is written with an uppercase "K." The Kanban Method uses kanban and kanban boards, just as Association Football ("soccer") uses footballs. All first-class elements of the Kanban Method are also proper nouns: Kanban Cadences, Kanban Values, Kanban Agendas, Kanban Lens, Kanban Litmus Test. Each of these is unique to the Kanban Method. The Kanban Lens defines "the way we'd like you to view your organization when using the Kanban Method." When you see "Kanban" on its own, capitalized, it is shorthand for "the Kanban Method" every time, with one exception: When it refers to my 2010 book, *Kanban: Successful Evolutionary Change for Your Technology Business* (2010; also called the Blue Book), it is simply *Kanban* (in italics).

1

A Conscientious Manager's Dilemma

My Motivation for Adopting Virtual Kanban Systems

In early April of 2005, I had the good fortune, together with my wife and young children, to take a vacation in Tokyo, Japan, during cherry-blossom season. To enjoy this spectacle, I made my second-ever visit to the East Gardens at the Imperial Palace in downtown Tokyo. It was here that I had a revelation—kanban wasn't only for manufacturing!

The Imperial Palace Gardens' Epiphany

On Saturday, April 9, 2005, I entered the park via the north entrance, crossing the bridge over the moat close to the Takebashi subway station. My second daughter, just three months old, was strapped to my chest, her older sister in a stroller pushed by alternately by her mother or auntie, both Tokyo natives.

The East Gardens of the Imperial Palace lie within the ancient walls of the historical castle of Edo, traditionally the home of the ruling warlord of Japan, known as the Shogun. Following the Meiji restoration of 1868, and the end of Tokugawa Shogunate with the capitulation of the Shogun, Tokugawa Yoshinobu, the Emperor of Japan moved his residence from Kyoto to Tokyo and occupied the castle. At that point, it became known as the Imperial Palace. The place where the gardens now stand had been the interior of the castle courtyard, filled with houses and workplaces belonging to members of the royal court. Fundamentally medieval in nature and unneeded after the Meiji Restoration, the castle courtyards were demolished and laid as gardens during the late 19th century. Today, these are open to the public and are some of the most unique and beautiful parks in the Greater Tokyo area.

That morning, many Tokyoites were already taking the opportunity on a sunny Saturday morning to enjoy the tranquility of the park and the beauty of the *sakura* (cherry blossoms). The practice of having a picnic under the cherry trees while the blossoms fall around you is known as *hanami* (flower party). It's an ancient tradition in Japan—a chance to reflect on the beauty, fragility, and shortness of life. The brief life of the cherry blossom is a metaphor for our own life, and our short, beautiful, and fragile existence amid the vastness of the universe.

The cherry blossoms provided welcome contrast against the gray buildings of downtown Tokyo, its hustle and bustle, throbbing crowds of busy people, and traffic noise. The gardens were an oasis at the heart of the concrete jungle. As I crossed the bridge with my family, an elderly Japanese gentleman with a satchel over his shoulder approached us.

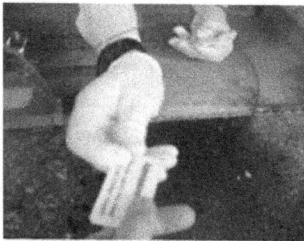

Reaching into his bag, he produced a handful of plastic cards. He offered one to each of us, pausing briefly to decide whether my three-month-old daughter strapped to my chest required a card. He decided she did and handed me two cards. He said nothing, and, as my Japanese is limited, I offered no conversation. We walked on into the gardens to look for a spot to enjoy our family picnic.

Two hours later, after a pleasant morning in the sunshine, we packed up our picnic things and headed toward the exit at the East Gate at Otemachi. As we approached the exit, we joined a line of people in front of a small kiosk. As the line shuffled forward, I saw people returning their plastic entrance cards. I fished around in my pocket and retrieved the cards I'd been given. Approaching the kiosk, I saw a neatly uniformed Japanese lady inside. Between us was a glass screen with a semi-circular hole cut out of it at counter level, very similar to an admission booth at a cinema or amusement park. I slid my plastic cards across the countertop through the hole in the glass. The lady took them in her white-gloved hands and stacked them in a rack with others. She bowed her head slightly and thanked me with a smile. No money changed hands. No explanation was given for why I'd been carrying around two white plastic admission cards since entering the park two hours earlier.

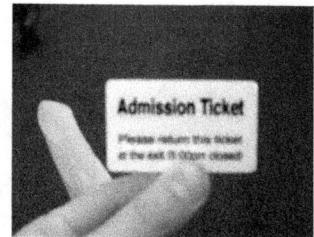

What was going on with these admission tickets? Why bother to issue a ticket if no fee was charged? My first inclination was that it must be a security system. By counting all the returned cards, the authorities could ensure that no stray visitors had remained inside the grounds when they closed the park in the late afternoon. Upon quick reflection I realized that it would be a very poor security system. Who was to say that I'd been issued two cards rather than just one? Did my three-month-old count as luggage or a visitor? There seemed to be too much variability in the system: too many opportunities for errors! If it were a security system, then surely it would fail and produce false positives every day. (As a brief aside, such a system cannot readily produce false negatives, as it would require the manufacture of additional admission tickets. This is a useful common attribute of physical kanban systems.) Meanwhile, the troops would be out scurrying around the bushes every evening looking for lost tourists. No, it had to be something else. I realized then that the Imperial Palace Gardens was using a kanban system! The limited supply of tickets (or kanban cards) ensured that the park would not become overcrowded—once the tickets were gone, no one could enter the park until someone left and returned their ticket(s).

This hugely enlightening epiphany allowed me to think beyond manufacturing with respect to kanban systems. It seemed likely that kanban tokens were useful in all sorts of management situations. As I've learned since, kanban systems appear to be applicable in any professional services, intangible goods, or knowledge worker industry. I've seen adoption in sales, marketing, finance, human resources and recruitment, web design agencies, advertising agencies, civil engineering and architecture firms, law firms, TV and movie post-production and editing, and many shared services in businesses as diverse as oil production and distribution, pharmaceuticals, and banking.

Managing at Motorola

Three years earlier, in 2002, I was an embattled development manager in a remote outpost of Motorola's PCS (mobile phone) division. Motorola, based in Chicago, had acquired our Seattle-based startup called 4thpass some months earlier. We developed network server software for wireless data services such as over-the-air download and over-the-air device management. These server applications were part of integrated systems that worked hand-in-hand with client code on the cell phones, as well as with other elements within the telecom carriers' networks and back-office infrastructure, such as billing. Our deadlines were set by managers without regard to engineering complexity, risk, or project size. Does this sound familiar? Our code base had evolved from the earlier startup company's product, where many corners had been cut in the rush to market. One senior developer insisted on referring to our platform as "a prototype." It was notoriously difficult to maintain and upgrade. We were in desperate need of greater productivity and higher quality in order to meet constantly increasing business demands.

In my daily work, back in 2002, and through my writing efforts on my earlier book,[2] two main challenges were on my mind: First, how could I protect my department of thirty

---

2. Anderson, David J. *Agile Management for Software Engineering: Applying the Theory of Constraints for Business Results.* Englewood Cliffs, NJ: Prentice Hall, 2003.

people from the incessant demands of the business and achieve what the Agile software development community referred to as a "sustainable pace"? And second, how could I successfully scale the adoption of an Agile software development approach across a business unit of approximately 250 people and overcome the inevitable resistance to change? I needed to do both of these things. I needed people in an effective, productive department who weren't exhausted from constant overloading and oppressive deadlines, and I needed the productivity gains I knew were possible with the successful adoption of Agile software development.

My Search for Sustainable Pace

The Principles Behind the Agile Manifesto[3] told us that "Agile processes promote sustainable development. The sponsors, developers, and users should be able to maintain a constant pace indefinitely." This was a compelling message for adoption of Agile software development methods for a conscientious manager leading a department, consisting of six project managers and twenty-four developers. Two years earlier, my team at Sprint PCS had become used to me telling them that "large-scale software development is a marathon, not a sprint." The pun was a deliberate mnemonic. We weren't "sprinting" at Sprint; we were running a marathon. If team members were to keep up the pace for the long haul on an eighteen-month project, we couldn't afford to burn them out after a month or two. The project had to be planned, budgeted, scheduled, and estimated so that team members could work reasonable hours each day and avoid tiring themselves out. The challenge for me as a manager was to achieve this goal *and* accommodate all the business demands.

In my first management job, in 1991, at a five-year-old startup that made video capture boards for PCs and other, smaller computers such as the Commodore Amiga, feedback from the CEO was that the leadership team saw me as "very negative." I was always answering "No" when they asked for yet more products or features when our development capacity was already stretched to the maximum. By 2002, there was clearly a pattern: I'd spent more than ten years saying "No," pushing back against the constant, fickle demands of business stakeholders.

In general, it seemed to me, software engineering teams and IT departments seemed to be at the mercy of other groups who would negotiate, cajole, intimidate, and overrule even the most defensible and objectively derived plans. Even plans based on thorough analysis and backed by years of historical data were vulnerable to unreasonable modification. Most project teams, with neither a thorough analysis method nor any historical data, were powerless at the hands of others who would push them to commit to completely unreasonable deadlines.

My feelings were that the software development industry had largely accepted crazy schedules and ridiculous work commitments as the norm. Software engineers were apparently not supposed to have a social or family life. Management guidance on how to

---

3. Beck, Kent, et al., "The Principles Behind the Agile Manifesto." http://agilemanifesto.org/principles.html

incentivize workers to stay at work and dedicate their entire lives to the cause of the latest project was legendary. The dubious leadership here came from Silicon Valley, the San Francisco Bay Area of California. Ideas such as having chefs from five-star hotels cook gourmet meals and providing laundry and even spa services within the workplace were all designed to keep workers in the office, working longer and longer hours. The blunt instrument of technology development management had been to work harder and longer rather than smarter. More intensity was apparently our only answer to insatiable demands for more features and functions.

I knew too many people whose commitment to work had undeniably damaged their social life and mental health. It was common for relationships with children and other family members to deteriorate, many irreparably. One program manager I knew at Microsoft actually kept and jokingly reported the "divorce rate per release" as a metric on how crazy things were getting. One department on SQL Server 2005 allegedly had a 30 percent divorce rate. Like all good humor, there was an underlying truth that made it deeply funny.

It's tough, though, for the general public to have sympathy for the typical software development geek. In Washington State, in the United States, where I lived for almost twenty years, software engineers are second only to dentists in average annual income. We might compare them to Ford assembly-line workers one hundred years earlier. It was also hard to sympathize with them over the monotony of their narrowly defined tasks or their mental wellbeing from performing such repetitive work, as they were paid five times the average US wage. It's hard to imagine anyone addressing the root causes of the physical and psychological ills developers routinely experience. More affluent employers have been apt to address symptoms by adding additional health-care benefits, such as massage and psychotherapy, and to provide occasional "mental-health" sick days. Many others simply turn a blind eye to employees taking mental-health days, and the bargain is understood on both sides—your employer will exploit you, and you are entitled to push back by taking sick days. The approach has always been to soothe the symptoms rather than pursue the root causes of the problems. A technical writer who worked with me at Microsoft circa 2005 once commented to me, "There is no stigma about being on antidepressants; everyone is doing them!" In response to this abuse, software engineers tended to acquiesce to demands, collect their fancy salaries, and enjoy an affluent life filled with material possessions while suffering consequences that were difficult to assign directly to work-related stress.

Some years later, I found myself once again in a meeting at Microsoft with some of my former colleagues. Before the meeting started, we were catching up personally. One colleague explained to me how he was taking more time for himself, how he'd taken up snowboarding so that he could save his relationship with the youngest of his four children. He went on to explain that "the other three have written me off already." He'd spent their childhood at work, and they resented him for it. I stopped to wonder just how many other families' lives are wrecked by these problems of overburdening and the expectation of "presentee-ism" and heroic work ethic, how social pressure to be one of the team—regardless of the wider consequences—is wrecking lives?

I wanted to break that mold as a manager. I wanted to find a "win-win" approach that allowed me to say "Yes" to new work demands while protecting my staff by facilitating a sustainable pace of work. In 2002 I wanted to give back to my department—to give them back a social and family life—and to improve the conditions that were causing stress-related health issues, such as panic attacks, in developers still in their twenties. So, I decided to take a stand and try to do something about these problems.

Kanban has enabled me to solve this riddle; and hence, I toyed with subtitling this book "How to Be a Yes Man!" It almost sounds too good to be true!

My Search for Successful Change Management

Another thing on my mind was the challenge of leading change in large organizations. I'd been a development manager at Sprint PCS and later at Motorola. In both companies, there was a real business need to develop greater agility—to be faster and more responsive with our way of working. But in both cases I had struggled to scale Agile software development methodologies across more than one or two departments or a small portfolio of projects. While scaling Agile adoption has been a hot topic over the past decade, writing in 2022, I'd already failed at it twice by 2002—twenty years earlier! While much of the Agile community at that time was struggling with how to motivate teams of six people, I'd already learned how challenging it was to scale adoption to hundreds of people.

I assumed that I needed greater positional power to compel people to follow my lead. I believed that I'd failed because I didn't have that power in each case. I was unable to simply impose change on a large group of people. In both jobs, I was trying to influence change at the request of senior leadership, but without any positional power over that wider group. Sure, I was a department manager, but I had been asked to influence change across a business unit. I needed to influence peers to make changes in their departments similar to those I had implemented with my own. Getting those managers on-board wasn't hard—they all wanted to be seen as helping, to look good in the eyes our boss. However, their staff were a different matter. These other departments resisted adopting techniques that were quite clearly producing better results with my own group. There were probably many facets to this resistance, but the most common theme was that every other department's situation was different. My department's techniques would have to be modified and tailored to others' specific needs. By mid-2002, I concluded that enforcing a prescriptive software development methodology or defined process at a large scale, a scale of a 250- to 450-person business unit, simply didn't work. It didn't matter how good the prescribed methodology was; it would meet with resistance from a significant portion of the workforce when applied at scale.

While researching and writing my 2003 book, *Agile Management for Software Engineering*, I came to realize that, in some way, every situation is unique. The thesis of the book was intended to demonstrate, through the framework of Eli Goldratt's Theory of Constraints, that Agile software development methodologies produced better economic outcomes. It was my (admittedly over-optimistic) belief at the time that such an economic argument would be persuasive for senior management to support wider adoption of Agile approaches. The Theory of Constraints asks us to look for bottlenecks and to manage and reduce them in order to improve the economic performance of the business. Thinking about this concept continuously while developing the manuscript in 2002, I came to realize that every situation ought indeed to be treated as unique. The notion that a single defined process description could fit any situation was clearly flawed. Why should the constraining factor or bottleneck be in the same place for every team and on every project every time? Each organization is different: different sets of skills, capabilities, and experiences. Each project is different: different budget, schedule, scope, and risk profile. And every organization is different: a different workflow of activities operating in a different market niche or supplying a different set of customers. It occurred to me that this might provide a clue to the resistance to change. If proposed changes to working practices and behaviors did not have a perceived benefit, people would resist them. If those changes did not affect what those people perceived as their constraint, or limiting factor, they would resist. Simply put, changes suggested out of context would be rejected by the workers who lived and understood their own working context, the workflow of the service they provided, and how effective, or not, it was.

It seemed better to let an improved workflow evolve by eliminating one bottleneck after another. This is the core thesis of Goldratt's Theory of Constraints. I was completely sold on it as an answer to my search.

Goldratt's approach, explained in volume 2, *Implementing Kanban*, seeks to identify a bottleneck and then find ways to alleviate it until it no longer constrains performance. Once this happens, a new bottleneck emerges and the cycle repeats. It's an iterative and evolutionary approach to improving performance systematically by identifying and removing bottlenecks.

I recognized that I could synthesize this technique with some ideas from Lean Product Development. By modeling the workflow of a software development lifecycle and then tracking work flowing through a series of states and visualizing that workflow and the work within it, I could see bottlenecks. The ability to identify a bottleneck is the first step in the underlying model for the Theory of Constraints. Goldratt had already developed an application of the theory for flow problems, awkwardly called "Drum-Buffer-Rope." Regardless of the the name, I realized that a simplified Drum-Buffer-Rope solution could be implemented for software development.

This synthesis of concepts would give me a mechanism to drive evolutionary change. Wrapped inside a feedback loop such as the Five Focusing Steps from the Theory of Constraints, a system such as Drum-Buffer-Rope becomes an enabler for an evolutionary approach to improvement. Goldratt called this a POOGI (a process of ongoing improvement). It promised process improvement driven from a position of the current process as actually implemented—a "start with what you do now and evolve from there" approach to change. I was hopeful that this held the answer to my search for successful change management. I was hopeful that the Theory of Constraints approach offered a solution for successful, institutionalized change—change that sticks!

The Three Challenges of Scaling Agile

To drive unique adaption of process for each specific situation would require active leadership on each team. This was often lacking. Even with the right leadership, I doubted that significant change could happen without a management framework in place and guidance on how to tailor a process definition to fit different situations. Without this to guide a leader, coach, or process engineer, any adaptation was likely to be imposed subjectively. This was just as likely to raise hackles and objections as imposing an inappropriate process template. I continue to believe that a lack of effective leaders with appropriate skills, training, and experience is one of three core obstacles to scaling Agile software development implementations.

Second was lack of organizational maturity, a lack of an appropriate organizational value system—a credo. Without that, there is an inability to manage risk and to make tough decisions with long-term benefits, focusing only on the short-term, making tactical choices and disregarding longer-term consequences, and an inability to manage change effectively.

The third issue was simply that people resist the imposed changes even when attempts are made to tailor processes for specific situations. I've come to believe that a process-centric approach to improved business agility is wrongheaded—scaling Agile methods is doomed to failure. More than twenty years of real-world experience and evidence appears to suggest this may be true. Where large-scale implementations of Agile methods appear to have worked, and there are very few, I suspect that my three criteria were addressed: they had strong leadership, a mature organization, and they approached the implementation incrementally, with a "roll your own" approach rather than following a specific defined methodology or framework.

From Drum-Buffer-Rope to Kanban Systems

Returning to my earlier inspiration from Goldratt, with his theory of constraints and his bottleneck-driven POOGI approach, I was receiving conflicting advice—from respected sources such as Donald G. Reinertsen—and the suggestion was that knowledge worker workflows were subject to excessive variability. That meant that it was difficult to identify bottlenecks, and that the bottleneck would rarely remain in one place, that the systems of flow would not stabilize. I didn't actually witness this firsthand until 2007 when I witnessed two managers on my team arguing during a staff meeting that each of their departments was "the bottleneck." Variability in the nature of our work was causing the bottleneck to oscillate from one function in the workflow to another. Reinertsen's intuition and advice appeared to be correct. However, it was fully two years after Don raised his concerns before I had this empirical evidence to reinforce it.

If the next paragraph seems a little confusing and technical, bear with me. The detail and esoteric differences, as we've learned this past decade, really aren't so important.

There was another concern: Generically, Drum-Buffer-Rope is an example of a class of solutions known as pull systems. Pull systems limit the work-in-progress (often abbreviated to "WIP"), or inventory in a workflow process, resulting in deferred commitment on upstream requests. They use a signaling mechanism to indicate when capacity is available to pull new work into the system. A kanban system is another example of a pull system. Kanban systems are more robust to variability in local cycle times or unevenness in flow because they limit WIP at each step in a workflow, whereas Drum-Buffer-Rope seeks to limit work-in-progress in front of a bottleneck by adding a buffer with a single WIP limit, described metaphorically as "the rope," which limits the WIP from the input to the system up until that buffer in front of the bottleneck. WIP beyond the bottleneck is not limited in a basic implementation of the system. To complete the metaphors in the name, the "drum" is the pace at which work is completed in the bottleneck. A drumbeat, every time an item is finished in the bottleneck station, provides the signal to pull new work into the system at the head of the rope.

Drum-Buffer-Rope creates pull at the pace of the bottleneck and prevents the whole system from becoming overburdened: It creates stability. However, in its simplest form it is not robust to variability in cycle times or unevenness of flow upstream from the bottleneck. In the event that the bottleneck stalled, work already started would continue flowing toward it. Restarting the bottleneck process becomes problematic, as it may be overwhelmed by work overflowing its protective buffer. While this argument is technical and esoteric, I was persuaded by Donald Reinertsen[4] that unevenness of flow throughout the process is a valid concern in knowledge-worker pursuits such as software development. Hence, kanban systems are a more appropriate form of pull system in this domain. Kanban also proved considerably easier to explain: Although its name uses a Japanese word, the name provoked far fewer questions than the metaphorical "Drum-Buffer-Rope." Explaining the metaphor behind Drum-Buffer-Rope, an allegory about a troop of Boy Scouts hiking on a narrow mountain path, was cumbersome and I struggled to gain credibility with it.

---

4. See "Foreword to *Kanban*," page ix.

It appeared "Kanban" was sticky while, in my experience, "Drum-Buffer-Rope" tended to turn people off.

However, considering all of this in 2004, there was still a significant concern that professional services work was very different from tangible goods industries such as manufacturing or supply chain management. There was no precedent for using kanban systems in fields such as software development. It was easy to level criticism that the use of kanban systems was an inappropriate choice for professional services pursuits.

It would be quite some years before there was sufficient evidence and social proof that the use of virtual kanban systems for professional services, intangible goods industries, and knowledge workers' activities would be generally accepted. This is the story of how Kanban was exapted from twentieth-century manufacturing into modern twenty-first-century business operations. This is the origin story of what came to be known as the Kanban Method.

Takeaways

- Kanban systems are from a family of approaches known as *pull systems*.
- Eliyahu Goldratt's Drum-Buffer-Rope application of the Theory of Constraints is an alternative implementation of a pull system.
- The Five Focusing Steps in the Theory of Constraints is an example of an evolutionary approach to improvement driven by identifying bottlenecks.
- Eliyahu Goldratt called such an evolutionary approach a POOGI (or "process of ongoing improvement"). The motivation for pursuing a pull-system approach was two-fold: to find a systematic way to achieve a sustainable pace of work and to find an approach to introducing workflow changes that would meet with minimal resistance.
- The Imperial Palace Gardens in Tokyo uses a kanban system to control the size of the crowd inside the park.
- The quantity of kanban signal cards in circulation limits work-in-progress.
- Kanban systems can be used to improve flow through a system in any situation in which there is a desire to limit the quantity of things inside a system.
- New work is pulled into the process when a current work order or task is completed and returns its signal card.
- Kanban solved the dilemma of finding an approach to both sustainable pace and introducing changes for improved economic performance without significant resistance and inertia.

2

A Former Athlete's New Challenge

The Motivation for Kanban at Microsoft in 2005

"Kanban only works with small, co-located teams!" This was a widely held belief around the time I published *Kanban* (the Blue Book) in 2010—a belief that lingers to this day. It is, of course, a myth! It was an assumption based on an understanding that standing up "looking at the board" was the core, essential element of the approach. Consequently, there were plenty of so-called experts willing to state publicly and categorically that Kanban didn't work with geographically distributed organizations. If people couldn't stand together in front of the board, it was posited, then clearly Kanban had nothing to offer. The huge irony of this myth is revealed in the next two chapters, which tell the story of how we got started with Kanban. . . .

Dragos Dumitriu is a friendly, jocular, Romanian-American with a winning smile and an enthusiasm for life that seems to compel people to like him and attract them to follow his lead. Tall, bald, solidly built, and spreading only slightly with the onset of middle age, he cuts a dashing figure in his handmade, tailored European suits and expensive sunglasses. Though twenty-plus years living in the United States has softened it, he still has a distinct eastern-European accent. As a package, there is something just a little intimidating about Dragos: something that says "I'm in charge; there will be no nonsense!" You can imagine smalltime gangsters running the other way at the sight of him as he emerges from a large, dark BMW in downtown Bucharest.

His physique is a legacy from his past as a young athlete on the Romanian Olympic team. As a young adult, Dragos owned and managed a fitness center in his native Romania and worked as a stunt double in movies and as a personal bodyguard. He's the personification of a "larger than life character." Moving to New York with his then-wife, a successful doctor, he took a low-paying job in a psychiatric hospital and two years later had risen to manage it. Following his wife to Fargo, North Dakota (a remote city in the north-central part of the United States, perhaps best known for the movie and spin-off TV show of the same name and infamous for its bitterly cold winters), he joined Great Plains Software as a project manager. Already well into his thirties, it was his first experience in the IT industry.

Following Great Plains's acquisition by Microsoft to create what is now known as Dynamics, Dragos transferred to Seattle in 2003 and found himself in the IT division as a program manager. The following year, ambitious for a challenge, he volunteered to take command of the small sustaining engineering team in the XIT business unit—a team that was known for having the worst customer satisfaction record across all of Microsoft's IT organization.

XIT Sustaining Engineering

At the time, Microsoft was divided into seven different businesses units. All were treated as separate businesses. In addition, there was a corporate headquarters unit that provided shared services such as human resources, finance, facilities management, and security to those seven businesses. The IT department of this corporate shared services function was known as XIT (or "cross IT," indicating the nature of the shared services they provided to the customer-facing businesses).

Dale Christian, who would later serve as CIO of Avanade and, later still, as CIO of The Bill & Melinda Gates Foundation, was XIT's general manager. Its sustaining engineering team was a small team tasked with minor feature upgrades and bug fixes "off-cycle" and outside of major releases and application upgrades. From an accounting perspective, costs attributed to that team were considered an operating expense, whereas costs associated with project teams working on major project portfolios were considered a capital expense. These are two different budgets, and while capital expense is an asset, operating expense is purely cost. This had an impact on both policy-constraining behavior and decision making.

The team Dragos volunteered to lead was located in Hyderabad, India, in a so-called captive center or campus, built by the outsourcing firm TCS specifically for Microsoft. A few short years earlier, Microsoft had made a strategic decision to outsource its IT functions. IT wasn't core to Microsoft's mission or its identity; rather, it was an enabling function. It was reasonable, therefore, that IT could be provided as a service from afar. It was hoped that existing developers and testers working in IT on Microsoft's campus near Seattle could be repurposed to work on products within one of the other seven business units. Most of this switch happened in 2003, so what remained of IT was largely a vendor-management organization consisting mainly of individual contributors with the job title "program manager." Dragos's job was to lead and manage the small, six-person Sustaining Engineering team working in Hyderabad.

For context, Seattle is, depending on the time of year, either twelve-and-a-half or thirteen-and-a-half hours behind Hyderabad. This time difference creates both challenges and opportunities when managing vendors in India remotely from the West Coast of the United States. The advantage is that things can happen overnight. The disadvantage is that synchronous communication such as conference calls are challenging to schedule, and that when it is Friday in Seattle, it is already Saturday and the weekend in India. There are effectively only four days per week available for managing across this time difference.

As mentioned already, the Sustaining Engineering team had the worst record for customer service across all of Microsoft's IT departments. This organization had stubbornly refused to improve. After the switch to a new team offshore, things had not improved at the TCS facility in Hyderabad. All of the personnel had changed, the management had changed, and the service was now provided by a vendor with a master services agreement, yet still there was no improvement. So hopeless was the performance of XIT Sustaining Engineering that the program manager position had been vacant for some months—no one wanted it.

Into this scene Dragos arrived—ambitious, always up for a challenge, a born leader, and keen to make a mark. Hoping to be recognized and rewarded with greater responsibilities in the future, he volunteered for the job. A few of his colleagues thought he was crazy.

At this point, it's worth reflecting on why I spent so many words familiarizing you with Dragos. I am laying the foundation to dispel another myth: that Kanban works only when it is led by remarkable, larger-than-life characters like Dragos. The results Dragos achieved, as described in Chapter 3, are remarkable. Heck, I wrote two chapters of a book about them! It's been easy for people to dismiss these results as uniquely attributable to his character and not the method he was following. As you'll see toward the conclusions of Chapters 3 and 4, this simply isn't true. Dragos doesn't have to be in the room for you to garner the same scale of results. But you need to follow his method, his way of thinking. You need to follow the Kanban Method. Yes, leadership is definitely required, but you don't have to be a former Olympian for the Kanban Method to work for you.

Dragos was the program manager for XIT's software maintenance service known as Sustaining Engineering. They were responsible for maintaining the software for the XIT business unit. His team provided two basic services: minor upgrades (known as change requests) and defect fixes. The team (shown in Figure 2.1), consisting of three software developers, three testers, and a local department manager (second from left in the photograph), developed minor upgrades and fixed production bugs for about eighty cross-functional IT applications used by Microsoft staff throughout the world.

I had joined Microsoft's Developer Tools division in September 2004, and hence Dragos and I were colleagues in different business units. We had yet to meet.

Figure 2.1 Dragos pictured with the XIT Sustaining Engineering team in Hyderabad, circa February 2005

> **Why Athletes Make Great Employees**
>
> A friend of mine is a former Winter Olympian from the Austrian team. She competed in the luge at the Salt Lake City Olympics in 2002. Nowadays, she's a coach for the Austrian national team in Innsbruck. Chatting with me in 2009, she advised me that when looking to hire new personnel for my business, "Always look out for athletes."
>
> "They have discipline. They know how to set goals. They are motivated. They know how to measure performance, and they take an organized approach to training and improving performance."
>
> I thought of Dragos, how well he fitted this description and how valuable these characteristics were to his role at Microsoft.

The Problem

By the summer of 2004, senior management and customers were out of patience. Something had to be done! Dragos volunteered to take charge. He loved this sort of challenge. He spent his first few weeks observing, learning, understanding, and examining data from their tracking system. He wasn't tasked with filling the shoes of his predecessor. He was expected to do more than just fill the position and crank the handle of the existing broken process. Dragos was told to make changes—to fix whatever it was that was broken.

He quickly understood that customer dissatisfaction was rooted in long lead times, unreliable delivery, and broken promises for what seemed like small, highly achievable, and often important changes and bug fixes. His team maintained applications such as the human resources employee records system and the payroll system. These were used by finance to enable salary payments to most of Microsoft's global workforce. To understand the nature of their work, let's consider a strawman business initiative and how it might impact XIT's applications. Imagine that Microsoft plans to open a new office in San Juan, Puerto Rico. Puerto Rico is a protectorate of the United States; its currency is the US dollar. In many ways, Puerto Rico is similar to one of the states of the United States. Hawaii had similar status until 1959, when it became the fiftieth state of the United States.

A business initiative such as opening a new office in San Juan will create impact for all of XIT's corporate shared services customers: finance will need to make payroll for Puerto Rican employees; human resources will need to store employee records for those employees as well as facilitate recruitment on the island; facilities management will need to provide an office building and allocate space to departments and offices to individuals; while security will need to secure the premises and have a capability to print employee badges and enable scanners on entrances and exits.

In this scenario, requests might be "support Puerto Rican address format in the employee records system" or "support Puerto Rican tax withholding for payroll for Puerto Rican employees." These will break down into details such as "Add Puerto Rico to the drop-down menu of States of the United States on the employee address form." Any lay person familiar with using personal computers could understand that from a business owner's perspective these seem like simple little changes. Why, then, were they taking months? And why was the XIT group constantly breaking delivery promises? It is easy to understand the frustration of the customers in finance, HR, and the other shared corporate services.

One of the organizational dysfunctions was that often the high-level business objective or initiative behind a request was opaque to the workers in XIT. A business initiative, for example, "Let's open an office in Puerto Rico," would manifest as several requests for support from someone in any of the shared IT services, such as facilities management, finance, HR, and so on, who would in turn work with their product manager to push requests for changes to IT systems through to the Sustaining Engineering team. Requests would therefore appear in isolation, apparently independent, when in fact there may have been value in understanding them as a dependent set. Workers in Sustaining Engineering were set up as order takers, and the orders were for small changes, delivered in short order. However, context was missing.

Fixing this bigger, more strategic dysfunction was not part of Dragos's remit, nor was it immediately obvious as a deeper, root cause of the dysfunction. Dragos's job was to make Sustaining Engineering better order takers, to make them fit enough to deliver what was asked of them.

Current Capability

The Sustaining Engineering team had an average five-month lead time on change requests, and this, along with their backlog of requests, was growing uncontrollably. Not only was the average lead time already unacceptable, but it was likely that for any one item the lead time from commitment to delivery was six weeks to greater than one year. As a service, they were slow and unpredictable. They had a habit of promising delivery dates and then failing to meet them.

Constraints

The Sustaining Engineering programmers and testers working for TCS were following the Software Engineering Institute's Personal Software Process/Team Software Process (PSP/TSP) methodology. Microsoft mandated this contractually with TCS. This choice had been made by Jon De Vaan, Vice President of Microsoft's Engineering Excellence group. Jon reported directly to Bill Gates in his role as Chief Architect as well as Chairman of Microsoft. Jon De Vaan was a big fan of Watts Humphrey[5] of the Software Engineering

---

5. https://en.wikipedia.org/wiki/Watts_Humphrey

Institute at Carnegie Mellon University. Humphrey had been recognized for his contribution to the profession of software engineering as a recipient of the National Medal of Technology, awarded by the President of the United States. Humphrey was the creator of the PSP/TSP, and De Vaan had been looking for an opportunity to experiment with it at Microsoft. Unable to gain traction for it on product teams, he had been granted the opportunity to run his experiment with the IT division. Consequently, TCS was contractually obligated to follow it. Jon De Vaan was an early developer at Microsoft and a trusted friend of Bill Gates. Sometime later, when the Windows Vista project went off the rails and had to be reset as Windows 7, it was to Jon that Bill turned as the person to lead the recovery. In 2004, as head of Engineering Excellence, no one was going to challenge the preferences of Jon De Vaan. This meant that changing the process used by the Sustaining Engineering team, changing their software development lifecycle method, was not an available option. This constraint turned out to be a stroke of luck! Dragos was forced to follow a "start with what you do now" approach. Insisting on installing an Agile methodology was never an option.

The perception was of a team that was badly organized and poorly managed. As a result, senior management was not disposed to provide additional money to fix the problem.

Sustaining Engineering were order takers for small, short-order requests seen in isolation; they were a cost center; their hands were tied regarding their choice of working processes; and management was unwilling to provide additional funding to enable improvements, as there was no appetite to throw more people (and money) at the problem.

By sheer coincidence, Dragos had discovered my first book, *Agile Management for Software Engineering*. Impressed with what he'd read, he asked for my advice. I arranged to visit him in his office in building 115 on Microsoft's campus in Redmond, Washington, in the leafy green eastern suburbs of Seattle. The interaction, interview, and analysis described below has been formalized into the first steps of the STATIK (systems thinking approach to introducing Kanban) method. This method is described more fully in volume 2, *Implementing Kanban*.

Visualize

To begin to understand the problems, I asked Dragos to sketch the workflow. He drew a simple stick-figure drawing describing the lifecycle of a change request, and as he did so, we discussed the problems. Figure 2.2 is a facsimile of what he drew. The PM figure represents Dragos.

Requests were arriving uncontrollably. Four product managers represented and controlled budgets for the customer functions named previously, such as Finance, Human Resources, Facilities Management, and Security. Requests were for small upgrades but also included production defects (problems discovered in the field by end users). These defects had not been created by the maintenance team, but by the application development project teams. These project teams were working on the major project portfolio, and their work was considered a capital expense, or an asset. Those application development teams were generally broken up one month after the release of a new system, after the end of the so-called "warranty period," and the source code was handed off to the Sustaining Engineering team for further maintenance. While many readers will recognize this dysfunctional pattern, we weren't in a position to do anything about it. Our job was to make the Sustaining Engineering team better and faster at fixing bugs, not to help XIT as a whole by reducing the quantity of defects created. This was, therefore, another constraint. We were not in a position to shape demand or enact changes that would reduce demand. Sustaining Engineering were order takers.

It is important to be pragmatic and avoid idealistic wishful thinking, that "If only we were able to influence the whole business unit, have position power to make wider changes, and hold sway over senior managers, then. . . ." In management jobs, you have to build trust and earn respect through accomplishments within your own sphere of influence, within your own constrained boundaries. If you are successful at this, then you may be rewarded with greater responsibility and greater scope. Patience is required. It simply isn't feasible to jump directly to fixing the big problems and making grand changes across an entire business unit.

Some of these ideas are now captured as core values and coaching guidance in the Kanban Method: Pragmatism and patience are contained in the catchphrase, "There is no wishful thinking in Kanban."

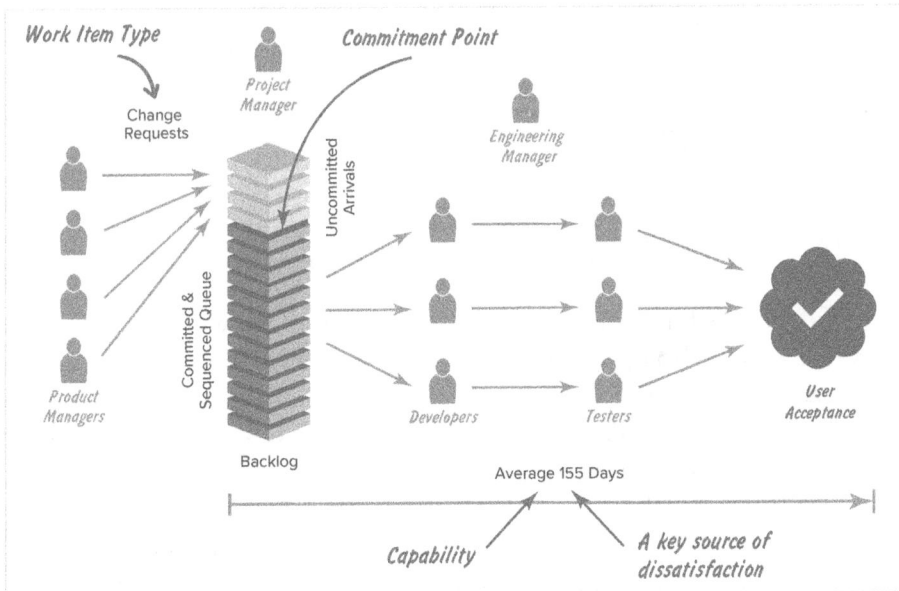

Figure 2.2 XIT Sustaining Engineering workflow

Demand and Capability Analysis

When each request for a change or defect fix arrived from a product manager, Dragos would send it to India for an estimate, as illustrated in Figure 2.3. The policy was that estimates had to be made and returned to the business owners within 48 hours. This would facilitate making some return-on-investment (ROI) calculation and deciding whether to proceed with the request. Once a month, Dragos would meet with the product managers and other stakeholders, and they would reprioritize the backlog and create a project plan from the requests.

Due to the service level agreement to return estimates within forty-eight hours, estimates preempted existing planned work already in progress. Effectively, gathering information for future speculative work was treated with greater urgency and importance than completing existing planned and committed work.

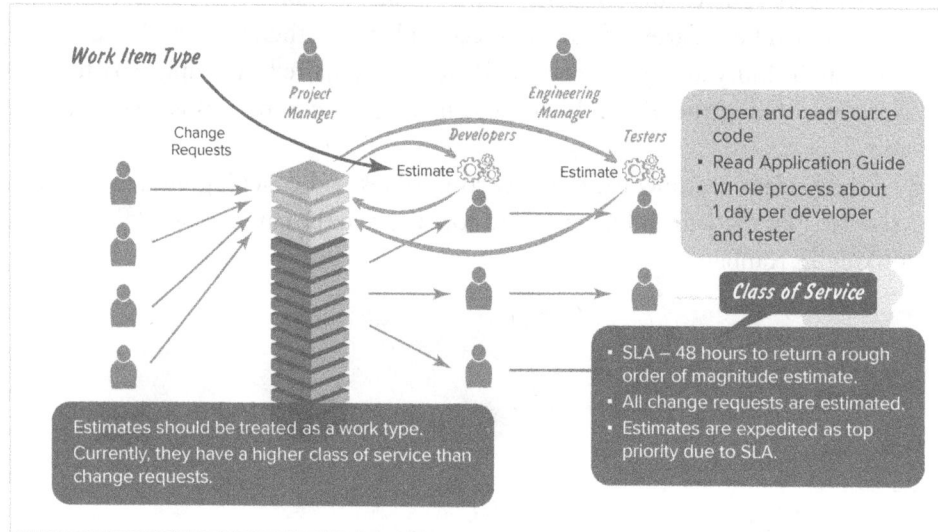

Figure 2.3 How requests for estimates disrupted planned work

The effort of creating estimates for new, incoming work was consuming a lot of time. Despite being referred to as "rough order of magnitude" (ROM) estimates, the customer expectation was actually for a very accurate estimate, and team members had learned to take great care in preparing them. The root cause of this was that estimates were used both as input to ROI calculations, and hence prioritization decisions, and as a means to cost a request for the purpose of interdepartmental budget transfers.

Bizarrely, payment for the work done by XIT Sustaining Engineering was made based on the estimate rather than the actual time spent doing the work. It appeared from our analysis that Microsoft corporate departments were effectively "paying" XIT in advance for each request. While this seemed truly bizarre, we decided to let it go unchallenged. Pragmatism must prevail: You need to pick your battles, and a candid discussion with a VP of Finance who had made the policy decisions on how Sustaining Engineering work should be accounted for (i.e., as an operating expense), and how it might be paid for from requesting business unit budgets, was not something that either of us relished. We didn't have the pay grade or the respect within the firm to even suggest such a meeting. Like the contractual requirement to use the Software Engineering Institute's PSP/TSP methodology, the finance policies were, at least for us, an immovable object, a constraint around which we had to work. We had to be successful despite these rules. It wasn't acceptable to point the blame at them and wash our hands of further responsibility.

Each of these high-precision estimates was taking about one day for both a developer and a tester to produce. The fear of getting it wrong was driving them to do analysis and design work just to develop an estimate. Of course, this analysis and design work was thrown away and not preserved such that it might be reused later.

At this time, the demand for estimates ranged from eighteen to twenty-five per month. We quickly calculated that the estimation effort alone was consuming seven or eight working days per person each month. Consequently, 33 to 40 percent of capacity was consumed assessing the viability of uncommitted work. At least one-third of capacity was used to speculate about future work in preference to coding and testing current, committed work. There was no governance over the number of requests for estimates, and hence, the impact of estimating was potentially unlimited. Estimating these new requests pre-empted existing work and caused delay. Given that it was ungoverned, it had the potential, though apparently it had never happened, to completely halt all current, committed work. Consequently, estimating randomized the plans made for any given month and resulted in work being completed behind schedule. In fact, demand for estimation was sufficiently high, and its impact pre-empting committed work so great, that XIT Sustaining Engineering were incapable of delivering anything against plan. Their current delivery capability was effectively 0 percent on-time.

While the demand for estimates was eighteen to twenty-five per month, the number of items being delivered was around six per month,[6] as shown in Figure 2.4. The backlog, which had eighty or more items in it as of October 2004, was growing, although not as quickly as it should have been compared to the demand for estimates. What was going on?

---

6. In two of the three quarters shown in Figure 2.4, the delivery rate is approximately double, around twelve per month. This gives a false impression of capability. During this six-month period, Microsoft management had doubled the staffing level in an attempt to reduce the backlog and allow TCS, taking over as the vendor, to start their contract with a relatively small backlog. From July 2004, staffing had returned to historical levels and the delivery rate returned to similar historical levels of approximately six items per month. Unfortunately, we do not have a chart of this earlier period.

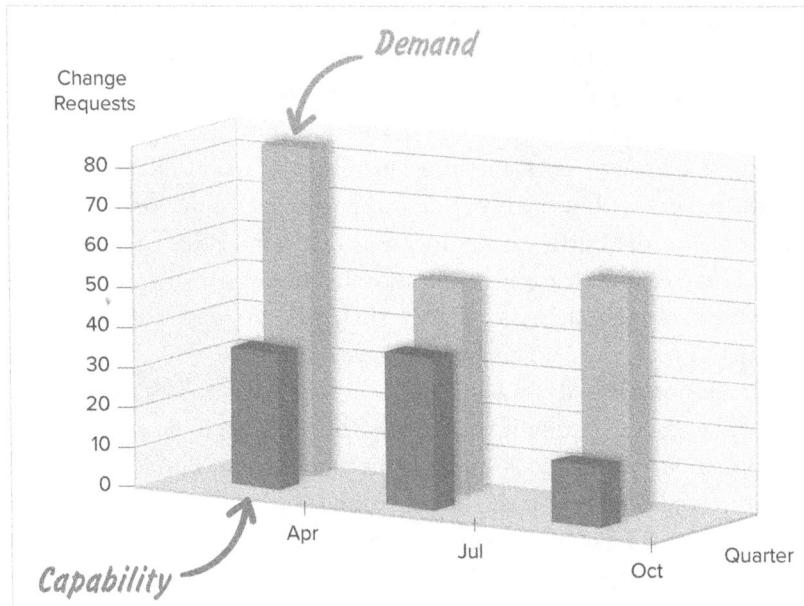

Figure 2.4 Demand for change requests versus capability to supply over the previous nine months

Analyzing Previous Work

A study of all items closed, whether complete, discarded, or abandoned mid-flight, showed that 48 percent of requests submitted were never actually delivered. This explained why the backlog wasn't growing as rapidly as might have been expected. Nevertheless, the growth was typically greater than six per month. Of the items never delivered, 26 percent represented items discarded during planning because either they had a poor ROI or they were "too big." Items estimated as needing more than fifteen days of engineering had to be redirected to a major project in the portfolio so that they could be accounted for as capital expense. This governance rule was intended to enforce the notion that maintenance work, accounted for as operating expense, was only ever for small items. Historically, the "too bigs" were only 2 percent of demand. Hence, low ROI represented 24 percent of demand. The remaining 22 percent were abandoned and closed with the reason "overtaken by events." This was often caused by the decommissioning of an application or intranet site. For example, in 2003, there was a huge earthquake and subsequent tsunami off the coast of Sumatra, Indonesia. The tsunami wave took the lives of over 250,000 people in Indonesia, Thailand, Sri Lanka, and Southeast India. At the time, Microsoft had created a website to enable employees to make donations, and these were distributed to charities such as the Red Cross. This site was no longer required some eighteen months later, and it was decommissioned. Other such examples were often seasonal in nature or for one-off events.

We can summarize our demand and capability analysis as follows:

- Speculative work requiring an estimate and business case: 18–25 per month
- Actual committed work, planned and sequenced: 9–13 per month
- Work actually delivered each month: approximately 6 items

We can summarize delivery capability as:

- Lead time was, on average, 5.5 months and growing at a rate of at least 0.5 months per month.
- Items delivered against original planned and committed dates were approximately 0 percent.

Although only six or so items were delivered each month, the entire backlog was reprioritized and replanned each month. And although approximately twelve items were discarded or abandoned, a similar number were committed, sequenced, and added to the plan implemented as a Gantt Chart in Microsoft Project. In Kanban language, work was committed early, at the monthly planning meeting after the request was submitted. At the time of commitment, each item would have a proposed delivery date. Around six items would be delivered over the next month. However, the committed backlog would be at least eighty items. New requests would have arrived in the meantime, and all the undelivered work would be reprioritized at the next monthly planning session and then the new plan with new dates for each item recommunicated to stakeholders. It was likely that a typical request would be replanned four or five times prior to delivery. This was a key factor in customer dissatisfaction and lack of trust in the Sustaining Engineering service. They were simply not capable of keeping their promises.

The problem was two-fold: They were committing too early to too much; and even for the immediate month ahead, they were overcommitting because the disruptive effect of the requests for estimates wasn't taken into account.

Flow Efficiency

The requests were tracked with a tool called Product Studio. An updated version of this tool was later released publicly as Team Foundation Server Work Item Tracking, which later morphed into the web service Azure Devops. The XIT Sustaining Engineering team was similar to many organizations I see in my teaching and consulting work—they had lots of data, but they were not using it. Dragos began to mine the data and discovered that an average request took eleven days of engineering (a combination of development and testing time), as shown in the histogram in Figure 2.5. However, lead times of 125 to 155 days were typical. More than 90 percent of the lead time was queuing or other forms of waste. They were only 8 percent flow efficient. While this sounds very poor, we've come to realize that often the starting condition for improvement is well below this. Hakan Forss[7]

---

7. Hakan Forss, Lean Kanban France, Oct 2013

and Zsolt Fabok[8] have both reported beginning flow efficiency numbers of 1 to 2 percent. These numbers are widely accepted amongst the Kanban coaching community as typical. The good news, whether we have 8 percent as we did in 2004, or a much lower number, is that there is a huge potential upside. Improving flow efficiency and decreasing lead times should be a matter of identifying and eliminating sources of delay.

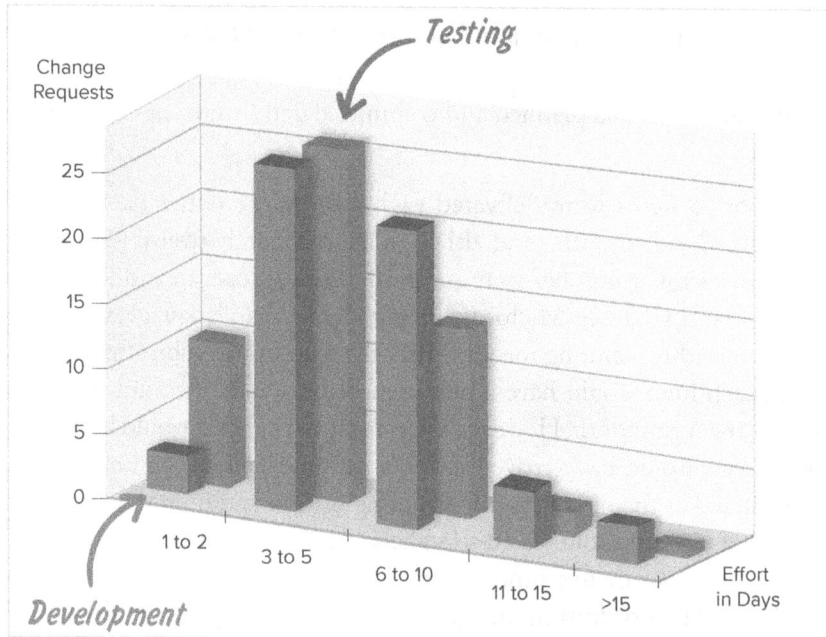

Figure 2.5 Histogram showing actual development and testing time per change request

An Additional Work Item Type

In addition to change requests and defect fixes, there was another type of work, known as production text changes (PTCs). These were text changes to on-screen dialog boxes or web pages. This had grown to include graphical or web page design changes and eventually expanded to involve modifying values in tables used to drive business logic in applications or XML files used for configuration or reference while an application was running. We later discovered that, for example, the tax tables for the payroll system, which calculate the income tax deductions to be withheld by the employer, fell into this category of work. The acronym PTC was meaningless! The common element was that these changes did not require a developer and were often made by business owners, product managers, or the program manager, but they did require a formal test pass, so they affected the testers. PTCs all had a common workflow. However, their nature and the business risks associated with one item compared to

---

8. Zsolt Fabok, Lean Agile Scotland, Sep 2012; Lean Kanban France, Oct 2012

another varied greatly: Changing a department logo on an intranet web page clearly doesn't carry the same risks as deploying the new withholding-tax tables in the payroll system. And this was another problem: PTCs were given their own class of service. They were all top priority—effectively, expedite requests. At the time, we didn't understand why. We didn't have enough insight into the true nature of PTCs. Inherently, it just seemed wrong. Why were so-called text changes being expedited? It was a red flag, but at the time we chose to ignore it. All we knew was that PTCs were disruptive, they pre-empted planned and committed work, and they affected our ability to deliver that planned work on time.

I asked Dragos about the nature of arrival of PTCs and the volume of demand. His response was that they were unusual— weeks would go by without a single request, and then without much warning, a whole batch would arrive. Their sporadic nature and demanded class of service made PTCs a problem, a problem that today we teach Kanban practitioners the skills to adequately understand and design for. In 2004, we ignored them. As described in the next chapter, we got away with it for two reasons: First, because the improvement in general performance was so great, there was capacity to cope with PTCs; and second, their arrival impact was much less disruptive—merely a ripple—because of the WIP control and deferred commitment benefits from using a kanban system.

From Understanding a Problem to Designing a Solution

Now that we understood the problems and the constraints within which we had to work, the focus turned to what we might do about it. What Dragos chose to do, and how he enabled it to happen, is explored in Chapter 3.

Takeaways

- The first step to improving workflow for a service is to sketch and visualize it.
- Conduct demand and capability analysis to understand the nature of the workflow.
- Identify and understand sources of customer dissatisfaction.
- Analyzing flow efficiency helps us to understand the potential improvement possible.
- Typically, flow efficiency is very low (e.g., 5 percent or less) before any interventions are made.

3

"Do you think they'll go for that?"

Design and Implementation of Kanban at Microsoft XIT

"So, our proposal is that we're going to stop estimating, and stop planning, and ask them to trust that this will magically result in everything being delivered within thirty days?"

"Yes! Do you think they will go for that?"

Dragos and I looked at each other across his office, in building 115 of Microsoft's campus in Redmond, Washington. It was a dark, dreary, cloud-covered, rainy day in the fall of 2004.

"No. Probably not!"

This is the story of what Dragos did and how he got it done. The results are now legendary. The delivery rate of change requests jumped by 230 percent, while lead times fell from an average of 5.5 months to a mere 12 days, and on-time performance rose to 98 percent against a 25-day service level agreement.

Dragos was promoted, and later headhunted, when Dale Christian shifted from his position as general manager of XIT to CIO at Avanade. In two moves, in two years, Dragos went from program manager of a six-person team—only two pay grades above a university graduate at Microsoft—to Senior Director for Global IT Operations of the Accenture/Microsoft joint venture company. The XIT Sustaining Engineering service team went from having the worst customer service record within Microsoft's IT group to the best, and Dragos was rewarded with the division's process improvement award for the second half of 2005.

How Policies Affected Performance

The team was following the required process, which included many bad policy decisions that had been made by managers at various levels, often in isolation and without due consideration for the wider impact on the service as a whole. It is important to think of a service and its workflow as defined by a set of policies that govern behavior. Someone has the authority to override or change policies; they are under management's control. For example, the policy to use PSP/TSP was set at the executive vice-president level, one rung below Bill Gates, and this policy would be hard or impossible to change. Policies on accounting and budget transfers were made by a mid-ranking executive in the finance department, and these policies would also be difficult to change. Policies on prioritization and the use of ROI calculations in businesses cases were made by the program management office (PMO) and were required of product managers. While not impossible to change, neither Dragos nor I had the pay grade or the influence to effect change there. However, many other policies, such as the policy to prioritize estimates over actual coding and testing, were developed locally and were under the collaborative authority of the immediate managers. It is possible that these policies made sense at the time they were implemented, but circumstances had changed, and no attempt had been made to review and update the policies that governed the team's operation. There was scope to change some policies and effect improvements in performance despite the other constraints.

No Estimates

After some discussion with his colleagues and manager, Dragos decided to enact two initial management changes. First, the team would stop estimating. He wanted to recover the capacity wasted by estimation activity and use it to develop and test software. Eliminating the schedule randomization caused by estimating would also improve predictability, and the combination would, he hoped, have a great impact on customer satisfaction.

However, removing estimation was problematic. It would affect the ROI calculations, and customers might worry that bad prioritization choices were being made. In addition, estimates were used to facilitate inter-departmental cost accounting and budget transfers. Estimates were also used to implement a governance policy. Only small requests were allowed through system maintenance. Larger requests, those exceeding fifteen days of development or testing, had to be submitted to a major project initiative and go through the formal PMO portfolio management governance process. We will revisit these issues shortly.

Estimates were disruptive and affecting ability to deliver against promised dates. The lack of predictability was affecting customer satisfaction. Had Dragos chosen to fix this one issue of predictability, perhaps he would have made a different choice. Eliminating estimates was a choice made to get back at least one-third of capacity that was being spent on them and improve predictability. There were actually four choices available to us for consideration: stop estimating; time slice estimation activities separately from value-added committed work delivery; isolate estimation with a specialist role of "estimator"; or develop a hybrid system of passing a specialist estimator role around from one team member to another with a fixed cadence, such as weekly. Consider each of these approaches in turn ...

To stop estimating altogether is the most radical choice. It requires that we introduce a service level agreement. This gives back wasted capacity, but it requires a new agreement, a new contract, with the customers. It is the boldest choice.

The time-slicing approach of allotting estimating, prioritizing, and planning into a fixed time period and then task switching between customer-valued work and such planning is the approach used in the Agile software development lifecycle methodology Scrum. To have made such an approach work at XIT, Dragos would have needed to allocate eight days per month for estimating and planning and then spend the remainder of the month coding and testing. This approach would have improved predictability and helped dramatically with customer satisfaction, but it did nothing to address the approximately one-third of capacity being sucked away by estimation effort.

- The choice of assigning a specialist could also have worked quite nicely in this case. Dragos could have informed the local manager at TCS in Hyderabad that one of the developers and one of the testers were to be permanently assigned to analysis and design in order to provide estimates. A simple policy change! This would have prevented the other two developers and two testers from being disrupted and resulted in significant on-time delivery improvement. However, it would also have made it abundantly clear that one-third of capacity was being used for estimating.

- The option of passing the estimation responsibility around from one team member to another, on a weekly basis, might have been more acceptable to the team than assigning a specialist, but it still didn't recover the capacity being wasted on estimation.

Only the choice to stop estimating altogether freed up capacity. Whereas customers were unhappy about unpredictable, unreliable delivery and broken promises, they were also unhappy about lead times. Lead times were growing because demand exceeded capability to supply. As a consequence, they needed to produce more. Recovering a third of capacity was a means to produce more and directly address the growing backlog and lengthening lead times. It presented an interesting trade-off: In exchange for replacing individual estimates and delivery date promises with a service level agreement (SLA), 50 percent more work would be completed, and there was some chance that the growing backlog could be tamed. With long delivery times brought under control, product managers and sponsoring customer departments like HR would likely find it fit-for-purpose.

Choosing not to estimate as part of the changes made at XIT Sustaining Engineering was a choice made because of specific circumstances, and it was a choice made while considering three other options. Any of the other options was possible and viable and would have contributed to fixing a significant issue with customer satisfaction. Regardless of which choice we had made, we would still have been using a kanban system. This story would still have represented the prototype for what developed into the Kanban Method.

In the early days, Kanban was often cited as the "no estimates" method. This created some fear and trepidation amongst a traditional project management audience, while raising tribal hackles in the Scrum[9] community, which had ritualized their Planning Poker and other estimation techniques. Choosing whether to estimate or not should always be a consideration for the policies that define a class of service. The risks associated with work should always determine whether it is better to proceed with what you know or delay to gather additional information before making a commitment. A request for an estimate is a request for information speculating about the cost or time required to complete a piece of work. This information may be useful for risk management in some situations, whereas in others, it makes little difference to the good governance of the entity and can therefore by avoided. With XIT, their customers were used to consuming IT services defined by service level agreements (SLAs). As a consequence, Dragos was in a position to make his customers a straightforward offer to trade: "If we switch to an SLA with a defined lead time expectation, in return, we will deliver to you around 50 percent more completed requests each year."

Limit Work-in-Progress

Dragos also decided to limit work-in-progress and pull work from an input buffer as current work was completed. The input buffer was sized to anticipate the maximum delivery rate within the one-week period between replenishment meetings; that is, it was just big enough to ensure that the developers were never starving for work and consequently never idle. He chose to limit WIP in development to one request per developer and to use a similar rule for testers. As the Personal Software Process (PSP) already recommended this practice, it was, in fact, the policy already in use. He inserted a small buffer between development and test to receive the PTCs and to smooth the flow of work between development and test, as shown in Figure 3.1. This approach of using a buffer to smooth out variability in size and effort is discussed in volume 2, *Implementing Kanban*. The buffer was arbitrarily sized at 5. We didn't know how big to make it, so we guessed and decided to empirically adjust its size as we observed how it worked. If a large batch of PTCs arrived,

---

9. Scrum is an example of a generic class of prescriptive processes known as Agile software development methodologies. In software engineering, a methodology is defined as a description of a process workflow, together with a defined set of roles to be played and the responsibilities those roles carry in executing the work. Software engineering methodologies describe which role performs which function, who they collaborate with, who carries responsibility and accountability, and how work is handed off from one individual, team, or group of collaborators to the next. Often, methodologies have specific and detailed guidance on techniques to be used for specific activities. Scrum is often described as a process framework because its definition and prescriptive activities are not exhaustive. Scrum needs to be augmented with other practices to become a complete methodology. Hence, what is defined is referred to as merely a framework—a skeleton or frame onto which a full process definition can be hung.

it is likely the buffer would overflow, stalling upstream development work. Developers would have to wait until the testers cleared the batch of PTCs—and kanbans became free in the buffer—to allow finished development work to flow forward.

> **Note:** This is a policy choice. One change request per developer at any given time is a policy. It can be modified later. Thinking of a service as a set of policies is a key element of the Kanban Method.

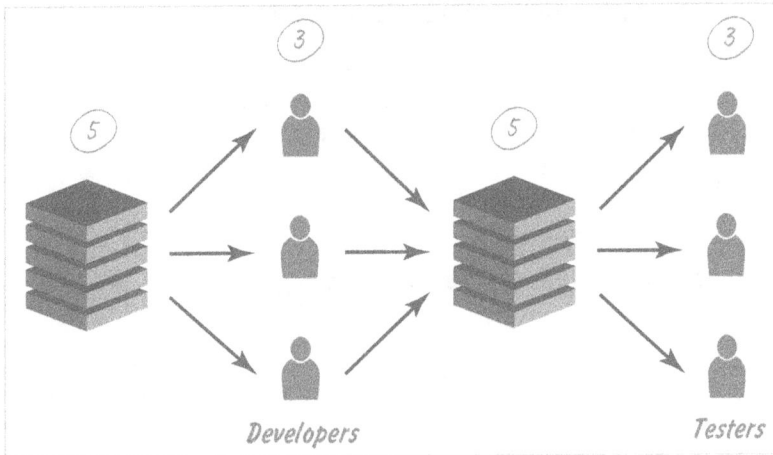

Figure 3.1 A kanban system for the Sustaining Engineering workflow

No Planning

Dragos wanted to abandon the monthly planning meeting and replace it with a more frequent meeting to replenish the kanban system. There would be no more Gantt charts and no more early commitment to everything in the plan. The backlog of requests would remain uncommitted until an item was pulled into the kanban system at the replenishment meeting by consensus among the four product managers and Dragos as program manager.

Dragos had to think about the cadence for interacting with the product managers. A weekly meeting to replenish the kanban system seemed feasible. It was planned as a conference call; the topic of the meeting would be the simple replenishment from the backlog, to empty slots—free kanban—in the input buffer. In a typical week there might be three slots free in that buffer. So, the discussion would center around the question, "Which three items from the backlog would you most like started next for delivery within twenty-five days?" It's a simple question, and it should facilitate a short meeting.

Dragos wanted to offer a guaranteed delivery time of twenty-five days from commitment—the point when a request was accepted into the kanban system and placed in its input buffer. This twenty-five-day service guarantee was considerably greater than the eleven days of average engineering time required to complete the job. The statistical outliers required around thirty days, but he anticipated very few of them; twenty-five days sounded attractive, especially compared to the existing lead time of around 140 days. He expected to hit that target with regularity, building trust with product managers and their customers as he went.

So traditional planning with a Gantt chart, with anticipated start and end dates for each request, and therefore specific promised delivery dates for each item, was to be discarded and replaced with a simple service level agreement with a twenty-five-day or less service level guarantee on lead time from commitment to delivery.

Sitting in Dragos's office, we had an understanding of the problems and a design for a solution. We looked at each other; Dragos was giggling,

> "So, our proposal is that we're going to stop estimating, and stop planning, and ask them to trust that this will magically result in everything being delivered within thirty days?"

> "Yes! Do you think they will go for that?"

> "No. Probably not!"

It was going to take more than a strong logical argument to get people on board.

Who might object and why?

Let's consider each of the changes in turn and think about how the proposal might be received in isolation.

First, we propose to stop estimating. Developers and testers find estimation disruptive, and it impacts their ability to do good, high-quality work. Also, they are professionally qualified in software development and testing; they have degrees and certifications in this subject. No one ever asked them to study, sit an exam, or acquire a certification in estimation. An ability to estimate is not core to their identity or how they derive their professional pride or self-esteem. If we tell the team in Hyderabad that we no longer require them to make estimates, they will celebrate.

Next, there is the program manager who facilitates making the plans and owns the plan constructed in a Microsoft Project Gantt chart. If we tell the program manager that estimates will no longer be produced and that Gantt charts are no longer required, there is likely to be some resistance. It is highly likely that the program manager has a self-image as a project manager, and many such people in that position are members of professional organizations such as the PMI[10] and hold credentials and qualifications such as the PMP,[11] for which they had studied and passed an exam. To suggest that we remove the practice of planning and producing a Gantt chart from these people would likely be interpreted as an attack on their identity, a show of disrespect, and an indication that their skills and, hence, they personally were no longer valued. However, in this case, the program manager was Dragos, the former Olympic athlete, stuntman, bodyguard, and psychiatric hospital

---

10. Project Management Institute

11. Project Management Professional

manager. He wasn't vested in any of this professional project manager identity. And so we got lucky—Dragos was the change agent—he was the instigator, not someone objecting and being obstructive. Had this not been the case, it could all have died there and then. Perhaps we wouldn't have Kanban as a management method adopted globally? Perhaps there would never have been a first edition of this book, or any other book on the topic?

Lastly, we have the product managers. Their role had three main aspects to it: managing the budget on behalf of their customer and business owners; assisting customers to elaborate requirements and performing business analysis; and providing good governance over the budget by building business cases and prioritizing the work based on optimizing the return on investment.[12] The equation used was as follows

$$ROI = \frac{\text{Business Value}}{\text{Cost}}$$

$$\text{Cost} = \text{hourly rate} \times \text{estimated engineering hours}$$

Without an estimate, there would be no value for the denominator in the ROI equation, and consequently, it would be impossible to calculate. Stopping estimation denied the product managers the ability to complete their business cases and to perform their prioritization function by stack ranking requests by ROI.[13] And this is a key reason, why we believed "they" would not go for it.

Would they go for a kanban system?

Our second proposal was to implement a kanban system to pull work from an uncommitted backlog. Rather than making early commitment, we intended to defer commitment.

In this case, the developers and testers are unmoved and unaffected by the change. So, we wouldn't expect any resistance. And once again, Dragos was the program manager and the change agent. However, this was a change for the product managers and their customers in each respective business unit. They were used to being given firm plans within a couple of weeks of submitting a request. However, they were also used to the idea that the plan was worth nothing and that the Sustaining Engineering team never delivered anything when promised.

Our approach to this was first to show them the data on abandoned and discarded requests. Only 52 percent of requests were ever delivered. Why commit to all of them when 48 percent of them never make it into production? This technique has proven powerful and persuasive in many implementations since then. It is particularly persuasive

---

12. This method of prioritization intended to maximize return on investment is described in the *Project Management Body of Knowledge*, published by the Project Management Institute, and it is widely adopted globally as the standard way to prioritize professional services and knowledge worker activities.

13. Note: This was usually performed in an Excel spreadsheet using the column sort function. ROI was simply a ratio achieved by dividing two numbers. Business value, it was assumed, could be reduced to a simple dollar amount. This is actually standard practice in product and project management.

when you direct that those affected do the data mining and discover for themselves just how many of their requests are never implemented. Sometimes it is necessary to put a definition, an explicit policy on "abandoned." What does it mean to be abandoned? If a request is older than six months, or twelve months, or thirteen months, or two years, then is it abandoned? Where is the organization's tolerance and threshold for "If we haven't gotten to it yet, we probably never will."? When you make this data explicit, it becomes hugely powerful.

The change to a pull system would be coupled with the adoption of a service level agreement, effectively aggregating delivery risk across all requests rather than making fragile, individual commitments based on speculation. The business units were used to consuming other IT services defined by a contract, a service level agreement, including guarantees on delivery lead times. So, in this case, we were asking them to switch modes and see this work differently. Rather than a series of mini-projects, instead they should view it as a continuous service. This argument appeared to work and raised little objection. Things had been broken for so long, why not try this alternative, yet familiar approach?

Lastly, we proposed to stop planning. Once again, this made little to no difference to the developers and testers. They were used to picking up their work from a sequence defined in a project plan. Instead, they would pick up their work from a buffer, defined in their existing tracking tool, Product Studio. And once again, the program manager was Dragos, so no resistance from him. What about the product managers? They were being asked to attend a weekly replenishment meeting rather than a monthly planning meeting. Other aspects of planning that they owned, such as preparing business cases and producing a prioritized backlog, would be unaffected, assuming we could resolve the ROI calculation conflict.

Actually, the planning meetings were long and laborious, with a large plotted Gantt chart on the table being marked up in pencil. These meetings weren't anyone's idea of fun, and they took many hours. A short, fifteen- to twenty-minute call once per week sounded like significant relief, assuming everything else worked effectively and they continued to look professional, competent, and effective in their roles.

Finally, we needed to consider Dragos's upline managers. What did they think?

By all accounts, Dragos's immediate manager had misgivings and was fearful of the consequences. The next two layers up simply died laughing, "You're going to stop planning and stop estimating and everything will be fine???" Once, they'd sobered up a bit, though, they were able to reason about it, "This service has been broken for a long time. A succession of former managers has been unable to fix it. Moving it offshore didn't fix it, either. This sounds utterly crazy, but we put you in the job to make changes. If these are the crazy changes you want to make, then at least we should give them a try." So, senior management were prepared to hold their breaths and wait and see.

However, there was still the issue of how to enable the product managers to continue making their business cases and prioritization decisions without an estimate. The solution to this was the spark of genius that, together with Dragos's diplomatic skills and personality, were to enable the first kanban system implementation at Microsoft.

Shuttle Diplomacy

Dragos arranged to visit each of the product managers in their offices individually, and then their immediate manager. He wanted to get each of them onboard with our proposal without peer group influence or social pressure causing them to close ranks and conservatively stick to their existing modus operandi. If he could get them onboard individually, then he'd hold a group meeting for the official kickoff of the change initiative and the rollout of the kanban system.

Dragos brought the basics: a sketch of the workflow and the proposed kanban system, Figure 3.2, together with a description of the replenishment meeting and the chart showing the distribution of engineering effort for requests over the past year (previously shown in Figure 2.5 and repeated here for your convenience as Figure 3.3).

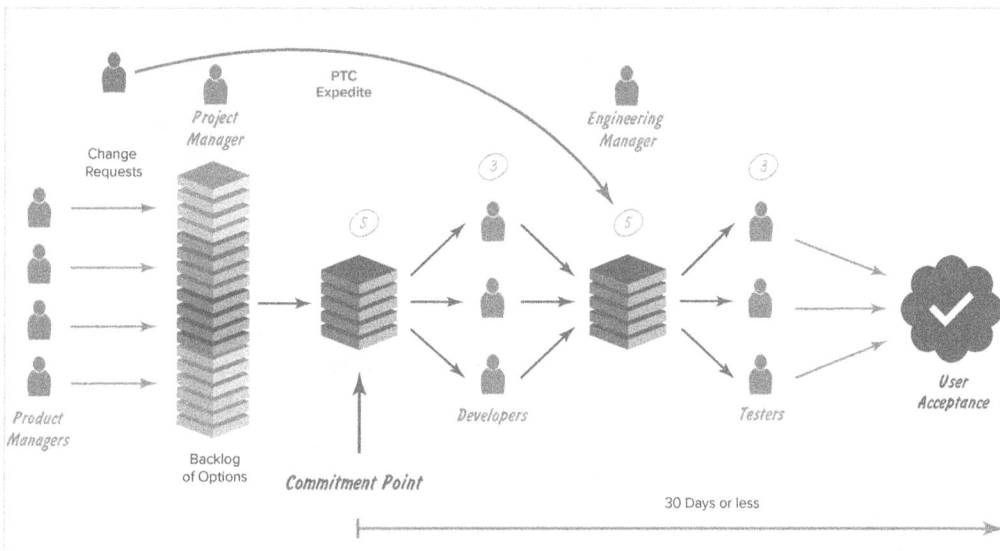

Figure 3.2 The full solution proposed for the XIT Sustaining Engineering workflow

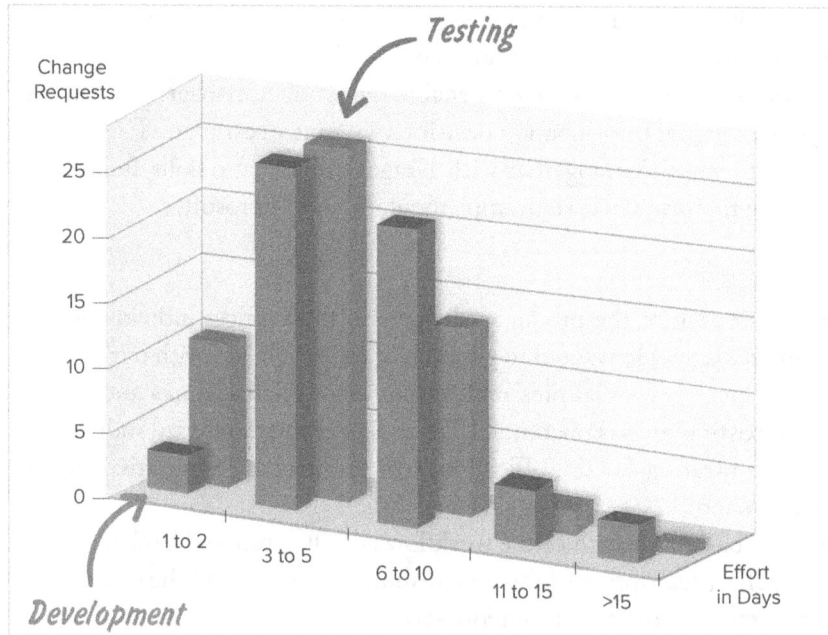

Figure 3.3 Histogram showing actual development and testing time per change request

Dragos showed each product manager that the distribution of effort was within a relatively narrow range: Most requests fell within the range of three to ten days of development and testing, with a mean of just under six. Given the volume of requests and that we fully expected this volume to increase dramatically, Dragos suggested that it was reasonable to replace a specific, deterministic—though still speculative—estimate with an average extracted from recent historical data based on actual hours spent. An average of actual hours spent is a fact, whereas an estimate for any individual item is merely speculation.

$$ROI = \frac{\text{Business Value}}{\text{Average Cost}}$$

Essentially, if the product managers were willing to accept that cost varied within a tight range and effectively ignore this variation, all the other benefits of improved productivity and predictability could be enabled. We weren't asking them to change anything about their own jobs or how they worked. Their identity, self-esteem, social status, respect within the organization, and professionalism weren't being questioned or threatened in any way. Instead, we were asking them simply to accept average cost as a fact and its value as good enough to enable them to make effective prioritization decisions.

Actually, this technique works well when there is significant asymmetry in the problem. When all business values significantly outweigh any cost incurred, the outcome of a stack ranking of the ratios is not very sensitive to variation in the cost. Cost can effectively be ignored. Where cost estimates have true value is when this asymmetry doesn't exist, and costs are actually relatively close to the payoff labeled "business value." Ironically, this condition of relatively symmetric payoff and cost is quite common in IT systems for shared services and back-office functions such as finance and human resources. So, estimates of project costs are important when governing an IT portfolio for back-office systems. However, with system maintenance and sustaining engineering teams, small requests often have a huge impact—such as deploying the tax tables for the new fiscal year—and hence the asymmetric payoff requirement is most certainly met in this case. In 2004, however, we weren't that sophisticated, and neither were the product managers. They all bought the argument and agreed.

The game was on! Kanban was green-lit for deployment at Microsoft's XIT Sustaining Engineering department. It was October 2004.

Implementing Changes

So, the changes were enacted. Dragos had their instance of Product Studio instrumented using stored procedures in its database to enforce the kanban system's WIP limits. It would signal the ability to pull work when there were free slots, and database triggers would send automated emails. He cancelled the monthly planning meetings and scheduled weekly conference calls to replenish the kanban system. New work requests were no longer sent to Hyderabad for estimation.

It began to work. Requests were processed and released to production. Delivery times on new commitments were met within the twenty-five-day promise. The weekly meeting worked smoothly, and the input buffer was replenished each week. Gradually, XIT Sustaining Engineering began to build trust with the product managers. By the first quarter of 2005, customers began to see requests deployed to production quickly and within the promised SLA.

Evolutionary Relics

An evolutionary relic is something left behind by evolution that no longer serves any purpose but, for which there isn't a mechanism to remove it: Biologists call them vestigial organs. Humans have several vestigial organs: Our coccyx bone on the end of our spine is the obviated connector for a tail, and our appendix is left over from an herbivore species from which we evolved into modern humans. There is some argument that our gallbladder may be a similar relic. It seems we aren't quite sure what it is for, but just like our appendix, if it goes wrong it can be rather serious and life-threatening. Evolutionary processes leave behind artifacts and behaviors that are hard to explain and serve no purpose.

Paul Klipp, an American from Chicago, living in Krakow, Poland, and founder of Kanbanery, a kanban software tool, explained the concept on his blog[14] on March 6, 2013, after attending the Kanban Coaching Professional (KCP) Masterclass.

---

14. http://paulklipp.com/blog/evolutionary-change-better-than-a-kick-in-the-nuts/ used with kind permission

I'll enlist the help of a giraffe. His name's Fred.

Like all mammals, Fred has a larynx controlled by his brain, and Fred is the product of evolutionary change. Fred's larynx is just inches from his brain, because it's at the top of his neck and so is his head, as you might expect. Fred's getting impatient, so he bellows for me to get to the damn point. His brain got impatient first and sent the impulse to bellow right down that nerve to his larynx. A short trip? Not really. Silly evolution decided that the best way to route a nerve between one thing on the top of his neck and another thing on the top of his neck was to wrap it around his aorta first.

Fred's brain
Fred's larynx
Fred's heart

Here's Fred's laryngeal nerve; it's about 15 feet long.

Now, who decided THAT was a good idea?

That's where evolution gets you. It's a hell of a lot better than being a fish, at least from the giraffe's point of view, but the evolutionary path from fish to giraffe has some constraints. The corresponding nerve in a fish makes sense. A straight line between a fish's brain and its gills passes the heart, so the nerve crossing behind the heart is pretty sensible. Here's the thing, though. Evolution starts with the existing processes and systems and changes them incrementally. Re-routing a nerve is not an incremental change; it's a revolutionary change.

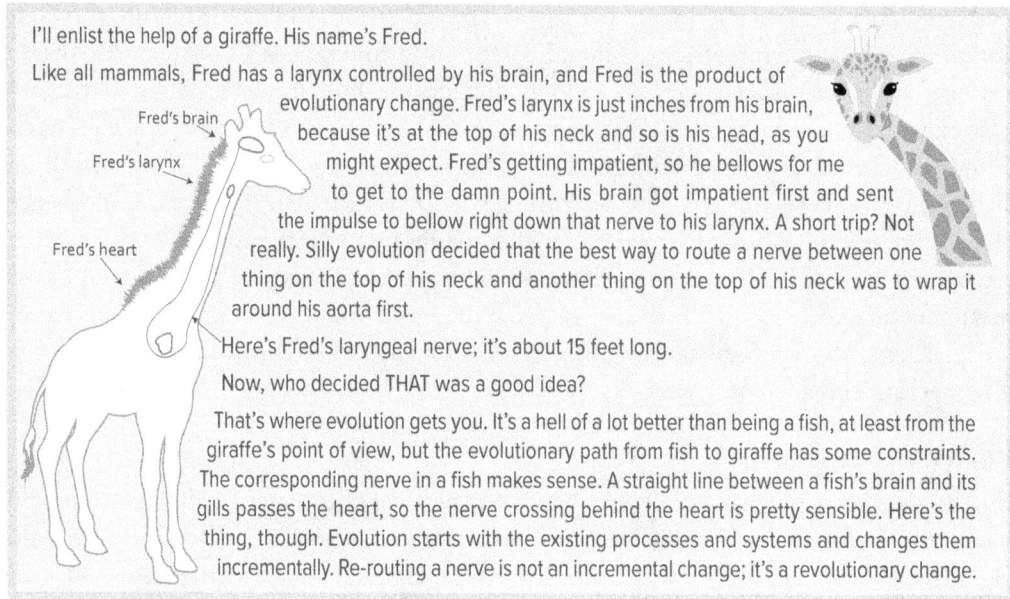

If true evolutionary processes are at work, awkward solutions evolve over time. You wouldn't intentionally design a nerve to run down a giraffe's neck and back up again. It isn't logical or efficient, but it is robust. The concept of "survival of the fittest" in evolutionary biology indicates that a solution was fit for its environment. For us, we seek to evolve fit-for-purpose business services. Being fit-for-purpose is likely to indicate an ability to survive and continue. The ability to respond to stress in the environment and continuously evolve to remain fit for the ever-changing environment is what Nassim Nicholas Taleb labeled antifragility. Kanban as a means to wire a business with evolutionary DNA provides a means to antifragility.

Meanwhile, if you walk into a company and everything is too neat and tidy, and all of the processes are efficient, lean and devoid of artifacts or activities that seem to serve little purpose, have little or no value, and may have been obviated by circumstances of new techniques, then you are looking at a designed environment—the process consultants have been in, designed a new process, installed it (perhaps through the use of positional power), and then left. These designed solutions are fragile, and the businesses using them are likely to be fragile. Why?

When resistance is overcome using positional power, it is highly likely that employees are acquiescing, while their behavior is actually passive-aggressive. When management's attention is turned to something else, they'll quietly revert to the old ways. They had no ownership in the changes, and they haven't internalized them. It hasn't become "how we do things around here." It isn't part of their identity individually or as a group.

Evolutionary change is robust, while designed and managed change is fragile. The Kanban Method is fundamentally based in the belief that wiring a modern business with the means and mechanisms for evolutionary change—to have the evolutionary DNA that is able to respond to a changing environment and changing expectations, to evolve and remain fit-for-purpose—provides the resilience and robustness that organizations need to survive and thrive. The Kanban Method provides the operational means to maintain a fit-for-purpose organization that is built for survival.

Prioritization: The Evolutionary Relic at XIT Sustaining Engineering

Returning to Dragos's story, recall that he wasn't asking the product managers to change how they were working: they would continue to make business cases and calculate ROI using their own estimate of business value and the IT engineers' estimate of costs. They would continue to column-sort their spreadsheet to provide a stack ranking of change requests from highest to lowest ROI. They had accepted the viability of using an average value for cost, effectively meaning that all change requests were ranked by their business value.

Meanwhile, they'd bought into deferred commitment; they had no objection to switching from the time-consuming monthly planning meeting to weekly replenishment meetings.

However, as soon as we start with Kanban, their prioritization work instantly becomes an evolutionary relic. Why? At a replenishment conference call, they may be asked to "pick the one item you'd most like for delivery within the next twenty-five days." This isn't a request for the item with the highest return on investment; rather, it is a request based on urgency or timeliness. An item deemed important, but perhaps not with the highest ROI, is likely to get selected. For example, "Support Puerto Rican address format for employee information within the employee records application." This isn't a request with a particularly high ROI. How do we even calculate the "business value" of such a request and put a dollar value on it? Even if we do cook up some method to devise a number, it's unlikely to produce the highest ROI. And yet, it will get picked! Why? Because the Puerto Rican office is planned to open at the end of next month and we will need to be able to record details of the new employees hired for that office.

Kanban replenishment questions are about urgency and timeliness, not return on investment. Product managers may have a spreadsheet filled with data, stack ranked and column-sorted by the ROI calculation, but when it comes to the crunch, and making a decision during the replenishment conference call, they'll find that the item they most want for delivery in twenty-five days or less is most likely not the item in row two of the spreadsheet. Consistently, they'll find that their top picks are coming from further down their list.

Their efforts to prioritize have been obviated. They are now selecting items from their pool of available options based on the cost of delay of those items. What is the cost of delaying the new Puerto Rican office because we can't onboard the employees? Cost of delay isn't the same as return on investment. Effectively, both methods are now in use: cost of delay and return on investment. For selection purposes, one has obviated the other. The practice of calculating return on investment continues, yet it has become an evolutionary relic.

This approach of leaving (some) existing practices in place while introducing new practices to replace them is a standard technique in applying evolutionary change. Effectively, ROI and cost of delay are two species for the purpose of prioritization or, to use less ambiguous and more precise language, sequencing of work. These two methods, the incumbent and the insurgent, will compete, just as two biological species compete to be fittest for the environment.

An evolutionary-change approach in the workplace is used to reduce resistance. We don't ask individuals or groups to give up a particular practice, such as prioritization based on ROI, because "we don't think they'll go for that!" Instead, we let the old practice continue while we introduce into the environment the practice that we anticipate becoming its successor. If the new practice, such as selecting and sequencing work based on urgency or timeliness through an understanding of cost of delay, is successful, then we expect the older practice of sequencing based on return on investment to die out. However, with stubborn environments, often where there is a tightly knit, highly cohesive social group with a conservative, risk-averse culture, or where a practice is particularly strongly associated with the identity, self-esteem, ego, or social group status of individuals, the old practice tends to stick around. Although the old practice has been obviated and no longer plays a role in successful outcomes, it survives. Time spent on it is wasteful overhead, and yet it remains. It's an evolutionary relic—something hard to explain left behind by evolutionary change in action.

The Abandonment Guillotine

What happens to items that are never sufficiently important or sufficiently urgent—items that simply never get selected in a replenishment meeting? A few months after the initial roll out, Dragos recognized that a new policy was needed: Any item older than six months was purged from the backlog—closed as "abandoned." There was now an explicit abandonment guillotine policy. If it wasn't important enough to be selected within six months of its arrival, it could be assumed that it wasn't important at all. Such policies work on the assumption that every request for work has a mother—the person who initiated the request. If the mother truly cares and the item is truly important, it will be resubmitted.

Dropping Estimation: One Further Obstacle to Adoption

Recall from the previous chapter that there was a governance rule concerning operational versus capital expenditure: Work requiring more than fifteen days of engineering must be routed to a project in the major project portfolio and accounted for as capital expense. If we don't estimate, how would we know whether something is too big or not?

This was solved by accepting that some such items might sneak through. We refer to this as the "credit card security" solution. Credit card companies don't try to completely prevent fraudulent transactions on credit cards—doing so would make it so challenging to use a credit card that many of us would revert to cash or find other modern means of making payments. Instead, credit card companies build an allowance for fraud into their business models and pay for it using the margin they charge the merchant for accepting credit card payments. When any of us use our credit cards, a percentage, often 3–4.5 percent, is retained by the card company and not paid out to the merchant. Some of this money is insurance against fraudulent transactions. Credit card companies worked out that it was better to risk some bad things happening rather than completely eliminate the possibility, which would shrink their business significantly.

Historical data told us that these "too big" items were less than 2 percent of total requests. Hence, retaining the estimation effort to eliminate this 2 percent risk was bad economics. We were spending 30 to 40 percent of our capacity on estimation. If the governance rules on accounting were the only remaining reason to retain estimation, it was a very bad bargain—who would pay $40 to insure against a potential loss of $2? Instead, we decided to let the "too bigs" into the system and catch them later.

Developers were instructed to be alert, and if a new request they started to work on appeared to be so large that they estimated it would require greater than fifteen days of effort, they should notify their local manager. If the item was confirmed with high confidence to be too big, then it would be rerouted to the major project portfolio. The risk and cost of doing this was less than one-half of 1 percent of available capacity. It was a great tradeoff. By dropping estimates, the team gained back more than 30 percent of capacity at the risk of less than 1 percent of that capacity "wasted" by starting an item that was "too big." This new policy empowered developers to manage risk and to speak up when necessary.

> **Note:** This is a common theme in the Kanban Method. The combination of explicit policies, transparency, and visualization empowers individual team members to make their own decisions and to manage risks themselves. Management comes to trust the system because they understand that the process is made of policies. The policies are designed to manage risk and deliver customer expectations. The policies are explicit, work is tracked transparently, and all team members understand the policies and how to use them.

What happened next?

The first two changes were left to settle in for six months. A few minor changes were made during this period. As mentioned, a backlog purge policy was added; the weekly meeting with product owners also disappeared. The process was running so smoothly that Dragos had the Product Studio tool modified so it would send him an email when a slot became available in the input buffer. He would then alert the product owners via email, who would decide among themselves who should pick next. A choice would be made, and a request from the backlog was replenished into the kanban system within two hours of a slot becoming available.

Looking for Further Improvements

Dragos began looking for further improvement opportunities. He'd been studying historical data for his team's tester productivity and comparing it with other teams within the XIT services at TCS in Hyderabad. He suspected that his testers were not heavily loaded and had a lot of slack capacity. By implication, the developers were a significant bottleneck. He decided to visit the team in India. He sat in their office for two weeks, observing. On his return, he instructed TCS to make a headcount-allocation change. He reduced the test team from three to two and added another developer (Figure 4.6). This resulted in a near-linear increase in productivity: the throughput for that quarter rose from forty-five to fifty-six change requests completed and deployed to production. He had correctly assessed that there was slack capacity in test. Two testers were sufficient to handle the work coming from four developers.

Microsoft's fiscal year was ending in June 2005. Dale Christian, the general manager, and his leadership team were noticing the significant improvement in productivity and the consistency of delivery from the XIT Sustaining Engineering team. Finally, management trusted in Dragos and the techniques he was employing. My phone rang:

> "David, it's Dragos. Dale loves what we are doing. He sees the results. They've been reviewing the annual budgets and I've been told I can hire two more people. So, I'm about to email TCS and ask them for two more developers."

> "I don't think I would do that," I replied.

> "No?"

> "I think there is a danger that two testers can't handle the workload arriving from six developers. I think, based on my admittedly only superficial understanding of your data, that two more developers will turn testing into a bottleneck and you won't get all the benefits you are expecting. My gut feeling is that you should go for one of each—a new ratio of five developers to three testers. I think that will work."

I was using my knowledge of the Theory of Constraints and bottlenecks to give this advice. As mentioned previously, this approach is explained in more depth in volume 2, *Implementing Kanban*.

Dragos added one more developer and one additional tester in July 2005. By the winter of 2006, the results were significant, as shown in Figures 3.6 and 3.7.

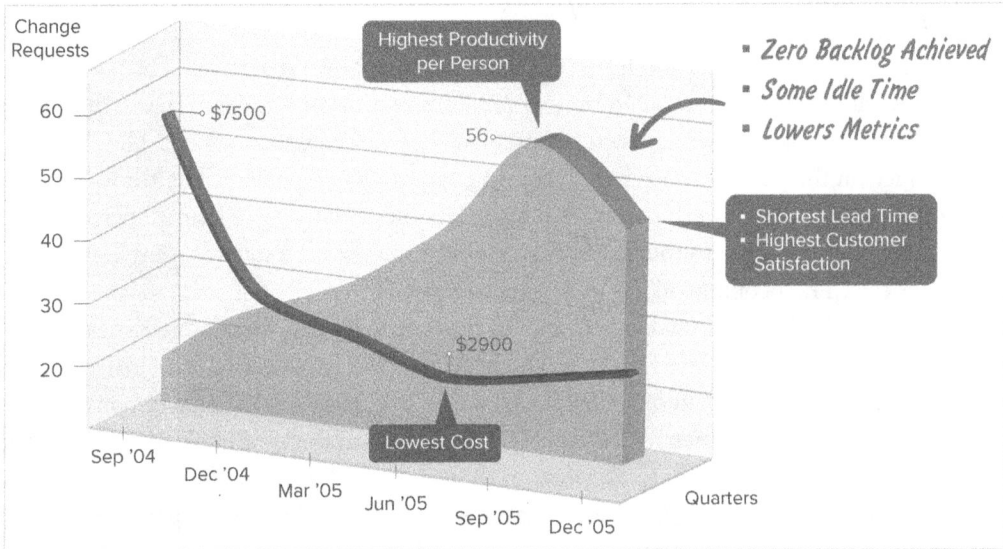

Figure 3.6 XIT Sustaining Engineering delivery rate of change requests versus cost per change request

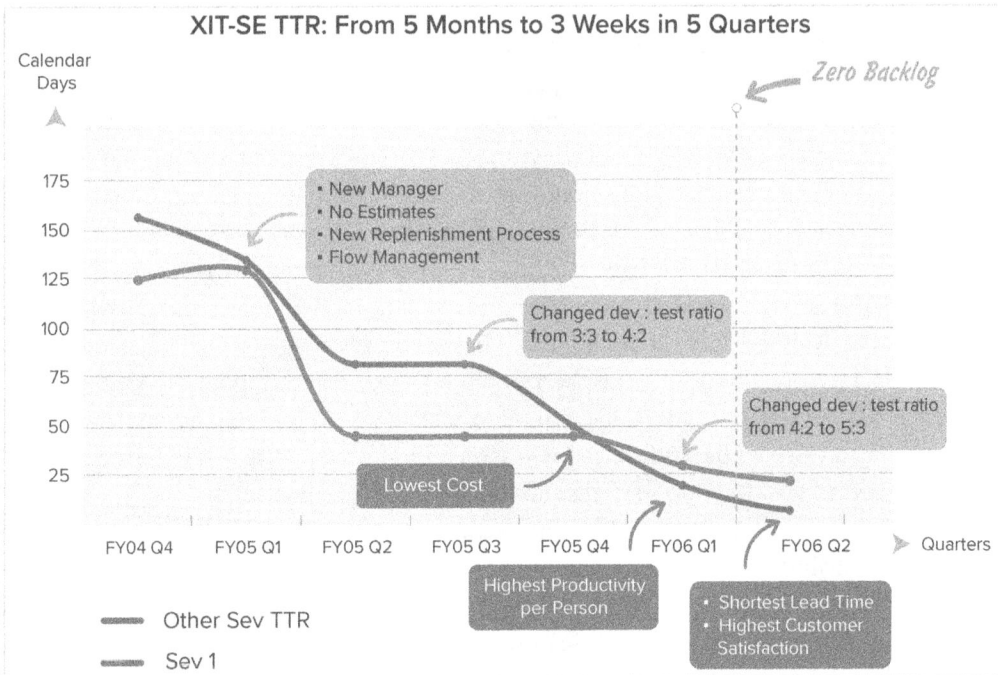

Figure 3.7 XIT Sustaining Engineering time to resolve (TTR), or average lead time per change request from commitment to deployment

Results

The additional capacity was enough to increase throughput beyond demand. The result? The backlog was eliminated entirely on November 22, 2005. By this time, the team had reduced the lead time to an average of fourteen days against an eleven-day engineering time. The due-date performance on the twenty-five-day delivery time target was 98 percent. The throughput of requests had risen more than threefold, lead times had dropped by more than 90 percent, and reliability improved almost as much. No changes were made to the software development or testing process. The people working in Hyderabad were unaware of any significant change. The PSP/TSP method was unchanged, and all the corporate governance, process, and vendor-contract requirements were fully met. The team won the Engineering Excellence Award at Microsoft for the second half of 2005. Dragos was rewarded with additional responsibilities, and the day-to-day management of the team was handed off to the local line manager in India, who relocated to the United States to work on the Microsoft campus in Seattle.

These improvements came about in part because of the incredible personality and managerial skills of Dragos Dumitriu, but the basic elements of Kanban were key enablers: mapping the workflow, analyzing the flow of work, setting WIP limits, and implementing a pull system. Without the flow paradigm and the kanban approach of limiting WIP, the performance gains would not have been possible. Kanban enabled incremental changes with low political risk and low resistance to change.

By the fall of 2005, I began reporting the results initially via my blog, then at a Theory of Constraints conference in Barcelona, and again in the winter of 2006 at a Lean Product Development conference in Chicago. That year, others began to pick up the concept and replicate it. Most notably, Eric Landes at automotive component manufacturer Robert Bosch's South Bend, Indiana, facility, where he replicated our results with a team doing software maintenance of intranet applications. At the time, what we referred to as "a virtual kanban system for software engineering" was gaining broader adoption and awareness. It wasn't yet the full Kanban Method as we know it today. That wouldn't emerge until 2007, as described in Chapter 4. However, the results at Robert Bosch validated that the approach was replicable and that it did not require leadership from a former Olympian and trained bodyguard like Dragos for it to work. What it did need was someone, like the figure in the cartoon on the cover, prepared to say, "Let's do something about it" and take some action.

The XIT story shows how a WIP-limited pull system was implemented on a geographically distributed IT service using offshore resources and an outsource vendor. The implementation was facilitated with a software tracking tool. There was no visual board, and many of the more sophisticated features of the Kanban Method described later in this book had yet to emerge. Nevertheless, what manager could ignore the possibility of similar results? Adopting a "start with what you do now" evolutionary approach to change using kanban systems was clearly an approach worthy of reporting publicly for others to replicate and something that we both wanted to try again!

Takeaways

- The first known and documented virtual kanban system for intangible goods and professional services work was implemented with the XIT Sustaining Engineering software maintenance team at Microsoft, starting in 2004.

- It was implemented with an offshore team at TCS in Hyderabad, India.

- It used an electronic tracking tool called Product Studio.

- Work-in-progress (WIP) limits were imposed using policy and so-called triggers in the database. Sometimes this is referred to as a virtual kanban system, as no physical signal cards (kanbans) were used. There was no visual board.

- The process was described as an explicit set of policies.

- The first Kanban implementation at Microsoft improved productivity more than threefold, dropped lead times by 92 percent, and improved on-time delivery to 98 percent.

- Policies affect performance. Some policies set by senior executives must be treated as constraints and can't be easily changed.

- Stopping estimating was a choice. Other options were available: Isolate the disruption of estimation in a time slice; isolate the disruption of estimation using a specialist estimator role; or combine the other two options with a specialist role that rotated among team members. These other options were rejected because they improved predictability but didn't recover any wasted capacity.

- Input buffer sizing should anticipate the maximum anticipated delivery rate in the time period between replenishment meetings. The goal is to ensure that the first activity in the workflow is never starved of new work to start, and its workers are consequently never idle.

- A buffer between two activities may be desirable to smooth flow due to variability in local cycle times in each activity.

- Sometimes initial buffer sizing can be arbitrary. From empirical observation over ten years, a WIP of five is often a good starting position. From there, the size can be adjusted up or down as observations are made about how heavily it is used.

- Abandoning traditional planning and switching to deferred commitment and a service level agreement for delivery expectations is a core concept in Kanban. Traditional planning often encourages early commitment, leading to replanning and rescheduling work. This can be a source of dissatisfaction for customers.

- Once a proposed kanban system is designed for a service delivery workflow, it is important to anticipate who might object to making the switch.

- Generally, people who will raise objections are those who have their identity, self-esteem, or social status anchored in the skillful execution of a specific practice. A suggestion to change or remove such a practice will likely meet with resistance.
- Shuttle diplomacy—meeting with individual stakeholders to explain the proposed changes—is highly recommended. Get individuals to agree and commit to the changes before holding a group kickoff meeting.
- Evolutionary change processes can leave behind strange historical artifacts or obviated practices. Generically, we refer to these as evolutionary relics. In biology, they are called vestigial organs.
- An approach to changing a practice that will invoke resistance and defensiveness from some individuals is to introduce the new, hopefully replacement, practice alongside the incumbent and let the two techniques "compete" for fitness. The fitter alternative will survive and thrive, while the other may wither and its use may die out.
- The use of a time limit on submitted requests is useful to prevent backlogs growing to a large and unmanageable size. The time limits are known as Abandonment Guillotines.
- Sometimes there may be an advantage to letting something bad happen, so long as it can be detected quickly and its impact minimized. This may be more desirable than spending a lot of effort up front to prevent the bad thing from happening at all. Risk avoidance can be more expensive and wasteful than risk mitigation. This concept is referred to in Kanban guidance as the Credit Card Fraud Solution.
- When adding people or automation equipment to a service delivery workflow and kanban system, it is important to consider where to place the additions so as to avoid accidentally creating a bottleneck that limits the value and improvement produced.

4

Down with Democracy!

Kanban Magic: Emergent, Evolutionary, Social,
Cultural, and Process Change

"I still haven't found what I'm looking for!" I was explaining why I
was leaving Microsoft to take up the position as Senior Director
of Software Engineering at Corbis in downtown Seattle—a company
wholly owned by Bill Gates. While the use of a kanban system at
Microsoft had shown great promise, by the summer of 2006 I was still
looking for a means to enable evolutionary change. I was still looking for
that "process of ongoing improvement" I had envisaged in 2002, while
writing *Agile Management for Software Engineering*. The role at Corbis
would provide me with an organization of around 150 people in IT in
which I could test out my latest ideas. As I explained in an interview
with Microsoft's MSDN Channel 9, I wasn't going to install an Agile
method at Corbis; instead, I was going to start where they were and let
improvements evolve.

While the Theory of Constraints community talk about POOGIs,
the Japanese have a word in their language that captures the concept:
kaizen, which literally means "continuous improvement." A workplace
culture where the entire workforce is focused on continually improving
quality, productivity, and customer satisfaction is known as a "kaizen
culture." Kaizen is primarily associated with Toyota. Very few businesses
have actually achieved a true kaizen culture. When trying to understand
the concept and where we might have observed it, we could point to
Formula 1 motor racing teams as an example.

One of my more recent clients, a Chinese telecom equipment and consumer electronics company, has an executive vice president who aspires for the firm to be seen as "the Toyota of the 21st century"—the archetypical kaizen company in professional services and knowledge worker industries. Companies like Toyota have almost 100 percent employee participation in their improvement programs. On average, each employee gets one improvement suggestion implemented every year as part of ongoing improvement. There are very few businesses that can emulate or better this claim.

In the software development world, the Software Engineering Institute (SEI) of Carnegie Mellon University defined the highest level of their Capability Maturity Model Integration (CMMI)[15] as Optimizing. The CMMI model was originally inspired by Toyota in the 1980s. Maturity Level 5, the highest level, was intended to describe an organization that could emulate Toyota's culture within systems engineering and software companies, with a primary focus on government system procurement and space and defense industry contractors. Around 1990, no such firm existed. CMM[16] Maturity Level 5 was aspirational. The model built from level 1 through 5 to describe the behavior of organizations that actually existed and provide a road map to move toward a more Toyota-style culture. The execution against this goal over the past thirty years has fallen short. The CMMI literature said little about company culture or how to affect it; instead, it focused on practices with an assumption that if you prescribe it, people and companies will adopt it. More recently, the Kanban community has developed its own maturity model, described in our recent book, *Kanban Maturity Model: A Map to Organizational Agility, Resilience, and Reinvention*, written by Teodora Bozheva and me. This new maturity model came about by observing the vast variety of Kanban implementations around the world over the past decade and capturing many case studies. We began to observe patterns in Kanban implementations and styles of kanban boards. We were able to correlate these patterns to observable levels of organizational maturity. As a consequence, the new Kanban Maturity Model has emerged to provide a road map to deeper implementation and higher levels of organizational maturity. Unlike the CMMI, Kanban has a lot to say about culture, change management, and the psychological and sociological reasons that people and organizations resist change. In the five years since its launch, the Kanban Maturity Model has demonstrated considerable success in helping more organizations achieve a kaizen culture, improve their business agility, and enable them to offer continually fit-for-purpose products and services in the markets they choose to serve.

---

15. Since publication of the 1st edition, Carnegie Mellon has divested the CMMI business from its Software Engineering Institute (SEI). It is now an independent business, the CMMI Institute, and was acquired by the nonprofit training business ISACA. However, the maturity model was defined during the prior period when the CMMI was part of Carnegie Mellon University, in Pittsburgh, Pennsylvania.

16. (as it was known at the time)

Kaizen Culture

To understand why it is so hard to achieve a kaizen culture, we must first understand what such a culture would look like. Only then can we discuss why we might want to achieve it in our organization and what its benefits might be.

In kaizen culture, the workforce is empowered. Individuals feel free to take action, free to do the right thing. They spontaneously swarm on problems, discuss options, and implement fixes and improvements. In a kaizen culture, the workforce is without fear. To enable a kaizen culture, managers must be tolerant of failure. If experimentation and innovation are done in alignment with organizational values, and with the goal of process or performance improvement, it should be encouraged: Not every change will produce an improvement; not every experiment will be a success. However, if there is fear of punishment for making changes or failed experiments, there will be no spontaneous initiatives to make improvements. Kaizen cannot exist where there is a culture of fear. In a kaizen culture, individuals are free (within some limits, usually explicitly defined policy constraints) to self-organize around the work they do and how they do it. Visual controls and signals are evident, and work tasks are generally volunteered for ("pulled") rather than assigned by a supervisor. A kaizen culture involves a high level of collaboration and a collegial atmosphere where everyone looks out for the performance of the organization and the business and does so altruistically, putting the common good before their own personal benefit. A kaizen culture focuses on systems-level thinking while making local improvements that enhance overall performance.

A kaizen culture has a high level of social capital. It is a highly trusting culture where individuals, regardless of their position in the decision-making hierarchy of the business, respect one another and each person's contribution. High-trust cultures tend to have flatter structures than lower-trust cultures. It is the degree of empowerment that enables a flatter structure to work effectively. Hence, achieving a kaizen culture may enable elimination of wasteful layers of management and reduce coordination costs as a result.

Many aspects of a kaizen culture are in opposition to established cultural and social norms in modern Western culture. In the West, we are brought up to be competitive. Our school systems encourage competition in academics and in athletics. Even our team sports tend to encourage the development of heroes and teams built around one or two exceptionally talented players. The social norm is to focus on the individual first and to rely on outstanding individuals to deliver victory or to save us from peril. It is little wonder that we struggle in the workplace to encourage collegial behavior and systems-level thinking and cooperation.

Kanban Accelerates Organizational Maturity and Capability

The Kanban Method is designed to minimize the initial impact of changes and reduce resistance to adopting change. Adopting Kanban should change the culture of your organization and help it mature. If the adoption is done correctly, the organization will morph into one that adopts change readily and becomes good at implementing changes and process improvements.

When you first implement Kanban, you are seeking to optimize existing processes and change the organizational culture rather than switch out existing processes for others that may provide dramatic economic improvements. This has led to the criticism[17] that Kanban merely optimizes something that needs to be changed. However, there is now considerable empirical evidence[18] that Kanban accelerates achieving high levels of organizational maturity and capability.

When you choose to use Kanban as a method to drive change in your organization, you are subscribing to the view that it is better to optimize what already exists, because that is easier and faster and will meet with less resistance than running a managed and engineered formal change initiative with a defined and designed future process, often labeled and named as a business goal. It is common for such bold change initiatives to be given dramatic and heroic-sounding names, though one of my more recent clients, more by accident than design, had named theirs the "Butterfly Project" because one way to get funding for an improvement idea was to label it as "part of the butterfly." Kaizen cultures don't have improvement programs and defined, named projects with budgets and goals. A kaizen culture just is! Kaizen cultures get on with improvement like business as usual. Driving improvement is everyone's business, every day.

While senior managers and consulting firms are addicted to defined and managed change initiatives—a concept introduced and perfected by McKinsey & Company—such radical change is actually harder, costlier, and less likely to stick than incrementally improving what already exists. Also, understand that the collaborative-game aspects of Kanban will contribute to a significant shift in your corporate culture and its maturity. This shift will later enable much more significant changes, again with lower resistance, than if you were to try to make those changes immediately. Adopting Kanban is an investment in the long-term capability, maturity, and culture of your organization. It is not intended as a quick fix.

Together, we can better understand the benefits and pitfalls of a kaizen culture through our second Kanban story, spanning from 2006 through 2008 at the stock photography and intellectual property rights business Corbis, based in downtown Seattle. The implementation spanned most of the approximately 150-person IT department in a global company with offices in New York, London, Paris, Hong Kong, and Tokyo, and around 1,300 employees in total. I had taken the role of Senior Director of Software Engineering, reporting to the Chief Information Officer.

---

17. Larman, Craig and Bas Vodde. *Scaling Lean & Agile Development: Thinking and Organizational Tools for Large-Scale Scrum.* Boston: Addison Wesley, 2008.

18. Willeke, Eric, with David J Anderson and Eric Landes (editors). *Proceedings of the Lean & Kanban 2009 Conference.* Bloomington, IN: Wordclay, 2009.

Corbis: The Not So Rapid, Unresponsive Team That Didn't Exist

When I introduced a kanban system at Corbis, in 2006, I did so for many of the mechanical benefits that were demonstrated with Microsoft XIT in 2004 through 2006 (as described in Chapters 2 and 3). The initial application was the same—IT applications software maintenance. I was not anticipating a significant cultural shift or a significant shift in organizational maturity. I did not expect what we now know as the Kanban Method to evolve from this work.

Back in 2006, it wasn't yet clear that kanban systems were a natural fit for IT services work, but a kanban system form seemed to fit well with the functional problems of maintenance work. I didn't go to Corbis with the intent of "doing Kanban." I did go there with the intent of improving customer satisfaction with the application development department within the IT division. It was a happy coincidence that the first problem to be addressed was the lack of predictability concerning delivery from IT software maintenance.

Background and Culture

In 2006, Corbis was a privately held business, with around 1,300 employees worldwide. It controlled the digital rights to many fascinating works of art as well as representing approximately 3,000 professional photographers, licensing their work for use by publishers and advertisers. It was the second-largest stock photography company in the world. There were other lines of business, too, the most notable of which was the rights-licensing business that controlled the rights, on behalf of families, estates, and management firms, to the images and names of personalities and celebrities. The IT department consisted of about 150 people split between software engineering and network operations/systems maintenance. The workforce was augmented from time to time with contract staff to work on major projects. At its peak in 2007, the software engineering department employed 105 people, including thirty-five contingent staff in Seattle and another thirty at a vendor in Chennai, India. Most of the testing was performed by this team in Chennai. There was a very traditional approach to project management: Everything was planned in a dependency tree of tasks and rolled up by a program-management office. It was a company with a conservative culture, in what had been a relatively conservative and slow-moving industry, prior to the arrival of so-called penny stock vendors offering images for license at prices as low as $1, and later the arrival of web services such as Flickr that encouraged any amateur digital photographer to share their photographs with a global audience. While strategically there was some urgency to change in order to compete with these disruptive influences, Corbis was remarkably slow moving, and its IT group exhibited very low organizational maturity, offering poor quality and predictability. It was a source of much frustration to many business owners across the company. At the time I arrived in September of 2006, the approach to project management and the software engineering lifecycle were conservative and traditional.

The IT department maintained a diverse set of approximately thirty systems. Some were fairly typical accounting and human-resource systems; others were exotic, and at times esoteric, applications for the digital rights–management industry. There was a wide range of technologies, software platforms, and languages supported. The company had grown by acquisition, and consequently there was a heterogenous set of technologies and some duplication, such as two accounting systems. The workforce was incredibly loyal; many people in the IT department had been with the company more than eight years, some with as many as fifteen years of service. Not bad for a company that was about seventeen years old. The existing software development process was a traditional, waterfall-style software development lifecycle (SDLC) that had been institutionalized over the years with the creation of a business analysis department, a systems analysis department, a development department, and an offshore testing department, all managed by a department manager on my staff in Seattle. Within these departments there were many specialists, such as analysts whose background was accounting and whose specialty was financial applications. Some developers were also specialists, for example, J.D. Edwards's programmers, who maintained the J.D. Edwards accounting software.

None of this was ideal; but it was what it was. Things were the way they were. When I joined the company, there was some expectation and trepidation that I would impose an Agile software development methodology and use my positional power to force people to change their behavior. Although this might have worked, it would have been brutal, and the impact during the transition would have been severe. I was afraid of making things worse, afraid that projects would grind to a halt while new training was provided and staff adapted to new ways of working. I was also afraid of losing key personnel, knowing that the workforce was fragile due to the excessive levels of specialization. I chose to introduce a kanban system, get the systems-maintenance work back on track, and see what happened from there.

The Need for a Software Maintenance Function

Software maintenance (or "RRT" for "Rapid Response Team," as it was known internally) had been funded by the executive committee with an additional ten percent budget for the software engineering department. As you might guess from reading Chapter 2, this was operating expense budget and therefore affected the profit and loss statement directly. Ten percent was as much as the executive team were willing to charge to operating expenses in any given year. This equated to five additional people—the full-time development staff being approximately fifty. These people were hired in the spring of 2006, prior to my arrival. Due to the diverse nature of the systems involved and the existing high degree of specialization within the department, it was decided that, unlike the XIT Sustaining Engineering team at Microsoft, a dedicated team of five people to do maintenance work would not be a good solution. So, five additional people were added to the general staff pool: one project manager, one analyst, one developer, and two testers. This introduced an additional complication: It was necessary, from a governance perspective, to show that the additional five people were actually doing maintenance work and hadn't simply been sucked into the major-project portfolio. However, on any given day, those five people could be any of the approximately fifty-five people from the application development group. RRT was a role to be played rather than a permanent assignment.

One solution would have been for everyone to complete complex timesheets to show that 10 percent of the team's hours were being spent on maintenance activities. This would have been highly intrusive and would have added an administrative burden to the department, but it is typical of how middle managers respond to such a challenge. Another approach was to introduce a kanban system: We would demonstrate, through a combination of a WIP limit and transparency onto workflow, that five people were always assigned to software maintenance.

An expectation had been set, when arguing the business case for the funding, that a maintenance team would enable Corbis to make incremental releases to IT systems every two weeks. Major projects had typically involved major system updates and new systems releases once every three months. But as the business matured and the nature of these systems became more complex, this cadence of quarterly major releases had become intermittent. In addition, some of the existing systems were effectively end-of-life and were really due for complete replacement. Legacy-system replacement is a major challenge, and it typically involves long projects with a large staff until a parity of functionality is reached and the old system can be turned off as the new one is brought online.

So, the maintenance releases were the one area within Corbis IT where kanban could enable some form of business agility.

Small Projects for Maintenance Wasn't Working

The existing system to deliver maintenance releases, the system that was broken, was to schedule a series of short, two-week-long projects. This fitted well within the existing paradigm for the project management group and their traditional approach to their work based upon the Project Management Institute's (PMI) *Project Management Body of Knowledge*. However, it carried significant overhead in both coordination costs and transaction costs. When I first arrived, the negotiation of scope for a two-week release cycle was taking about three weeks. The front-end transaction costs of a release were greater than the value-added work. It was taking about six weeks to get a two-week release out the door.

Implementing Change

It was clear before making any changes that the status quo was unacceptable. The current system was unable to deliver the required level of business agility. System maintenance gave us an ideal opportunity to introduce change. Maintenance work was generally not mission critical. It was nevertheless highly visible. Business owners had direct input to prioritization, and their choices were highly tactical and important to short-term business goals. System maintenance was something everyone cared about and wanted to work effectively. And finally, there was a compelling reason to make changes: Everyone was unhappy with the existing system. The developers, testers, and analysts were all aggravated with the time wasted negotiating scope, and the business people were hugely dissatisfied with the results. The only people relatively happy with the status quo were the project managers and their group manager, who were working in accordance with their professional credential, the Project Management Professional (or PMP), granted to them for passing an exam from the PMI. They didn't take responsibility for project failure, nor were they ever held accountable. Their role was to crank the handle on the bureaucracy and point the finger of blame at the department managers when expectations were not met. If there was going to be resistance, we would expect it to come from the project managers. Everyone else was eager for change.

Working with Rick Garber, the lead of the process improvement team, we designed a kanban system with scheduled biweekly releases, planned for 1:00 p.m. every second Wednesday, and with scheduled replenishment meetings with the business owners, set at 10:00 a.m. every Monday. Effectively, we set a weekly replenishment cadence and a biweekly delivery cadence. The frequency of these events was determined through collaborative discussions with business owners and downstream partners in IT operations and based on the transaction and coordination costs of the activities. A few other changes were made. We introduced an Engineering Ready (input) buffer with a WIP limit of five items and then added WIP limits throughout the lifecycle of analysis, development, build, and system test. Acceptance test, staging, and ready for production were left unlimited, as they were not considered capacity constrained and were, to some extent, outside our immediate political control.

Primary Effects of the Changes

The effects of introducing a kanban system were, at one level, unsurprising, yet at another, they were quite remarkable. We started to make releases every two weeks. After about three iterations, these were happening without incident. The quality was good and there was little to no need for emergency fixes when the new code went live in production. The overhead for scheduling and planning releases had dropped dramatically, and the bickering between the development teams and the project management office had almost completely disappeared. So kanban had delivered on its basic promise. We were putting out high-quality releases very regularly, with a minimum of management overhead. Transaction and coordination costs of a release had been drastically reduced. RRT was getting more work done and we were delivering that work to the customer more often.

It was the secondary effects of a kanban system that were all the more remarkable.

Corbis: Lackluster Results Bring Emergent Cultural Change

Unanticipated Effects of Introducing Kanban

It was mid-January 2007; we'd just made our third delivery under the new kanban system. Darren Davis, a development team manager and the lead responsible and accountable for the operation of RRT and its kanban system, a role we now call "service delivery manager," was sitting across from my desk at our regular weekly one-to-one meeting. "It's working," he told me. "We're getting releases out. People like it. Customers are happier. However, we are just not seeing the productivity improvements you achieved with XIT at Microsoft."

"What do you suggest?"

"I'd like to put a board on the wall and visualize the process. Let everyone see what is going on."

This technique of visualizing software development work using a board with index cards stuck to it, where each card represented an individual request for functionality, had started several years earlier, amongst a community known as the Extreme Programmers. They called these boards "card walls." Darren was asking permission to use an Extreme Programming card wall, but have it model and visualize our RRT workflow, with each ticket on the board representing a change request.

I agreed that it was a good idea, and Darren proceeded to set it up. He started holding morning standup meetings around the board for fifteen minutes at 9:30 a.m. each day. The physical board had a huge psychological effect compared to anything we got from the electronic tracking tool we used at Microsoft and had adopted at Corbis. By attending the standup each day, team members were exposed to a sort of time-lapse photography of the flow of work across the board. Blocked work items were marked with pink tickets, and the team became much more focused on issue resolution and maintaining flow. Productivity jumped dramatically.

With the flow of work now visible on the board, I started to pay attention to the workings of the process. As a result, I made some changes to the board. My team of managers came to understand the changes I was making and why I was making them, and by March, they were making changes themselves. In turn, their team members—the individual developers, testers, and analysts—started to see and understand how things worked. By early summer, everyone on the team felt empowered to suggest a change, and we'd observed the spontaneous affiliation of (often cross-functional) groups of individuals who would discuss process problems and challenges and make changes as they saw appropriate. Typically, they would inform the management chain after the fact. This is seeking for-giveness behavior rather than delaying waiting for permission. Seeking forgiveness allows us to move faster, to move with agility. It is a behavior associated with greater social capital. It's evidence of a higher trust culture. What had emerged over approximately six months was a kaizen culture in our application development group. As anyone from a pool of around fifty-five staff could play a role in RRT on any given week, we now had an entire department that felt empowered. Fear had been removed. My staff now took pride in their professionalism and in their achievements, and they were clearly motivated to do even better.

Sociological Change

Since the Corbis experience, there have been other, similar reports from around the world. Rob Hathaway, at the time a consultant with the firm Indigo Blue, in London, was the first to truly replicate these cultural change results with IPC Media, a publishing firm that owns a number of famous periodicals such as *New Musical Express* (NME). When I visited IPC, I saw five uniquely different kanban boards, supporting thirty to fifty people. The cultural changes were sufficiently impressive that it was the director of marketing who took the stage at the UK Lean conference in London that autumn to present their case study.

The fact that others had been able to replicate the sociological effects of Kanban observed at Corbis made me believe that there was a causation and that the outcome was neither a coincidence nor a direct effect of my personal involvement. It was validating proof that neither David nor Dragos needed to be in the room in order for the approach to work!

I've thought a lot about what brought about these sociological changes. Extreme programmers and others using Agile software development methodologies had the benefit of visual boards for almost a decade, and yet kaizen culture had generally not emerged. This is evidenced by the observation that their processes seldom vary far from the prescribed definitions in the textbooks. If evolutionary change was happening in uniquely different organizations, we'd have expected divergence from textbook definitions and a lot of diversity in workflows. However, that hadn't happened. On the other hand, organizations following the Kanban Method appeared to achieve a kaizen culture. Organizations adding Kanban to their existing adoption of Agile software development found a significant improvement in social capital amongst team members. It made me ask, "Why could this be?"

My conclusion was that Kanban provided transparency into the work, but also into the process (or workflow). More than just a To Do, Doing, Done visualization of work state, Kanban provided visibility into how the work flows through a series of value-adding activities. It provides service level insights beyond the narrow, local concerns of a single team performing a single function. Kanban enabled every stakeholder to see the effects of his or her actions or inactions. If an item was blocked and someone was capable of unblocking it, Kanban showed this. Perhaps there was an ambiguous requirement. Typically, the subject-matter expert who could resolve the ambiguity might expect to receive an email with a request for a meeting. After a follow-up call, they would arrange a meeting to suit their diary, perhaps three weeks later. With Kanban and the visibility it provided, the subject-matter expert would realize the effect of inaction, prioritize a meeting, perhaps rearranging his or her schedule to make it happen, and avoid further delay.

In addition to the visibility into process flow, work-in-progress limits also force challenging interactions to happen sooner and more often. It isn't easy to ignore a blocked item and simply work on something else. Kanban encouraged behavior known as "stop the line" or *Andon* from Toyota's *Jidoka* system for quality control. It encouraged swarming behavior across the workflow. When people from different functional areas and with different job titles swarm on a problem and collaborate to find a solution, thus maintaining the flow of work and improving system-level performance, the level of social capital and team trust increases. With higher levels of trust engendered through improved collaboration, fear is eliminated from the organization.

Work-in-progress limits coupled with classes of service (explained in volume 2, *Implementing Kanban*) also empower individuals to make selection, sequencing, and scheduling decisions on their own, without management supervision or direction. Empowerment improves the level of social capital by demonstrating that superiors trust subordinates to make high-quality decisions on their own. Managers are freed from supervising individual contributors and can focus their mental energy on other things, such as process performance, risk management, staff development, and improved customer and employee satisfaction.

Kanban greatly enhances the level of social capital across an organization. The improved levels of trust and the elimination of fear encourage collaborative innovation and problem solving. The net effect is the rapid emergence of a kaizen culture and a high maturity organization capable of meeting customer expectations, managing risk, and delivering superior economic results.

Viral Spread of Collaboration

Kanban clearly improved the atmosphere in the software engineering department at Corbis, but it was the results beyond that group that were the most remarkable. How the viral spread of Kanban improved collaboration around the company is worth reporting and analyzing.

Corbis: Viral Spread of Cultural Change

Each Monday morning at 10:00 a.m., Diana Kolomiyets, the project manager responsible for coordinating the IT systems maintenance releases, would convene the RRT replenishment meeting. The business attendees were typically vice presidents. They were officers of the company who ran a business unit and reported to a senior vice president on the executive committee. Corbis was still small enough, at only 1,300 people, that it made sense for such a high-ranking manager to attend the weekly meeting. Equally, the tactical choices being made were often sufficiently important that they really needed the direction of a vice president to influence a good choice.

Usually, each attendee received an email on the Friday prior to the meeting. It would state something like, "We anticipate that there will be two slots free in the queue next week. Please examine your backlog items and select candidates for discussion at Monday's meeting."

Bargaining

In the first few weeks of the new process, some of the attendees would come with an expectation of negotiating. They might say, "I know there is only one slot free, but I have two small ones, can you just do them both?" This bargaining was rarely tolerated. The other attendees at the meeting ensured that everyone played by the rules. They might reply, "How do I know they are small? Should I take you at your word?" or counter with, "I've got two small ones too. Why shouldn't I get my favorites selected?" I refer to this as the "Bargaining Period," because they weren't in denial of the WIP limit and capacity constraints of our workflow. However, they believed those were elastic and could be bent a little. They were prepared to probe this elasticity by negotiating.

The behavior we observed of other attendees, the business customers at RRT replenishment meetings, kept everyone accountable. They were not prepared to tolerate this bargaining behavior or negotiate any elasticity in the concept of a unit of work—something to which a kanban would be assigned. This peer group enforced good behavior, and the IT group as service provider no longer had to push back or point to the formal agreement as a defense. The WIP limit held firm. This would happen again and again, as you will see in several of the Corbis anecdotes related later in this book.

Observing the behavior of the customer group—the replenishment meeting attendees at Corbis—led to some general guidance. I believe that it is better to aggregate demand from several customers together and deliver it via a bigger shared services group than it is to have a small team provide service to a single customer. It's worth noting that this represents the antithesis of conventional guidance in the Agile software development community, where a single product owner per delivery team (or pipeline) is preferred. Instead, with Kanban, when there is a larger shared service, servicing multiple customers, those customers have a vested and shared interest to ensure that everyone plays fairly. Bullying and manipulative behavior are dampened. Consequently, the service delivery workflow gains relief from what has historically been a source of overburdening.

Other evidence supporting the use of larger shared-service groups emerged later in the story of the Kanban Method. This led directly to more advanced kanban board design patterns, which enabled enhanced labor pool liquidity, as seen at Maturity Level 5 in the Kanban Maturity Model. One firm from southern Florida described the process as "putting the departments back together," having previously broken them up into several small Agile teams. It proved much more effective to have shared-service kanban systems supported by twenty-four to thirty-six people rather than four to six small independent teams.

Democracy

After about six weeks, and coincidentally around the same time that the development team introduced the use of the physical whiteboard, the replenishment meeting attendees introduced a democratic voting system. They spontaneously volunteered this, as they'd become tired of bickering with each other. The bargaining at the meeting was wasting time. It took a few iterations to refine the voting system for the new democratic system, but it settled down to an agreement where each attendee got one vote for each free slot—each free kanban—in the queue that week. At the beginning of the meeting, each member would propose a small number of candidates for selection. As time went by, proposing requests got more sophisticated; some people came with PowerPoint slides, others with spreadsheets that laid out a business case. Later we heard that some members were lobbying their colleagues by taking them to lunch. Deals were being done: "If I vote for your choice this week, will you vote for my choice next week?" Underlying the new democratic system of prioritization, the level of collaboration between business units at the vice-president level was growing. Although we didn't realize it at the time, the level of social capital across the whole firm was growing. When leaders of business units start collaborating, so, it seems, do the people within their organizations. They follow the lead from their leader. Collaborative behavior coupled with visibility and transparency breeds more collaborative behavior. I refer to this period as the "Democracy Period."

Down with Democracy

Democracy was all very well, but after a further four months, it seemed that democracy hadn't always elected the best candidates. A considerable effort was expended implementing an e-commerce feature for the Eastern European market—apparently there was a huge market for high-quality stock photography amongst ad agencies in the Ukrainian capital of Kiev. The business case looked stellar, but its candidacy was suspect from the beginning, and some had questioned the quality of the market research data. After several attempts, this feature had been selected and was duly implemented. It was one of the larger features processed through the RRT system. It involved a new system capability to list a country catalog in a foreign currency. Corbis had no interest in managing the currency volatility risk in Ukrainian Grivna, and instead, prices were to be listed in Polish zloty. This involved an underlying change to the system architecture, and many people got involved. The Ukrainian country catalog change request got widely noticed. Two months after launch, our Director of Business Intelligence did some data mining on the revenue generated. It was a fraction of what had been promised in the original business case, and the estimated payback period against the effort expended was calculated at nineteen years. Due to the transparency that Kanban offered us, many stakeholders became aware of this, and there was discussion about how precious capacity had been wasted on this choice when a better choice might have been made instead. The Ukrainian country catalog request effectively ended the democracy period.

Collaboration

What replaced it was quite remarkable. Bear in mind that the selection committee at replenishment meetings consisted mostly of vice president–level employees and officers of the company. They had broad visibility into aspects of the business that many of us were unaware of. Therefore, at the beginning of the meeting, they would ask, "Diana, what is the current lead time for delivery?" She might reply, "Currently we are averaging forty-four days into production." And then they asked a simple question: "What is the most important tactical business initiative in this company forty-four days out from now?" There might be some discussion, but typically there was swift agreement. "Oh, that'll be our European marketing campaign launching at the conference in Cannes." "Great! Which items in the backlog are required to support the Cannes event?" A quick search might produce a list of six items. "So, there are three slots free this week. Let's pick three from the six and we'll get to the others next week." There was very little debate. There was no bargaining or negotiation. The meeting was over in about twenty minutes. I've come to refer to this as the "Collaboration Period." It represents the highest level of social capital and trust between business units that was achieved during my time as Senior Director for Software Engineering at Corbis.

What we had lived through represented a company-wide improvement in organizational maturity. From bargaining to democracy to cross–business unit collaboration and company-wide alignment, we'd seen a progression in behavior that would map from Level 1 or 2 through to Level 4 or 5 on the Kanban Maturity Model (see Chapter 13). Behavior had moved from a self-serving, "What's in it for me?" as an executive or "What's in it for us?" as a business unit to an altruistic "How can I help the wider business achieve the best possible results?" and a belief that what is good for the business as a whole will hopefully reflect back upon me, as a vice president, and my business unit. Many times, I've referred to this anecdote as one example of "Kanban Magic"—the amazing ability of Kanban to generate secondary social or psychological benefits without direct intervention. Kanban replenishment meetings for shared services have a direct impact on selection and sequencing of work, and they have an oblique influence on social capital, collaboration, trust, alignment, and congruent action. Achieving deep levels of organizational maturity seems to happen better through oblique approaches rather than a direct approach of setting a goal to achieve a level, as evidenced by the Kanban and CMMI case studies that emerged around 2010. Deeper maturity achieved faster was observed from adopting Kanban rather than creating a direct goal of achieving a given CMMI maturity level.

Cultural Change is Perhaps the Biggest Benefit of Kanban

It was interesting to see this cultural change emerge and to see how it affected the wider company as employees followed the lead of their vice presidents and started to collaborate more with their colleagues from other business units. This change was sufficiently profound that Gary Shenk, newly promoted to CEO in 2007, called me to his office to ask if I had any explanation. He told me that he had observed a new level of collaboration and collegial spirit in the senior ranks of the company and that formerly antagonistic business units seemed to be getting along a lot better. He suggested that the RRT process had something to do with it and asked if I had any explanation for it. While I am sure that I wasn't as articulate back then, I convinced him that our kanban system had greatly enhanced collaboration and, with that, the level of social capital among everyone involved.

The cultural side effects of Kanban were quite unexpected and in many ways counter-intuitive. He asked, "Why aren't we doing all our major projects this way?" Why indeed? Thus, with senior executive enthusiasm, we set about implementing Kanban in the major-project portfolio. We did this because Kanban had enabled a kaizen culture, and that cultural change was so desirable that the cost of changing the many mechanics of prioritization, scheduling, reporting, and delivery that would result from implementing Kanban across our entire portfolio was considered a price worth paying.

Takeaways

- *Kaizen* means "continuous improvement."
- A kaizen culture is one in which individuals feel empowered, act without fear, affiliate spontaneously, collaborate, and innovate.
- A kaizen culture has a high degree of social capital and trust among individuals, regardless of their level in the corporate hierarchy.
- Kanban provides transparency on both the work and the process through which the work flows.
- Transparency of process allows all stakeholders to see the effects of their actions or inactions.
- Individuals are more likely to give of their time and collaborate when they can see the effect it will have.
- Kanban WIP limits enable "stop the line" behavior.
- Kanban WIP limits encourage swarming to resolve problems.
- Increased collaboration from swarming on problems and interaction with external stakeholders raises the level of social capital within the team and the trust among team members.
- Kanban WIP limits and classes of service empower individuals to pull work and make prioritization and scheduling decisions without supervision or direction from a superior.
- Increased levels of empowerment increase social capital and trust among workers and managers.
- Collaborative behavior can spread virally.
- Individuals will take their lead from senior managers. Collegial, collaborative behavior among senior leaders will affect the behavior of the whole workforce.

5

Obliquity!

More Kanban Magic: Operations Review

*O*bliquity,[19] by the economist and writer for the *Financial Times*, John Kay, describes how businesses counterintuitively do better when they don't try to approach their goals directly. While the book carries many examples, a recurring thread in his narrative retells the demise of Britain's largest and most successful manufacturing company, Imperial Chemical Industries (ICI). ICI had a portfolio of businesses similar in nature to America's DuPont: a collection of chemical and pharmaceutical businesses, perhaps best known for its paint brand Dulux and its pharmaceutical division that developed beta-blockers. The portfolio included Alfred Nobel's explosives business, The Nobel's Explosive Company, where my father worked for thirty-two years until his retirement at age fifty-seven in 1992. The local factory adjacent to my hometown had employed over 35,000 people at its peak. By then it had shrunk to around 700. So, Kay's story had a personal element for me.

ICI no longer exists! It went from one of the two richest companies in the United Kingdom to oblivion in just fifteen years: While other divisions were divested or closed, the butt of the firm survived as a specialist manufacturer of scents and perfumes. If you've enjoyed the scent in your hotel elevator recently, it may well have been an ICI product you were experiencing. Kay believes the humiliation of ICI, the crown jewel of twentieth-century British industry, was both understandable and avoidable. He traces the demise to two related events: the acquisition

---

19. Kay, John. *Obliquity: Why Our Goals Are Best Achieved Indirectly*. 1st ed. New York: Penguin, 2011.

of a minority shareholding by activist investor and corporate raider Lord Hanson and how the board of directors reacted to Hanson's challenges.

In 1991, Hanson acquired enough shares in ICI to challenge the board's leadership at the annual shareholder meeting. Hanson was a corporate raider, or "asset stripper." His tactic was to buy minority holdings in companies and then force the board of directors to break up the company and sell off the bits. If a conglomerate business was undervalued, its shareholder value could be instantly released by the breakup, providing a fast and profitable return for investors. Americans reading this text may be more familiar with Hanson's American equivalent Ivan Boesky. Although Hanson didn't win his challenge, ICI's board of directors, sufficiently rattled by it, chose to divest their pharmaceutical business as Zeneca (now Astra Zeneca, one of the largest drug companies in the world). This left the chemicals business, including the explosives business, with the ICI brand.

Traditionally, ICI followed a set of values and a mission statement, which in 1990 contained the key phrase "responsible application of chemistry." In other words, commercialization of chemical science was in scope regardless of the field or application. This meant that holding businesses such as The Nobel's Explosive Company was entirely congruent with their mission, and experimenting with drugs and developing a pharmaceutical portfolio was equally congruent. Following Hanson's attempted raid and breakup, the board changed the mission, in 1991, to a much more direct statement: "to be the industry leader in creating value for customers and shareholders." There was no mention of chemistry at all. Over the next five years they set about divesting more businesses and acquiring other, more profitable ones. The stock price rose accordingly, and it kept investors docile. Kay contends that ICI had lost its soul—it had lost its purpose and driving force to do cool stuff with chemistry and bring scientific innovation to commercial availability. Ten years later, in 2007, the rump of the business was acquired, and ICI ceased to exist as an independent entity. It took sixteen years to decline from the best to gone.

The title of his book, *Obliquity*, was suggested to Kay by Sir James Black, the Nobel Prize–winning chemist who discovered beta blockers while working as a researcher at ICI in the 1960s, who had come to believe that companies' goals were often best achieved without intending them. As described in Chapter 4, oblique approaches can be counterintuitive, and the results are emergent. Outcomes can be reconciled retrospectively, but action does not guarantee a certain outcome. Oblique approaches require some act of faith, some belief in a set of values, or a vision, a mission, or a purpose. Without an explicitly defined purpose, it is hard, perhaps impossible, to pursue oblique approaches. The concept of obliquity seems to mean "Do the right thing, within the scope and bounds of our vision, mission, or purpose—our reason to exist," and "Do not expect direct or immediate returns; just accept that you have done the right thing and that eventually you believe you will be rewarded for it."

This chapter presents some more examples of obliquity in action with Kanban and examines the Kanban Magic that derives from using the operations review.[20] Operations review is designed to be used at the scale of a product unit or business unit or line of business portfolio or a large department within a large corporation, or at the entire business level for a small or medium-sized business. Operations reviews typically consider the operational effectiveness of organizational units of 100 or more people, up to perhaps 600 or 800 people. Beyond that, there would be multiple instances of such meetings within an entire business.

My first experience and exposure to an operations review was during my time at Sprint, where my boss, John Yuzdepski, instituted it for his business unit of 350 people. Yuzdepski, a former NATO military officer and air force pilot, modeled the concept on NATO Readiness Reviews—meetings that examine the readiness of armed forces and provide operational options available to politicians in times of tension or open conflict. Our operations reviews at Sprint were attended by around seventy people representing pay grades from team lead to vice president. At Corbis, in 2007, the operations review was adapted for the whole IT department of around 150 people.

Corbis: Preparing the First Operations Review

The Making of Managers

When I arrived at Corbis in September 2006, there was little to no visibility into the work coming through our software engineering department. As a management team, the group of six reporting to me were flying blind. For five months already, they'd been talking about installing the tracking software Microsoft Team Foundation Server. However, it hadn't happened yet, and there was no momentum. Toward the end of the month, at my weekly team meeting, I announced that we would hold our first operations review on the second Friday in December. I explained the concept of operations review: that each manager would present data on their departmental capability, demand, quality, and so forth, and that it was an opportunity to highlight dependency issues and problems that couldn't be solved by a single team or department.

After a day or two, I began to get individual visits from these managers. The conversation that follows is paraphrased and probably represents several original conversations, but the general idea is to show the impact as the concept and implications of operations review sank in . . .

"David, this meeting we're holding in December—do you want me to present at that meeting?"

"Yes, I do!"

---

20. Volume 2, *Implementing Kanban*, will develop and define Operations Review as one of seven Kanban Cadences, each of which provides a mechanism for feedback and improvement actions.

"Oh!"

"What would you like me to talk about?"

"It's straightforward: what does your department do? And how good are you at doing it? What demand are you seeing and where is it coming from? How well are you servicing that demand? And what is impeding you from doing better?"

"Oh, okay! Thanks."

And a day or two went by . . .

"David, the meeting in December, where you've asked me to present, what exactly did you mean? Could you give me some examples of what you expect?"

"What business are you in? What types of work does your department do? I expect you to be able to articulate that.

"Then, for each of those types of work, report: how many requests you saw in the previous month; how many you delivered; how long they took on average or as a set with a range of values; how much work you have in-progress; and how well you are meeting customer expectations.

"I expect no more than three to five slides with one chart on each slide. You'll have eight minutes to present, so about one minute per slide, plus time for a question or two or any observations."

I sketched a couple of basic charts similar to those described in detail in volume 2, *Implementing Kanban*.

"Oh, okay! Thanks."

And another day or two went by . . .

"David, the meeting in December where you've asked me to present data about my department's performance— where will I get that data?"

"Well, you could collect it manually. You are the manager: It isn't so difficult to track when work is started and finished and then from that to derive the other data needed."

The story in the sidebar, describing my first managerial job in 1991, serves as an archetype for what I expect of a manager: Bring transparency onto a problem; get data; analyze

---

The Value of Manual Data Collection

As an aside, my first true management job started in summer of 1991, after I graduated college, at a company called Rombo in the industrial "new town" development of Livingston in central Scotland, between Edinburgh and Glasgow. The name of the firm was an interesting evolutionary relic: their first product had been a plug-in ROM board for expansion firmware for some popular home computers of that era. They no longer made the ROM board and had moved on to picture, video, and sound capture devices and supporting software applications. When I joined the firm, it was five years old and employed thirty people, most of whom were in the electronics manufacturing section. The CTO and co-founder was the electronics designer, and the CEO had been the lead developer and architect, but he'd become too busy. I was hired to form a new software development team—only three developers, two of whom had attended college with me but were already hardened game developers with knowledge of several assembly languages and academic qualifications in electronics and computer systems architecture.

I was also assigned the "customer help desk" function. At the time, this was two youths approximately seventeen years old. These were school-leavers—kids who hadn't qualified for a place at a university. Youth unemployment was high in the United Kingdom during the 1980s and into the early '90s. The government had introduced a subsidy scheme with the intention of helping young people gain real workplace experience and skills. This program paid half of their, effectively minimum wage, salaries. Originally known as the Youth Opportunity Program (or YOP), it had been renamed the Youth Training Scheme (YTS) because someone on the YOP had become known in British slang as a YOPPER, and the whole program had developed a shoddy reputation. So, I had two YTS trainees on my help desk. Their job was to answer the phone when customers called with problems.

I had a chat with the more experienced of the two. Both were enthusiasts for technology. They enjoyed working at the company and they enjoyed the technology. It also seemed that they enjoyed interacting with our customers. They enjoyed the phone conversations and they were kept busy. They could describe typical problems that customers called about, and they had developed quite an expert list of causes and effects to fix customer problems. The system appeared to be working. However, what they couldn't tell me was how many problems there were, how often they occurred, or even how many phone calls they'd answered. For a "call center" it was the lowest maturity imaginable!

The leadership of the firm were concerned. Once upon a time there had been no help desk. When customers called, the founders, who were the developers, answered the calls and fixed the problems. And then there was one help-desk person. Now there were two. The demand for help-desk people appeared to be growing. There were several legitimate questions: What are these people spending their time on? Are we going to need more of them? And if so, when, and how much is it going to cost?

Flying blind, I decided that I needed visibility. So, I designed a call sheet form and printed a stack of them. I took them to my staff and explained that I wanted them to fill in a sheet for each call received. It was simple enough to fill out while they were on the call. It recorded the product SKU, the version, a description of the problem, advice given, and whether the problem was resolved satisfactorily.

At the end of each day, the stack of sheets was filed in a drawer. At the end of the month, I collected all of the sheets and took them home on a Friday evening. I spent several hours over the weekend collating them to produce a report of call volume by product and defect type. In the first month, data revealed that just one problem was producing 50 percent of our call volume. Our video capture board for the IBM PC was problematic to install.

Older readers will recall that peripherals used I/O ports assigned through a set of DIP switches on the PC motherboard. Although IBM made PCs, there were also many clone manufacturers, and there was no real standard for how I/O ports were assigned. Our product had been designed to use a port that was typically unused—but not always. This problem was driving half of our call volume. While the setup and fix were described deep inside the product manual, users were not reading the manual, or if they were, they were not finding the advice they required. In response, we designed a single sheet of paper printed with the title READ ME FIRST in large type. It described how a user could check the I/O port settings and configure their machine appropriately. The product was shipped in a sleeved box and shrink-wrapped in plastic. We inserted the READ ME sheet inside the box sleeve. On opening the product, removing the shrink wrap, and sliding the box out of its sleeve, the READ ME FIRST sheet would fall out of the box. At the end of the second month, our call volume to the help desk had halved.

the data; determine clusters of problems; develop a fix for a root cause; implement the fix; get more data; demonstrate that the fix has worked, or repeat the process and try again with an alternative fix.

Throughout my career, I've had no compunction about telling a manager reporting to me to get out on the shop floor and collect data manually.

"Hmmm."

"Maybe it would be better if we had software to do the tracking?"

"Yes, that would save you a lot of time."

"So, we should install Team Foundation Server?"

"Yes!"

"Oh, okay! Thanks."

And a day or two more went by . . .

"So, David, I've been thinking about our conversation the other day . . ."

"Yes."

"This meeting is in December, right?" I nodded. "And if the meeting is in December, you'll want us to report data for November, right?" I nodded again. "And if we need data for November, then we need Team Foundation Server installed and up and running before then, right?"

"Yes."

"So, we need it ready to go by the last week of October, and this is the last week of September. So, we have four weeks to get it installed and configured and in regular use?"

"Yes."

"But, we've spent five months already and got nowhere."

"Indeed!"

That was a little Kanban Magic—a little obliquity. At no time did I tell my management team we needed to install Team Foundation Server, nor did I set any date for its commissioning and adoption. No direct order was given or target set. When you ask someone to star in their own eight minutes of fame in front of approximately one hundred colleagues, they realize that they need something to say, and everything else stems from there.

In Nassim Taleb's concept of antifragility, essentially, his observation on evolutionary theory, there is a concept of a "stressor"—when an antifragile entity is under stress, it is provoked to mutate, to improve, or to change. Asking someone to present on a stage is a stressor. It provokes changes in the person's behavior: They will either step up their game and deliver, or they will buckle under from the stress and retract into themselves. This is a litmus test for a manager—a test of whether they have what it takes to carry the responsibility they've been assigned, and of whether they have the leadership ability to be effective in their role.

What business are you in?

In Chapter 2, one of my first questions to Dragos was "What business are you in?" I wanted to know what his department did, and more, I wanted to know if he knew what business he was in.

It's surprising how many managers I meet, to this day, who struggle to answer this most basic question: "What business are you in?" Many of them believe their role as a manager is to behave as a "dating agent," a matchmaker—given the arrival of a task for their team, their job is to match the task with the most suitable worker and send them on a date together. They also often see themselves as traffic cops, directing the flow of work: Tasks arrive, and the manager's job is to route them in the most effective and efficient manner possible. Thus, when hearing the question, "What business are you in?" their mind conjures up this weird self-image of a matchmaking traffic cop—a matrimonial consultant in uniform!

My job as their coach or mentor is to help them transition out of this identity. I need managers to see themselves as responsible and accountable for a system that performs some form(s) of work. The system consists of policies that control it. Their job is to control the policies: to know when to override; to know when to change; and to know when to escalate to a higher authority. Their job is to ensure that the system, of which they've been placed in charge, is operating and flowing smoothly. I need managers to realize that it is the system that is in their charge, not the collection of people who report to them on the organizational chart. Operations review and those eight minutes in the limelight have an oblique role to play here, too.

Once again, the following conversation is a memoir; it paraphrases what may have happened in actual fact . . .

The conversation takes place in a private, one-on-one meeting in my office. These were the opportunities my managers had to discuss how things were going, lay out their issues and challenges, and seek my help. These also grew into what we'd now view as a degenerate service delivery review (SDR) meeting—degenerate because they have just two participants, when, ideally, we'd like the entire crew from a service delivery workflow in attendance at an SDR. SDR is discussed in greater detail in volume 2, *Implementing Kanban*.

"Can you give me some advice about what I should present at the meeting?"

"Sure. What business are you in? What types of work does your department do? Who are your customers? What do they ask you for? And how many do they ask for? What is the arrival rate of demand for each type?"

"You'll also want to report your delivery rate—how many you delivered in the same time period, and your work-in-progress and how it is trending. If it is growing, what is causing that and what might be done about it?"

"You'll want to report on quality. How much rework are you doing? What is your failure demand—things that have arrived only because you didn't do them well enough the first time?

"Later on, you'll want to report on dependencies and sources of delay and perhaps your flow efficiency, but let's start with the basics: what you do; how many; how fast; and with what quality."

This process of requesting a manager to present at operations review forces them to think about the right things. No one could imagine presenting on their matchmaking or traffic conducting. So, it turns out that operations review has an oblique role to play in self-image and identity change. Without explicitly coaching it, without having to first break down the existing self-image and helping the individual accept their new one, just simply asking them to present and giving some guidance on what to present catalyzes the change.

A request to present at operations review sends a signal about what you value. Implicitly, as a leader, you are communicating how you will value the contribution of a team lead or department manager. They internalize this. It tells them how their boss will value them and, mostly, they want to feel valued by their boss. Consequently, it adjusts how they assess their own self-esteem, their own self-image, and their social status amongst their peers. Asking them to present at operations review and, as the months go by, how they perform at those reviews, reforms their self-image and self-esteem. From dating agents and traffic cops, they transform into system thinkers who understand their role is to oversee and control a system that does work. They will be judged on how effectively and efficiently that system does that work. A little more Kanban Magic—a little more obliquity.

What we do is art; you can't measure it!

The manager of my system analysis department (we'll protect his identity) was passive-aggressive about the announcement of operations review. While he was publicly and vocally all for it, privately, he made it clear to me that it didn't apply to him: Systems analysis was an art form, and you couldn't measure it. Yes, he would present at the meeting, but he wouldn't be following the same format as the other managers on the team—data and metrics weren't for him or his team, nor for that matter was the Team Foundation Server tracking software.

When December arrived, he got up for his stint at the front. He had some pretty pictures. He had some stories. His report could have been my teenage daughter retelling what happened in the latest episode of *The Bachelor*. By the time the others had finished presenting, he looked like an idiot, not just to me, or my boss, but to his peers. The following month, without any direct intervention from me, his team was tracking their work with the software, and he had a set of slides with charts showing what business they were in; who was asking them for work; how much of it had arrived; what they'd done; and how effective it was (in terms of interruptions and issue resolution with developers caused by ambiguity—effectively poor initial quality). His behavior had changed; he'd fallen into line with his peers. He saw that there was a new value system in place, and while he perhaps didn't care whether I'd labeled him as a rebel or a troublemaker, he did care what his peers thought of him. It seemed that systems analysis could be tracked and measured and reported on after all. Yet another little bit of Kanban Magic, another example of obliquity in action.

Corbis: Operations Review, March 9, 2007

Ante Meeting

It's 7:30 a.m. on the second Friday in March. I'm at work early because this morning is our department's fourth monthly operations review. I'm joined by Rick Garber, the manager of our software process engineering group. Rick has the job of coordinating the ops review meeting and agenda. He's busy printing out the handout that contains the approximately seventy PowerPoint slides for today's meeting. Once the printing is done, we head over to the Harbor Club in downtown Seattle with a box of 100 handouts. Ops review is scheduled to start at 8:30 a.m. but a hot buffet breakfast is served beginning at 8:00. The invite includes all of my organization; that of my colleague Erik Arnold, including the process group, business analysts, and the project managers; and our Network & Systems Operation group led by Peter Tutak, though his people won't be presenting. They, after all, have to recover failed systems in production, so they feel the pain of our failure most. They also feel the greatest impact when we make new releases to production. So, arguably, they have the most to gain by actively participating.The invite also includes my boss, the CIO of Corbis, and a number of other senior managers, who are our business customers.

However, with some of our folks in India, some in other parts of the US, and always a few who can't make it for personal reasons, we expect around eighty attendees.

We found that offering food was a very strong oblique incentive to turn up early. At the first session, we served a continental breakfast, and we got feedback that a hot breakfast would be appreciated more. This was going to cost around $1,800 per month. Erik had the bold idea to ask our invited guest to sponsor it: hence, "this month's breakfast comes to you courtesy of our sponsor, the Marketing Department." It was a genius idea! We asked the VP of the department if he or she would like fifteen minutes to address our "all hands" meeting, explaining what they do and how IT can best assist them in getting it done, in exchange for sponsoring the breakfast. A sponsor charge of over $100 per minute. Amazingly, everyone who was asked accepted the invitation and paid up!

The group begins to arrive in good time to enjoy their breakfast. The room is on the top floor of a Seattle tower about a block from our own building and affords us all beautiful views of the city, the harbor, the piers, and Elliott Bay. The room is laid out with round tables, with six to eight people seated at each. We have a projector screen and a lectern at one end. Rick manages the schedule with precision. Each presenter has around eight minutes for their four or five slides. There are a few time buffers to allow for the variability that comes with questions and discussion. I kick things off promptly with a few opening remarks. I ask everyone to think back to the end of January and what we were doing back then. I remind everyone that we are here to review the organization's performance for the month of February. Rick has picked out a nice picture from the company archives to symbolize a theme for the month and to help jog memories, reminding everyone of a key activity from the month just past.

Set a Business Tone from the Beginning

I hand off the proceedings to Rick, who summarizes the management action items from last month and gives an update on the status. Next, we introduce our finance analyst, who presents a summary of the company performance for the month—the reason for delaying until the second Friday of the subsequent month was so that we could have the financial data after the books for the prior month are closed. She summarizes the budget details for both my and Erik's cost centers. We look at planned versus actual for all major budget areas, as well as headcount targets. We discuss open requisitions and encourage team members to submit candidates for open positions. Coming out of this first segment, everyone attending knows how well the company is doing and how well the software engineering group is managing against budget, and therefore, how much slack we have to buy new equipment such as large flat-screen monitors and more powerful computers. The purpose of leading with the financials is to remind everyone on the team that we are running a business; we are not just showing up each day to have fun with ones and zeroes with a group of friends. This is leadership by signaling: It communicates part of our cultural values.

Inviting Guests Broadens the Audience and Adds Value

The next speaker is a guest—a vice president from another part of the company. I had the bright idea that if we wanted our business customers to take an interest, we should show an interest in them and invite them to present. We offered each guest fifteen minutes. Each month, we had no trouble finding a candidate, so that month we heard a presentation on sales operations, the part of the business that fulfills customer orders and ensures delivery of product. Although some of Corbis's business was done on the web and fulfilled electronically, not everything the firm offers was delivered as a download; a whole department fulfilled more complex orders for professional advertising agencies and media firms. Over the next few months, our team learned about many aspects of the business, and senior leaders throughout the company learned what we did, how we did it, and how hard we were trying to deal with our issues.

I've said that Kanban had changed the culture at Corbis. Chapter 4 described the secondary emergent effects from replenishment meetings. Operations reviews had a similar secondary impact. By summer 2007, executives were openly talking about how well governed IT was, and we'd become the benchmark or archetype for governance and management discipline. I knew we'd changed the company when one afternoon, uninvited, that same vice president of sales operations from our March meeting walked into my office. "David! I need your help. I'm under some pressure to bring my department under control and get it running more effectively. Can you teach me how you are running these monthly meetings? I believe this is just what I need to turn my own unit around." Just another bit of Kanban Magic, another example of obliquity in action.

Main Agenda

Once our guest speaker finished, we moved on to the main portion of the meeting. Each manager had eight minutes for a presentation on their department's performance. We followed this with some project-specific updates from our program-management office. Each of the immediate team managers got up and spent five minutes quickly presenting their metrics: They presented information on defect rates, lead time, delivery rate, failure demand, flow efficiency, and, occasionally, a specific report that would drill into some aspect of their process that they were investigating for possible improvement. Then they took questions, comments, and suggestions from the floor for a few minutes.

This fourth month of the ops review, March 2007, was particularly interesting. The first ops review had happened, as mentioned earlier, in December. That first time, everyone came, almost 100 percent turnout. There was lots of curiosity, and afterward lots of comments like, "I have never seen transparency like this in my career," and "That was very interesting, I've never worked anywhere that shared information like this." The most actionable piece of feedback was, as previously mentioned, "Next time, can we have a hot breakfast buffet rather than cold?" The second month, people said, "Yes, another good month. Somewhat interesting! Thanks for the hot breakfast!" On the third month, some of the developers were asking, "Why do I need to get up so early?" and "Is this a good use of my time?" Enthusiasm was waning and attendance, while still high, was clearly fragile.

What happened next represents the defining crucible for an operations review: After three months of plain sailing, smooth flow, and almost faultless deliveries, there had been a significant problem, and now we were going to talk about it. The company had acquired a business in Australia, called Australia Picture Library (or APL). IT had been asked to switch off all the APL IT systems and migrate all fifty users to Corbis systems. The request had an arbitrary but urgent date. This date was based on an "economy of scale"–style cost savings that had partly justified the acquisition price, so there was a cost of delay involved. The request had arrived as a single item in our maintenance queue. It was big enough to have justified ten tickets, but we treated it as only one. The effect of an outsized item like this entering a kanban system is well understood in industrial engineering. It clogs the system and greatly extends the lead time for everything that comes in behind it. And so it was with us. Lead time jumped, on average, from thirty to fifty-five days. Queuing theory also tells us that reducing a backlog when already fully loaded takes a long time. We discovered later that it would take us five months to recover to our lead-time target of thirty days.

In addition, we had made a release that had required an emergency fix, the first such occurrence since we'd rolled out Kanban and operations reviews. So, there was lots to talk about.

All of a sudden, the room was alight with questions, comments, and debate. After three months of boring, good data, we had a story to tell. The staff were amazed that we (the managers) were willing to talk openly about the problems and what to do about them, and that ops review wasn't only about showing off how good we were, just presenting the good data; it was about addressing problems, facing up to our reality, and taking ownership and responsibility. None of the staff questioned again why we held the meeting every month.

The meeting ended with Rick summarizing the management action items from the morning's discussions and thanking everyone for coming. It was 10:30 and time to head back across the street to the office.

Respect for Managers and Managerial Action

Operations review communicates a much larger sense of "team"—all of a sudden, the team is a business unit with everyone collaborating to enable shared goals. A business unit exists to provide a set of services, and operations reviews provide transparency to those services and the current capability to fulfill them within customer expectations. Consequently, operations reviews improve the level of respect for managers and managerial action, and they develop trust in both directions—both up and down the organizational hierarchy. Operations reviews, through their transparency, focus on collaborative shared action, explicit assignment of responsibility, and clear accountability, and they improve the social capital across the entire organization.

Trust Goes Two Ways

To move with agility, senior managers need to be able to delegate, to enable and empower subordinates and employees to act with autonomy. However, empowerment often comes with a fear of loss of control—fear that the organization will operate without governance. Kanban offers the opportunity to provide autonomy without loss of control. Operations review, with its ability to examine and modify policies, plays an important role in business agility. Trust goes two ways: Managers must trust that commands are carried out as expected and that decisions and actions taken are within the authority of subordinates; and workers must trust that managers act in the best interests of everyone involved and that their actions improve the chances of organizational success. Workers need to see managers acting on the system, through policy changes, such that they are set up for success—working within a system that is capable of delivering on expectations. Workers must want to follow the lead of leaders because they trust their judgment and vision, while leaders must trust workers to follow their direction as intended. Operations Review plays a vital role enabling this mechanism.

◆

Operations Review: Keystone of a Kaizen Culture

There are a lot of important things to understand about Operations Review. I believe that it is the linchpin, or keystone, of the Kanban Method. It is an objective, data-driven retrospective on the organization's performance. It is above and beyond any one project, and it sets an expectation of objective, data-driven, quantitative management. Operations Review defines and embodies the new values of the organization and its leadership. It provides the feedback loop that enables deepening of organizational maturity and evolutionary change at large scale. It has a huge cultural impact and is core to driving adoption of a new value system.

Takeaways

- The concept of "obliquity" was postulated by the Nobel Prize–winning chemist Sir James Black, who discovered beta blockers while working for ICI in the 1960s.
- Sir James Black believed that company goals were best achieved indirectly.
- The economist and *Financial Times* writer John Kay made the term "obliquity" famous by adopting it as the title of his 2011 book.
- Operations Review is one of seven Kanban Cadences—meetings used as feedback mechanisms to evolve and improve operational workflows, policies, risk management, market strategy, customer segmentation, and service provision.
- Operations Review has played a unique role in demonstrating obliquity—achieving business objectives through indirect means.
- Bootstrapping Operations Review has focused line managers' attention on
  - Instrumentation of managed workflows
  - Understanding the business they are in
  - Comprehending service delivery effectiveness and the factors that influence it
- Serving food has improved attendance at Operations Reviews.
- Leading the agenda with financial data sets a business tone for the meeting and reminds everyone of current organizational objectives.
- Inviting an executive-level guest speaker from another business unit or service delivery partner broadens attendance and adds value, allowing attendees to gain insights beyond the operation of their own business unit.
- Attendance improves when there are known problems to discuss.
- Openly discussing known problems and defining corrective actions assigned to managers communicates to the staff that managers will be held accountable and that managerial action can improve conditions and performance for everyone.
- Operations Reviews communicate a much larger sense of team and collaboration on common goals. Social capital improves. Respect for the value of managers and managerial action improves.
- Operations Review is considered the keystone to the Kanban Method and the core element to enable enterprise-wide agility. It is the heart that pumps life into an enterprise-scale culture of continuous improvement—a true kaizen culture.

6

Scrumban Stories
The Rise and Fall of Scrum at Posit Science

During that year of cultural change at Corbis, Corey Ladas had joined our team as a process coach. I first met Corey in 2005 in his role as part of the Engineering Excellence team at Microsoft. He was one of a team who reported to Eric Brechner, who in turn reported to Jon De Vaan, the head of the group. Jon first appeared in Chapter 2 with his policy that Microsoft's IT department would follow the TSP/PSP software development methodology. Eric went on to lead development for parts of the Xbox One platform, where he introduced Kanban. Eric's experiences are captured in his 2015 book *Agile Project Management with Kanban,*[21] where he describes the very specific application of Kanban to large-scale software products.

In the spring of 2007, I persuaded Corey to come to Corbis. I needed help coaching the rollout of Kanban across our portfolio. He joined Rick Garber's process engineering team and started to work with different project teams at the Corbis HQ on Second Ave in downtown Seattle. One day he came to me and said, "I am finding that the projects where they are still using a traditional software development lifecycle (SDLC) process need different coaching from those who have adopted (the Agile software development methodology) Scrum."

What we were seeing was the emergence of what Corey later named "Scrumban"—the application of Kanban to a starting position where a project team or an organization consisting of many such teams (typically

---

21. Brechner, Eric, and James Waletzky. *Agile Project Management with Kanban*. Microsoft Press, 2015.

six to eight people per team) had already adopted Scrum as their way of working and coordinating with each other.

Already well established amongst enthusiasts for Agile software development, Scrum has since become widely adopted and popular in the technology industry globally. At the Agile conference in 2008, Corey presented his two flavors of Kanban guidance—for those using a traditional SDLC and separately for those who were already using Scrum. Simultaneously, he published a paper on the technique, and the term "Scrumban" entered the lexicon of software engineering methodologists—only to, almost instantly, become widely misunderstood. Scrumban meant, quite simply, the application of Kanban to a starting position where Scrum was already in use. It did not mean some hybrid of the two methods, selecting practices from each into some new prescriptive approach. It didn't mean take a bit of this and a bit of that, do the hokey-pokey and shake it all about, and you have something new and wholesome. Scrumban means "do all of Kanban and apply it in an environment that is already using Scrum." So strong was the mindset amongst methodologists in the software development world that many struggled to get their head around the concept of a tailoring approach that evolved a unique way of working for a specific situation. To them, any approach to software engineering management had to come as a designed, packaged, and defined prescriptive method. Their minds had been set by thirty years of such prescriptive methods. An approach to evolve your own "unbranded" solution was novel.

Writing fifteen years later, I know that this misunderstanding continues. A simple test for whether or not an organization understands Scrumban is to ask how many changes to their process have happened recently and can they describe a timeline of changes introduced since they "adopted Scrumban." If they look back at you with a confused, blank stare, they probably don't understand the concept of, and evolutionary nature of, Kanban. Kanban has always been the "start with what you do now" and evolve approach. You add Kanban to what is already there. When what is already there is the defined process called Scrum, then your story, like so many others, is a Scrumban story.

We see two common varieties of Scrumban stories in our work: The first is where Scrum has helped an organization initially but improvements have plateaued and stubbornly refuse to improve further; the other is where circumstances have changed, the market has moved, customer expectations have changed, and consequently the Scrum approach of two-week timeboxes, known as "Sprints," of planning, working, and checking in with stakeholders with a demonstration and retrospective on a biweekly cadence is no longer appropriate. In the first category, we often find that it takes a long time to recognize that things aren't improving. Managers often persevere with Scrum for months or years before they are ready to look for an alternative: Two years is typical, while up to four years isn't uncommon. I know this from the experience of receiving emails asking for help and reading the stories. "Things haven't improved any further for the past two years and we'd like someone to take a fresh look and suggest some new ideas." This is typical of such a situation.

With the second category, the timeframe is shorter. Quite simply, due to changes in context and circumstances, the two-week sprint approach isn't working and is causing stress, anxiety, and pain, resulting in dysfunctional behavior and tension among the team, managers, and customers. In both situations, there is motivation to find "an alternative path to agility"—to be able to move quickly, respond to change, and adapt to customer needs appropriately. Regardless of the motivation, given that the organization was already using Scrum, their choice to introduce Kanban in order to take them further means they, too, have a Scrumban story.

Corey has said, "Scrumban is a journey." To better understand that, here is one such journey, from one of the earliest Scrumban stories, Posit Science in San Francisco. Their story is primarily of the second type: Their circumstances had changed, and consequently, Scrum was no longer serving their needs. Their motivation was to find a new way of working, to meet the expectations of business owners, and to relieve their research and development organization of overburdening. They needed smoother flow, more predictable delivery, and a sustainable pace of work. Kanban proved a good and effective choice as a way forward.

Posit Science: Background—The Brain Aerobics Company

Dr. Michael (Mike) M. Merzenich, the founder of Posit Science, had a long history of scientific achievements. In the late 1980s, he was a member of the team that invented the cochlear implant, a device that enables the deaf to hear. In the 1990s, his career moved into neuroscience—specifically, the field of brain plasticity. He is the author of *Soft Wired: How the New Science of Brain Plasticity Can Change Your Life.*[22]

For much of his career, Mike Merzenich had known how important continuous learning is for adults. As a neuroscientist, he knew that the most important continuous learning was for the individual and the health of their brain, especially as it aged. Professor emeritus at the University of California, San Francisco, he had many achievements in his field. His devotion to and research of brain plasticity had earned him a spot in the National Academy of Sciences in 1999. Developing an understanding that brains are plastic and can be exercised and coached disrupted the long-held belief that human brains stop changing in early adulthood. It had long been assumed that after completing its development in young adults, the brain changed little, thus beginning its decline, deterioration, and demise. It was assumed that there was nothing medicine or technology could do to prevent it.

Mike and a few like-minded colleagues believed otherwise. They believed that brains are plastic, that they can be trained and molded, even in adulthood. That belief stemmed from the simple observation

---

22. Merzenich, Michael. *Soft-wired: How the New Science of Brain Plasticity Can Change Your Life.* San Fransisco, USA: Parnassus Publishing, 2013.

of people from different cultural contexts. While everyone would agree that children develop differently based on their nurturing and context, few had thought that to be true for adults as well. But as he had observed, older humans carried on diversifying more as time passed, learning new skills even later in life. They concluded that the brain is flexible and changing, its adaptability and plasticity never really disappearing. Could that plasticity trigger change that would negate deterioration, they wondered. Together with his team of researchers, Mike had dedicated his career to finding the precise triggers for that plasticity.

By 2004, he was ready to speak more publicly on the subject. He gave a TED talk[23] that February in Monterey, California. People do not forget because the brain has forgotten to remember, he explained. People lose their memory because the brain starts representing the things they are seeing and hearing and feeling less saliently. "When you're young and you see something surprising, your eyes are attracted to it. You are bright-eyed, literally. Your eyes take a series of snapshots that reveal information about what's out there." These snapshots leave a footprint in the brain, which keeps the machinery active. But as the footprint of what is seen or heard is less clear and vivid, the machinery behind it starts to operate less. Memory loss and neurological decline begin to take place as a result. Further on, the machinery becomes more and more inactive and eventually begins to die.

Mike, of course, believed there was an antidote to all this!

Simply keeping your mind active is not enough to fix it. To truly offset the demise of the machinery in your brain, he believed that what is necessary are very specific, challenging activities. Those challenges to keep your brain sharp could be in the form of continuous learning, such as taking up a foreign language or learning to play a musical instrument, such as the guitar, for example. Or, what he claimed would be the thing of the future—"brain aerobics."

Interactive games based on brain plasticity could engage the brain's natural learning mechanisms. Games created specifically to engage the otherwise deteriorating parts of the brain could offset the declining cognitive abilities. As the scientific community was improving its understanding of specific neurological issues, they felt more confident that training activities could be designed to harness the brain's plasticity to create and reinforce neural pathways for specific results. With computer technologies improving, those brain aerobics training methods could be more advanced and precise. Through the use of complex algorithms, they could monitor responses and adjust in a manner that heightened engagement and became customized to address individual deficiencies.

As with so many other enlightening TED talks, this one, too, seemed like pure science fiction to the audience. If it were true, if people could sustain their cognitive abilities just a while longer, that would be one of the most phenomenal discoveries of the century. However, Mike had already initiated the steps to make it a reality. Some months earlier, he'd founded Posit Science—the company that would commercialize "brain aerobics" with a series of interactive computer games.

---

23. http://www.ted.com/talks/michael_merzenich_on_the_elastic_brain

They had chosen the name "Posit" on purpose: It means "to put forward or advance" and reflected their hope to make a positive change in people's lives. "Science" also told us something—this wasn't superstition or belief, nor was it entertainment—this wasn't a games company; it was a scientific endeavor producing a medical-grade product designed to help people with dysfunction in their cognitive abilities either through aging or injury.

I first encountered Posit Science in 2009. There is only one other organization I've visited that had a similar feel to it based on how I experienced the culture, the employees, and what they said about why they had joined the firm and what they hoped to achieve there: The other was The Bill & Melinda Gates Foundation. The people at Posit Science all had joined for altruistic reasons. They had joined to do some social good—and to give something back to a wider society. Posit Science paid people well enough, but salaries were perhaps 15 percent under the market norm for San Francisco. This is true also of the Gates Foundation, where salaries are typically below the market rate for Seattle, and the employees all have some altruistic motivation for joining. In both cases, people joining these organizations believe in the mission, and it gives them each a sense of contributing to the greater good.

Posit Science as a tribe consisted of three distinct sub-tribes: the scientists, neuroscientists who had produced the original research; the game developers, who produced the product; and business people, who took that product to market. Regardless of their background, they all bought into the vision, mission, and purpose and believed in Mike Merzenich. While they were all being adequately remunerated for their work, they were all there for altruistic reasons, to give something back to society. If it was only about the money, they'd have been working somewhere else. So, there were three distinct social groups, but the purpose (the vision and mission) of Posit was the unifying factor that made them a highly cohesive super-tribe.

Together, the research team and the games developers strived to move technologies out of the laboratories and into the hands of people, where they could do the most good. Those who needed it most urgently, and of primary interest to Posit, were the elderly. Could computer-based training help them keep their "brains"? Could it enable them to be more childlike, grasping everything more vividly? Posit was developing a set of exercises called "The Brain Fitness Program."

What Dr. Merzenich and Posit Science were aiming to do with their brain aerobics program was to address all three key problems of brain decline: the slowing of the brain's processing speed; the weakening signals from the senses to the brain; and the decrease in production of key brain chemicals. They believed that by presenting the right stimuli, in the right order, with the right timing through intensive, repetitive, and progressively challenging programs, they could tackle all three. They believed that brain games and training was the solution.

No other species plays with objects and with language as much as humans do. We pursue a wide variety of entertainment for long stretches of time. We like enjoyment. That, of course, is no coincidence, as play is an important evolutionary tool. Physical, cognitive, and social development,a as well as general training for emergencies and disasters, have their roots in play or simulation games. As

Francis Steen of the University of California Los Angeles puts it, playing is an evolutionary adaptation for learning; it is a sort of a simulator that allows children and adults alike to imagine and try out different scenarios with little risk.[24] For Posit, those imaginary and playful scenarios could help bring much-needed changes in the brain.

The extraordinary and noble cause of Posit Science had attracted the attention of investors. The startup had received its first round of venture financing and begun operations on October 1, 2003. With the money in place, it was possible to assemble a global consortium of brain scientists to develop, test, refine, and validate exercises that rejuvenate the brain. In the first years, they tested those games in a few chosen retirement homes where they set up learning centers to observe the effects of the games on the residents. They looked for improvements in cognitive function—or lack thereof—stemming from their exercises. Scientists, determined to have clinically proven technology, needed substantial data that their brain training exercises worked before they commercialized their products.

To summarize the context: we have a newly formed, venture capital–funded startup with a powerful and unifying vision employing world-leading neuroscientists and successful game developers commercializing brand-new science in the highly regulated medical industry with a nascent and unproven market, located in the high-cost, high–burn rate center of the global technology industry, San Francisco, California. This is what defines them.

By the end of 2005, Posit had positive results. During the Society for Neuroscience Annual Meeting in Washington, D.C., Mike Merzenich presented results from one of the first studies on brain games. The study[25] showed that participants using the program had improved by ten or more years on average in neurocognitive status. The study had been conducted at Rossmoor, a retirement community near San Francisco, California, with 95 volunteers aged sixty-one to ninety-four. Researchers compared results from memory and cognitive assessment scores in participants enrolled in forty one-hour training sessions with both a control group using a computer and with a no-contact group. Participants using the brain plasticity–based training program had improved. Participants who had completed more difficult levels of exercises showed even greater improvements. Soon after, Posit Science released the first ever *Brain Fitness Program* CD-ROM. In March 2006, they began selling it through a partner network. The price tag was $395 for a single user. It was expensive, but the value far exceeded the dollars, or so Posit and its team of scientists believed.

This product launch represented the first major milestone, and punctuation point, in the history of Posit Science. Until then, they'd been in scientific mode—researching, experimenting, and slowly burning up their investors' capital. Now, in 2006, they were a commercial entity, seeking to make money from their product and, they hoped, one day become cash flow positive, no longer in need of investment to continue operations.

---

24. https://www.newscientist.com/article/mg21428610.300-human-nature-being-playful/
25. http://www.brainhq.com/news/brain-training-program-enhances-memory-cognition

Punctuation points in the history of an organization are always good opportunities to introduce change. Punctuation points can take many forms:

- Launch of a first product
- Taking an investment round
- Arrival of a new CEO or leader
- Key individual exit (typically a founder or a creator of intellectual property)
- Merger, acquisition, divestiture, takeover
- IPO (initial public offering—taking a company public from previous private ownership)
- Regulatory, legal, political or major economic changes (such as a financial crisis or a pandemic)
- Outsourcing and/or offshoring of work
- Company reorganization
- Retrenchment
- Arrival of a new disruptive competitor or business model (such as budget airlines in the 1980s and 1990s)
- Arrival of a disruptive innovation into a market (such as commercial jet aircraft into the flying boat and ocean liner transportation business, as happened in the late 1950s)

Famously, there is the expression "the first 100 days." It is used for example, to refer to the tenure of a new president and head of state, or a new leader in an organization. The 100 days starts with the punctuation point and runs for approximately three months. During this period, everyone is adjusting to the turmoil, and a new leader gets to blame his or her predecessor or the conditions that existed before they took control. As a consequence of the punctuation point—or the ever worsening conditions that existed prior to it, metaphorically, a "global warming" condition, a heating up that eventually forces change, provoking some engineered punctuation point such as a reorganization of a business—the new leader has an opportunity make changes without much resistance.

Posit had a new product in the market, but it had taken a long time to come to fruition, and the software code was unstable. The firm took the opportunity to hire a new head of software development, David Hoffman.

Hoffman quickly realized that Posit suffered from a common problem for young software companies: Their software code was fragile and hard to maintain, and the engineering of their product was such that it could be described as a prototype. This is typical of first-generation software products, where the focus has been on exploring the functionality and features needed to serve a market rather than on the integrity of the code and its underlying architecture. It was first documented by Fred Brooks in his classic work, *The Mythical Man Month*,[26] in which he said, "Plan to throw one away, because you will anyway." In other words, the first generation of a product always has code of poor internal

26. Brooks, Frederick P. *The Mythical Man-Month: Essays on Software Engineering*, Anniversary Edition (2 ed.). Reading, MA: Addison-Wesley, 1995.

quality, and the business discovers that it must scrap the code and start again for a second-generation product.

Until this point in its history, Posit Science wasn't a typical Silicon Valley startup. Since its founding, employees had worked normal, humane hours, which afforded them quality family time and a sustainable life. For people concerned with brain health, they knew all too well that it does not deal well with overburdening. Perhaps more than any other software development organization on the planet, Posit Science developers understood the damage they could do by working too hard while anxious, overburdened, and stressed. However, this comfortable work-life balance that had been a signature of the Posit story so far was now under stress and would soon break. The fragile code behind the *Brain Fitness Program* was generating a lot of rework as defects were discovered, and maintenance to add minor enhancements was much more problematic than anticipated. Meanwhile, Posit had started to work on a second-generation product, a set of games to be called *Insight*. As things got more complex, the heat started to rise. Work-life balance was slowly being eroded by the urgency of the work, and Hoffman's department was, consequently, growing anxious and stressed.

Hoffman decided he had to take action: It was time to start again, and they had to develop a new system architecture and a new, cleaner set of software code that would be much more robust and easier to maintain.He was creating his own, smaller punctuation point as a response to the global warming problem in his department. They scrapped the existing code base and started again for the new product, and took this opportunity to introduce a new way of working. The department adopted the Agile software development methodology known as Scrum. The product developers were motivated and ready for change. They embraced the opportunity with alacrity! Consultants and trainers arrived, and a popular Agile project management software tool was purchased to help everyone track work and report progress.

Posit Science: The Rise and Fall of Scrum (Part 1)

David Hoffman hired a project manager to lead the changes and help his organization get through all the work that was accumulating. It's at this point that Janice Linden-Reed enters this story and our story, the Kanban story. Janice had had a long career, beginning in the early 1990s, as a games designer, producer, and executive at firms such as Maxis and Total Entertainment Network (TEN). She joined Posit as a senior project manager, attracted to the firm by a close friend, a former games developer who'd joined the executive team at Posit. The work-life balance was the first thing she noticed. The games industry doesn't have the best reputation for maintaining a sustainable pace. She'd spent too many nights at previous jobs sleeping under her desk with a never-ending pile of work on top. Relatively speaking, Posit was much more relaxed.

With the decision to adopt Scrum, David Hoffman believed his people could work smarter rather than harder.

Adopting Scrum changed many things at Posit, from the layout of the office and the breakdown of work into smaller pieces that could be completed earlier to the variety of new meetings, such as the daily "scrum" and the periodic "sprint planning"; change swept the employees off their feet. It was difficult in the first year. They weren't used to the overwhelming transparency that came from using an Agile project-management tracking tool whereby everyone could see the state of all of their work at any time. None of the developers had been used to the close examination of their own work on such a regular basis, yet they had desperately needed to change how they were working. The old way wasn't sustainable. With time, they got used to it and things started to improve. With a better idea of what was going on, they delivered faster. The switch to Scrum was widely regarded as a good thing.

Scrum is ideal for low-maturity organizations looking to add process and bring some control to the chaos of their environment. One of the creators of the Scrum approach, Ken Schwaber, named his original website controlchaos.com. Ken knew exactly what sort of problems he was trying to solve with the design of Scrum, and David Hoffman's decision to adopt it at Posit was entirely appropriate.

Posit made only one alteration to the canonical Scrum definition: They agreed on a three-week time period for each "sprint" instead of the usual two. Part of Posit's process was "clinical validation testing." This wasn't testing the software for defects; rather, it was testing completed functionality—the actual brain game—to validate that it delivered on the underlying science. Clinical validation testing demonstrated whether the product delivered on the anticipated clinical outcomes and provided the expected medical benefits. This meant testing the product with patients to measure and validate expected improvements to their brain function. This takes time; the game initiates a chemical process in the brain to strengthen neural pathways. To see results takes at least a few days, possibly longer. Consequently, a minimum of one week was needed for clinical testing of new functionality. Given this overhead for every sprint, they decided that two weeks were needed to develop sufficient functionality to be worthwhile testing with patients, and hence, a third week was needed to gather the results of the tests. While Posit's products, and the general field of brain plasticity, were not yet regulated by the US Food and Drug Administration (FDA), Posit proceeded as if they were. Their training as scientists didn't allow them to cut corners on effectiveness. Their careers and reputations hinged on these brain aerobics games delivering on their clinical claims. There could be no compromise on clinical testing.

Scrum gave them a regular rhythm. They avoided too much overburdening. They had time and space to architect and code the *Insight* suite of games with much higher quality than the *Brain Fitness Program* that preceded it. *Insight* was launched successfully in 2007. Like so many Scrumban stories, Posit's story starts with an appropriate and successful adoption of Scrum.

Takeaways

- Scrumban is a name that implies the application of the Kanban Method to a service delivery workflow that has previously adopted the use of Scrum.

- Scrumban has two prime motivations: Improvement using Scrum has plateaued; or external circumstances have changed such that Scrum is no longer an appropriate fit and doesn't deliver the necessary levels of customer satisfaction.

- Scrumban isn't a process. Instead, it implies a journey. Scrumban suggests a story of how an organization evolves from using Scrum as a defined and prescriptive process methodology to its own uniquely evolved and tailored process solution.

- Posit Science is a brain-training game company employing some of the most pre-eminent neuroscientists in the world.

- Dr. Michael Merzenich, the founder of Posit Science, had a vision to extend the useful working life of the brain and improve the quality of life for older adults, enabling them to maintain their independence and basic cognitive functions longer.

- Both investors and prospective employees bought into this vision.

- Many employees at Posit Science believed they were doing a social good and altruistically giving back to society.

- Posit Science's brain-training games were clinically proven, medical grade products with an expensive price tag.

- The launch of their first product represented a punctuation point in the history of Posit Science.

- Posit took advantage of the first product release to appoint a new head of product development, who in turn hired the company's first project manager.

- The first product was poorly architected and the code base was fragile.

- For a second product launch, they developed a new system architecture and a new, cleaner set of code that was more robust and easier to maintain.

- There was a perception that Posit needed a better way of working, and the new head of development used his first 100 days to introduce the use of Scrum.

7

Proto-Kanban

Getting Started with Kanban in a Low Maturity Organization

Posit employed almost 100 people in downtown San Francisco; its burn rate in 2007 must have been well over a million dollars per month. There was an expectation that with two products in the market, revenue from sales would start to improve cash flow. The investors' money wouldn't last forever. If revenues did not improve, it was foreseeable that the business would run out of money. Executive attention began to switch from science and product development to finance and sales.

Posit Science: The Rise and Fall of Scrum (Part 2)

Janice made an effort to learn everything there was to know about Scrum so she could help the developers make better use of it. She grew to believe greatly in its teachings. She appreciated the predictability, the honesty, and the absence of fear. As much as she liked it, she gradually began to notice that the developers continued to experience many problems. There was still too much work to do. Aside from the creation of the games, the development group had myriad other things to do. Providing support to the users of the Brain Fitness program was one. Participating in the scientific research for the new games was another. Beyond that, they also worked with the learning centers at the retirement homes and needed to be aware of and adhere to FDA and other compliance requirements. They were assisting with the IMPACT study, a joint project of the Mayo Clinic and the University of Southern California, the most sophisticated study to date of the effectiveness of brain training games. On top of all that, developers also worked closely with the marketing and sales departments. The number of sources of demand and the impact it had on the day-to-day work of the developers were growing as time went by and both the product lines and the customer base grew.

Janice found that no matter how much she tried to help, all of these demands were overwhelming. She witnessed how unbearable it was becoming for the developers. Planning meetings were long and excruciating, sprints were disrupted with pre-emptive, urgent work, and the developers and testers were exhausted. Almost always too optimistic, the development team took on more than they could deal with and missed many deadlines, breaking promises as a result. The trust between the business people and the developers began to deteriorate. Questions about their ability to deliver lurked ominously in the atmosphere around their San Francisco office.

The sprint planning meeting every three weeks was dreaded by everyone. The situation worsened as the product backlog grew larger than ever. By the beginning of 2008, this wish list from business owners, customers, and regulatory stakeholders had grown to more than 800 requests. Sprint planning had become an intense event during which the developers would have to decide what to work on and what to leave until later. The challenge of selecting around forty items from an available set of 800-plus was overwhelming. Any new request for the backlog needed to be analyzed and broken down into so-called stories that were considered small enough to complete within one sprint. Then the stories had to be estimated to determine the anticipated number of hours of work. Next was a triage to pick the work to start immediately versus everything else that had to wait until later. There were seven stakeholder groups in each sprint planning meeting, with two representatives from each group, plus two developers, and Janice as facilitator. In a specialized field such as brain plasticity science, you might expect a highly specialized workforce, and once you add those business functions—including customer care—it is easy to see why so many people needed to attend. Everyone complained about these meetings. They were too long, too stressful, and seemed to add little value, as sprints were constantly being interrupted with new work that was urgent and critical. No one really wanted to be involved with it any longer; they simply wanted to work. Some people stopped attending altogether. As is often the case when people with valuable information fail to attend, participate in debate, and contribute to decisions, the result is poor-quality decision making. This leads to further complaints about bad decisions, and a vicious cycle ensues. Janice would try anything she could think of just to make the planning meeting a little bit more bearable. She would bring toys so that people could fiddle with them and relieve some of their frustration. Yet the meetings were so intense that the relief was too little to make a difference. Janice came to fear these meetings. She lost sleep over them. She suffered anxiety and trepidation about how each new sprint planning session would go.

What was happening at Posit was that their circumstances were slowly changing. They were, once again, (metaphorically speaking) in a global warming condition. Things were slowly heating up such that on a day-to-day basis no one would notice the changes, but seen over a longer time span, it was clear that the situation was deteriorating. The business pressure to have successful revenue-generating products was increasing as the investor funding ran down. There was greater complexity and much more urgency in their environment. The business had become reactionary to every revenue-generating or investment opportunity that came along. Planning every three weeks wasn't often enough. The conditions that had enabled a successful Scrum workflow no longer existed.

Too many blocked work items—due to preemption by something even more urgent and critical—meant increased multitasking. Deliverables were taking longer to complete, and releases were increasingly unpredictable. Developers were wearing out and overtired. Others in the company thought they were simply lazy. Relationships were strained. Janice felt that the assumption of laziness and lack of motivation was unfair and untrue. She wanted to help her department of developers. She felt direct responsibility. She initiated conversations to help understand what was wrong and how to make it better. She began researching whether other software development organizations were experiencing similar problems. She sought advice anywhere she could. She found the consultants and coaches hired from their Agile project management software vendor to be unhelpful. They blamed the developers, saying they did not adhere to all the rules of Scrum, that they lacked discipline. The consultants argued that Scrum could not be wrong if it was applied properly. It could not fail; if things were not working, then it could only be the fault of the people involved.

Janice felt this guidance from their external coaches was unsatisfactory, even insulting. This was a team of successful career games developers and Ph.D. neuroscientists. Wasn't it likely that they had needed a lot of discipline to achieve success in their careers? And if they could reverse the effects of brain aging, wasn't it also likely they were capable of reading and following a simple prescriptive process recipe such as the Scrum Guide? Janice knew how smart these people were, how devoted to the product they were, and how motivated they were to use their knowledge and experience to benefit those who might need help boosting their brain power. They were not lazy. They were not rebellious. It was shocking that their paid advisers treated them with such disrespect.

What Janice was hearing from the consultants was rooted in guidance from Ken Schwaber, co-creator of Scrum, who said, "Scrum is designed to work in a context. Your job is to create the context so that Scrum works for you."

This statement really defines Scrum as the antithesis of Kanban's start-with-what-you-do-now approach. Scrum requires that you change your context to facilitate the method of working. It's inward focused and self-serving in nature. From a developer's perspective: "Because I feel overburdened and stressed by the chaos around me, everything in my world must change to facilitate me doing my work without interruption and with high quality."

Kanban embraces the context you have and enables the way of working to evolve, adjust, and optimize to its environment. Scrum requires that you change the environment. For Posit, it seemed that they didn't control their environment, their market, or their impoverished circumstances; they were running out of money and desperate to keep their vision afloat, surviving any way they could.

What had enabled the success of Scrum at Posit a year earlier was that their world wasn't yet sufficiently chaotic. It wasn't yet sufficiently complex. While developing a single product and with plenty of investor capital to burn, the environment was relatively simple. Introducing three-week planning horizons and small batches of work to fit into those three weeks was just fine. As time went by and the scale increased—with more products, more customers and other stakeholders, and an ever-larger backlog of work on their wish list—and with ever-increasing pressure to chase revenue and business opportunities as investor capital was running short, Scrum simply broke down for them. It wasn't anyone's fault. It wasn't a lack of discipline. Nor was it an inability to control the environment and create the context in which Scrum would work successfully. Suggesting that Posit could have modified their environment to solve their problems, was, and would be to this day, wishful thinking. "If only we had deeper-pocketed investors and more patient capital behind us, then Scrum would work for us." "If only new business opportunities didn't arrive so frequently and unpredictably, requiring proofs of concept and demonstrations, scheduled at the client's convenience, then Scrum would work for us." There is no wishful thinking in Kanban, and if you find yourself saying, "If only . . . ," then you've already fallen from the path of pragmatism.

Janice kept on looking for explanations and ideas for how to help her developers. For months she used every free moment to watch webinars, read blog posts, and have discussions with some of the best in the field. On her commute to and from work she listened to various podcasts every day.

One day she stumbled upon a blog post that described problems like Posit's. In the post, the author explained how, in an attempt to solve their problems, they had stopped doing one of the essential practices of Scrum—they had dropped the use of timeboxed two-week sprints. Instead of worsening their performance—as they'd been warned by Agile software development consultants—it had helped them. The "permission giver" for this change had come from another blog post, a report of a presentation by Corey Ladas during the 2008 Toronto Agile conference. From Corey's session, the author had taken away the realization that there was another way forward if Scrum did not work for your circumstances: Using Kanban was *an alternative path to agility*. From just these two blog posts, Janice liked how Kanban sounded. Limiting work-in-progress (WIP) seemed a simple yet powerful concept.

Fascinated by the affirmation that the fault was not with the developers but in their method of working, it was Janice's turn to introduce a small punctuation point. She suggested Posit make a shift and introduce Kanban.

Posit Science: Kanban Gets Rejected

Janice was sure her colleagues would embrace any kind of improvement, but to her surprise, they rejected any change suggested. Perhaps Scrum had become too much a part of their identity? For two years, they'd had its rules and practices drilled into them by their external coaches. Scrum had become popular in the San Francisco Bay Area, and there was broader social pressure from fellow professionals to be seen as part of the movement. Meanwhile, they'd been criticized, belittled, and ridiculed for their inability to make it work for them. They'd been made to feel guilty for their lack of discipline. They didn't want to be seen as quitters. There was some risk of professional social ostracism for taking a different tack. Scrum had to stay.

It seemed to Janice that while Scrum had worked well in those early days, circumstances had changed such that Scrum's policies and practices were literally hurting the developers. And yet they resisted change. The idea of change seemed to be even more painful than their current situation. Taken aback, she continued to read everything she could find, trying to understand Kanban better.

She began noticing some of the ills described in nascent Kanban literature at the time. During the daily team meeting, it was clear that the developers were working on pretty much everything in the sprint, all at the same time. There was a lot of multitasking, and individuals were clearly over-burdened. It had never occurred to her just how problematic this was until she read about limiting the work-in-progress. While she could see the problems—and a solution—her team did not want to deviate from the definition of Scrum they'd been trained to follow.

Janice thought that Scrum did not say anything about limiting WIP. She had never heard that, nor had it been mentioned by any of Posit's professional external coaches. Actually, you have to look deep in Scrum literature, and back to its early days, to find advice from Jeff Sutherland, the other co-creator of Scrum, to find mention of focus. Team members are supposed to focus and not start too much work all at once. However, this guidance never specified a WIP limit or even the concept of a policy to limit WIP. It was just general guidance, loosely worded, suggesting that individuals shouldn't voluntarily overburden themselves. In 2008, it was rare to find a coach who even knew about, much less taught, this Scrum practice of focus.

Janice didn't give up. She kept on planting the seeds of the possible change and improvement. She waited for people to be ready for it. Eventually, David Hoffman intervened. He agreed that something needed to change. He would show the leadership the development department needed. Sometimes people need help to help themselves. They need leadership. He was willing to give it a try, to give Kanban a try.

However, there was still resistance and fear. The developers pushed back against a full Kanban implementation and a kanban (signal) system to pull work when they had capacity. Janice had to back off and reduce the scope of the changes. In October of 2008, she was able to make just three simple but important changes: She was able to extend their visual board to upstream analysis, intro-duce personal WIP limits, and drop the Ken Schwaber–style of estimating each request in hours of work, replacing it with a simpler system that simply asked for a "t-shirt size" ranging from extra-small through extra-large (XS, S, M, L, and XL). It was agreed by consensus that individuals would work on no more than three things at the same time: Their personal WIP limit would be three. This was visualized on the board by introducing small avatars—photographs of the team members mounted on magnets. Each person had three avatars, and they would place these beside tickets on which they were contributing some effort. Everyone could see who was working on what, who was collaborating together, and which tickets were currently being ignored. The changes to practices are summarized in Figure 7.1 while the new, extended board is shown in Figure 7.2.

	Before	After
Iterations	✓	✓
Scrum Master, PO	✓	✓
Sprint Planning	✓	✓
Daily Standup Meeting	✓	✓
Product Owner Accepts	✓	✓
Demo	✓	✓
Retrospective	✓	✓
Estimation	By task	By user story (T-shirt sized)
Other		Per-person WIP limit

Figure 7.1 Posit Science's Scrum implementation practices, October 2008

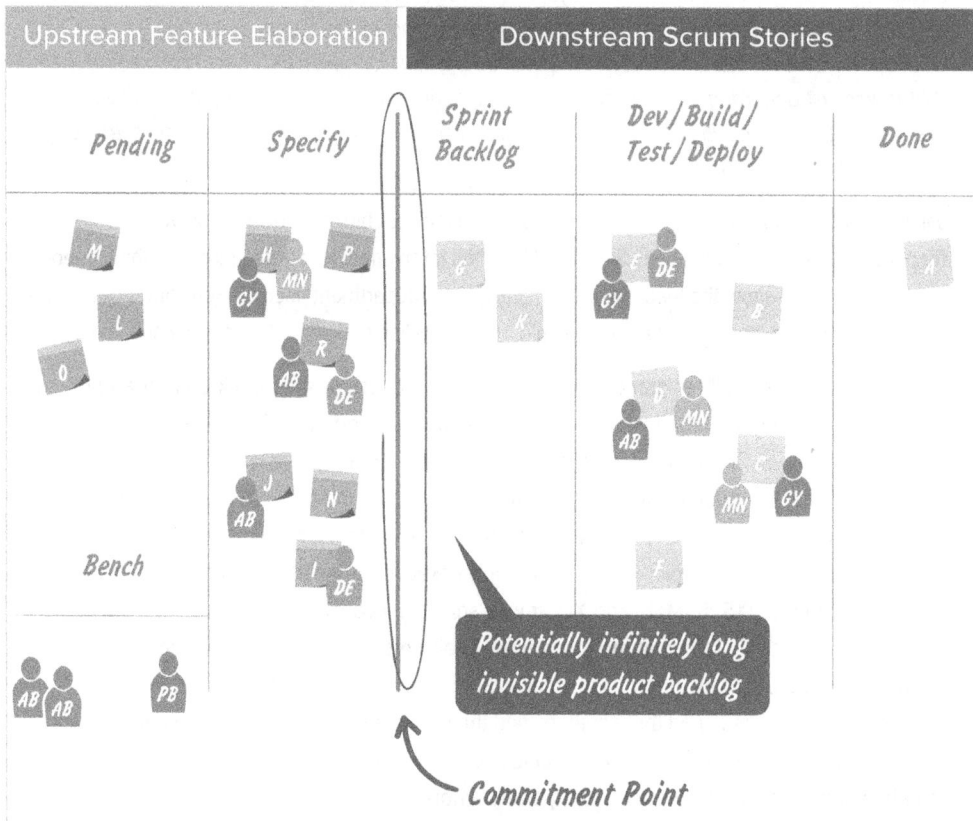

Figure 7.2 Posit Science's extended visual board, October 2008

On the extended board, the Scrum process is shown on the right-hand side, or downstream, while an upstream activity to elaborate customer requests—transforming a feature request into a set of user stories—is shown on the left-hand side. Tickets flow from left to right. Every third week, the sprint planning activity provided the commitment point. Stories selected for a sprint are committed, while the product backlog contains a potentially unbounded number of uncommitted stories. The product backlog isn't visualized on the board; rather, it is stored in the software tool.

This visual representation reveals some important details that were perhaps opaque previously: The people doing the elaboration work shown in the Specify column are, in fact, the same people doing development work. Hence, developers from the team multitask among estimated, planned, and committed work and unplanned, upstream, requirements-elaboration work. Requirements elaboration at Posit was unplanned, ungoverned, and disruptive. Part of the inability to deliver on sprint commitments was due to the distraction of working on unplanned requirements elaboration.

As a general rule, we never want to see a situation where workers cross a commitment point and multitask between planned, committed work and unplanned, uncommitted, optional requests. This is especially true when specific commitments to delivery dates have been made.

So, already we can see room for further improvement at Posit. The problem was that the developers were not yet ready for it. Perhaps standing in front of this board every day would help them to see what we could already see? Time would tell. Janice, now in the role of Kanban coach, had to be patient.

The idea behind the change in approach to estimation was to move away from unnecessary precision. It was causing a lot of pain, and the accuracy of the estimate was always questionable. A t-shirt size would provide a broad idea of how big each request was, especially for stakeholders who were not familiar with software development work. Being less precise was certainly easier and faster, and it tended to produce consensus. It was hoped that it would also be more accurate, enabling them to deliver on their promises. Janice communicated that the only important metric was, "Did we deliver what we promised?" Delivering on promises affects oxytocin levels in the brain. Oxytocin is the brain chemical associated with trust and some other emotions, such as love. By speaking the language of neuroscience with her neuroscientists, she hoped to make them understand and to move them to action. This entire department understood that the hypothalamus in the brains of both the trusting and the trusted would produce oxytocin when deliveries were made as promised. Each sprint completed with a matching promise of functionality would enhance the relationship between the stakeholders and the developers.

This October 2008 implementation at Posit (Figure 7.3) isn't a Kanban system. There are no WIP limits assigned to the workflow, and the end-to-end system is not relieved of overburdening. The work in the system can grow in an unbounded fashion, while within the sprint there is no restriction on how much multitasking may happen. Equally, work may be started and then set aside for periods of time. The work in the sprint backlog is bounded only by the planning, and its effectiveness is a function of the accuracy of the estimation process. While there is deferred commitment and pull, it is at the scale of a batch of work that ought to be completed over three weeks, while a true Kanban system works at the scale of individual requests, one kanban—one ticket—at a time.

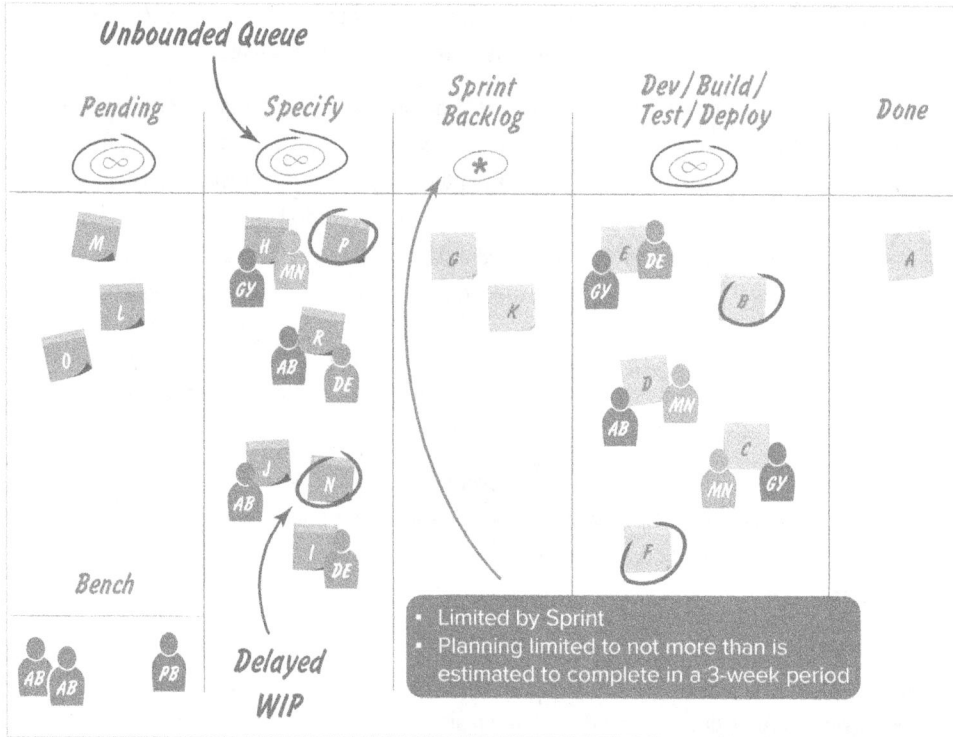

Figure 7.3 Protecting people from overburdening doesn't protect a workflow from overburdening.

Naming Proto-Kanban

This and other variants of partial implementations of Kanban have come to be known as "proto-Kanban," a term coined by the software engineering academic Richard Turner, formerly of the Stevens Institute. "Proto" implies evolutionary predecessor. These implementations are so named because of stories like this one, the Posit Science story. As you will see, this degenerate partial kanban system at Posit evolves into a full and proper implementation later. So, these degenerate implementations are, in fact, stepping-stones, and are an active part of the evolutionary process. Hence, this story isn't only a Scrumban story; it is also a proto-kanban story.

The term "proto-Kanban" has largely fallen out of use amongst the Kanban coaching community, in favor of "a low-maturity implementation" or, more simply, just "low-maturity

Kanban." This followed the arrival of the Kanban Maturity Model (KMM) in 2018. Together with Teodora Bozheva, I demonstrated that patterns of Kanban implementation correlated with distinct levels of organizational maturity. There, proto-Kanban implementations are typical of lower-maturity organizations. In cases where they evolve into full Kanban implementations, they illustrate that the organization, and its leadership, matured and demanded more of their processes and more of Kanban. In cases where the implementation didn't mature, didn't evolve, where it plateaued, this indicated that the organization and its leadership failed to mature. This plateauing problem, with an organization stubbornly stuck in a low-maturity mode of operation, is now recognized as one of the two most common failure modes of a Kanban implementation.

This record of the Posit Science story also illustrates one of the earliest examples of using a per-person WIP limit with a workflow that involves considerable scale—more than twenty people. At that time, autumn 2008, this approach was associated only with the nascent concept of Personal Kanban, which had not yet been codified or documented.

Takeaways

- Scrum worked well for Posit Science and enabled them to launch their second product within expectations.
- Complexity in their environment—supporting two products and chasing revenue opportunities while building a third product—created pressure and anxiety not previously seen at Posit Science.
- Sprint planning meetings became long, stressful, and emotional. Some people withdrew and stopped attending. Poorer quality decision making resulted from intermittent attendance.
- A "global warming" condition is a circumstance where something gets slowly, gradually worse in a manner that is imperceptible on a day-to-day basis but is much more evident over a longer period of time.
- The global warming condition at Posit was that it was becoming more and more reactionary to unfolding events and losing sight of long-term objectives.
- As Scrum began to break under the strain, Agile consultants insisted that the fault was with the people at Posit and not with the process. This analysis failed to accept that circumstances may have changed and that Scrum was no longer an appropriate choice.
- Janice Linden-Reed discovered Kanban through online discussion of the work of Corey Ladas and his Agile 2008 conference presentation about Scrumban.
- Janice's proposal to adopt Kanban was immediately rejected by the product development organization.
- After some time, the vice president responsible for the department agreed that something had to be done and that Kanban should be given a chance.
- Still, there was resistance. Only a partial implementation, with a per-person WIP limit, an extended board to include some upstream function, and a change to a less precise but perhaps more accurate style of estimation, was possible.
- Partial, or shallow, Kanban implementations are known as "proto-Kanban."
- Proto-Kanban implies an evolutionary predecessor.
- The term "proto-Kanban" was coined because shallow, partial implementations often lead, over time, to a full implementation.
- Posit Science was one of the first documented case studies to exhibit this proto-Kanban behavior and evolve into a full Kanban system.
- The term "proto-Kanban" has largely fallen out of usage in Kanban coaching circles.
- Proto-Kanban is associated with lower-maturity implementations of Kanban, and with Maturity Levels 1 and 2 of the Kanban Maturity Model (KMM).
- Per-person WIP limits seen in this case study are more commonly associated with Personal Kanban. However, use of per-person WIP limits has become an established part of typical proto-Kanban implementations.

8

Be Patient
Removing Objections to Enable Change

The business problems described in Chapter 7 hadn't gone away. Under financial pressure, politics became an issue within Posit, and different factions with opinions about how the firm should proceed began to emerge. There was pressure to move into the consumer space; one enabler for that would be a web-based implementation rather than the current products that had to be installed as native applications on a user's computer. Posit was still very much in the business of producing CD-ROMs containing native applications and shipping physical boxes through a distribution and retail channel.

Both the precision and speed a user attained was important to the games' clinical effectiveness. Data integrity was also vital—losing data, or confusing data from one user to another, would negate the clinical value of playing. These were computer games that were prescribed like drugs: "Play this game fifteen minutes each day and your peripheral vision should improve." They needed to be treated as both medical devices and drugs, the argument went. The staff at Posit were scientists involved in serious play, not entertainment.

Lumosity is now a well-known brand and one that readers may be familiar with. It has invested heavily in consumer marketing, especially television commercials. Lumosity makes brain exercise games, just as Posit does. They were and are peers. During the latter part of the first decade of this century, Lumosity was gaining ground while Posit was struggling for market adoption and revenue. The pressure to copy Lumosity's lead was strong. However, if you pause briefly and carefully read Lumosity's advertising or website, you'll realize that they make no medical claims as to the effectiveness of their product. Lumosity does not hold itself to the same clinical, medical-grade standard that Posit does. It's far easier to have a consumer product at an affordable consumer price when you don't hold yourself to the same regulatory regime. Without any doubt, Lumosity employs brain plasticity scientists, and their products are based on scientific underpinnings and good intentions, but aspects of non-functional quality on which Posit scientists were unwilling to compromise—such as precise timing of operation and clinical testing prior to launch—may have been areas where Lumosity was able to save cost and accelerate time-to-market.

Posit's identity as scientists and their vision and mission for their company—its purpose—was to make medical-grade products that reversed the effects of aging and repaired damage from trauma such as injuries sustained in automobile accidents or in combat. Lumosity presumably saw themselves differently—metaphorically speaking, more in the dietary supplements business rather than the prescription drug business. Although they were using scientific ideas, they didn't appear to have aspirations for robust clinical results. If their respective products were sold in a pharmacy, Posit's would have been over-the-counter or perhaps "prescription only," while Lumosity's would be off-the-shelf. Lumosity's willingness to compromise and develop a web-based platform enabled them to reach far more people and to mine a wealth of information from those web-based users. Consequently, their finances and valuation were in much better shape.

Posit Science: Things Heat Up and Motivate Further Change

InSight, Posit Science's new suite of games, was set to be just like the earlier Brain Fitness Program, delivered on a CD-ROM and priced similarly. Many people felt that it was expensive for its designated target audience. This issue would gradually become a bigger and bigger concern.

Janice continued to focus on the developers. Implementing a rudimentary proto-Kanban system was a small win for her and she saw that things improved a little. The developers were more focused and less anxious about whether they could meet their promises. While they felt relief from overburdening and enjoyed their three-items-per-person WIP limit, the changes did little to relieve the bigger problems of delivering whole projects against an expected schedule. The workflow was unpredictable and there was still too much work, including a portion that was unplanned—a reaction to current circumstances. The team continued to have a hard time coping. Janice realized that the most valuable role she could play was to help the developers realize what was really affecting their performance. If they could see and feel it, perhaps they'd be motivated to implement more changes, little by little. This was why she had liked Kanban in the first place. Its evolutionary nature seemed attuned to the nature of human behavior.

One of the ways she helped was to continually ask them during retrospective meetings how they felt—to let them express their frustrations in a safe environment. She started to change their vocabulary, introducing them to language such as "work-in-progress," "class of service," "cost of delay," and so forth. Armed with a better lexicon to express their troubles, they were able to see new ways to improve.

What continued to be problematic was selecting what to work on and what to leave until later. Asking business owners about priorities didn't help: Apparently everything was high priority. When priorities changed because something urgent hadn't yet been selected, the developers simply absorbed the request, taking on more and more work. While individually they were limited to multitasking across just three items, the workflow filled up with committed work. The problem described in relation to Figure 7.3 was real. After some months, they came to realize that they had to address the overburdening of the whole system if they were to improve their ability to deliver against customer expectations.

One source of demand was generated from tactical decision making by senior management. The pricing model that didn't much concern the development group became their direct problem. More than ever, there was pressure to chase the market. Potential clients and investors were actively pursued. In order to woo customers or investors, Posit leadership came with many requests for one-off demos and feature enhancements. Most of those had to be completed and presented against short deadlines. Unplanned, urgent work pre-empted committed work in-progress. This reactionary, opportunistic business demand could rarely wait the three or more weeks and be planned for a scheduled sprint. Posit needed every bit of business they could get, and no one could say no to these requests. Planning, estimations, and working in strict time boxes became more and more auxiliary and unnecessary in that context. Posit was breaking the rules of Scrum: Urgent and critical items were added to existing sprint commitments. This work was neither planned as part of a sprint nor delivered at the end of the sprint; rather, it was expedited to the customer whenever it was needed. Despite the emotional attachment to Scrum that had become so much of the developers' identity over the past three years, there was increasing recognition that its rules were not serving their needs. They were succeeding despite Scrum rather than because of it.

By the beginning of 2009, Posit was ready to embrace further changes. David Hoffman asked Janice if there was more change that could be implemented. Naturally, the answer was yes; so she started to facilitate team collaboration on a better process—one based on, not just inspired by Kanban.

Posit Science: New Insights on Priority, Urgency, and Impact

Posit was now actively working on its third product, DriveSharp, which consisted of three games. Through their research with elderly people, Posit's neuroscientists realized that one of the biggest problems faced by that demographic group is their deteriorating ability to drive, which was mostly due to two factors: failing peripheral vision and the inability to react quickly in more complex driving situations. Driving has always been associated with independence and, for this baby boomer generation, owning a car and the freedom to go wherever, whenever is something to which they attach great value. Being unable to drive means the loss of independence and reliance on others—it is a core identity issue. Fiercely independent people give it up sorely. A product that would enable people to continue driving long into their retirement and thus protect their prized independence was bound to do well in the market. Through the three games that were part of DriveSharp, Posit was aiming to extend independence and freedom for the Baby Boomer generation. This time, the channel to market would be in partnership with car insurance companies, with an offer that amounted to "sign up to play this game and receive a discount on your insurance." Who ever heard of seniors who don't love a discount? This product was a sure-fire winner. Consequently, the development team needed to focus on it immediately and deliver it quickly.

However, they were hindered by the continuing miscommunication between them and their stake-holders. Business owners would give them work items without much thought for how busy they were or what other stakeholders had asked of them. They said yes to everything and missed a majority of their deadlines. They felt miserable. The whole process was ruining relationships between people across the company. There had to be a better way than constantly saying yes and allowing everyone to believe their request was the most important one. The conversation needed to shift to under-standing business risks, which would facilitate discussions about urgency and impact, thus enabling a better understanding of when to start new work.

Although the long-term goal was for a more mature organization that could meet customer expecta-tions and business objectives, Janice had to start with small, realistic plans. She focused on issues people were raising at retrospective meetings. She looked through her notes and made a list of sources of dissatisfaction. She would address these one by one.

A recurring source of the team's dissatisfaction was often referred to as "fragmentation." Constantly changing priorities meant developers were continually pre-empted and pulled in different directions. This prevented them from focusing and completing work with high quality or in a timely manner. There was low satisfaction and little sense of achievement. Janice knew this was a hot button with the team, so she offered to alleviate their complaints by "smoothing the flow" and preventing interruptions and changes of direction.

Janice is looking directly at the emotional pain point—fragmentation—constant interruptions, low sense of achievement, probably lowered self-esteem, frustration, and a lack of pride of workmanship. When she proposes the new kanban system solution, she sells it to the team as a new "flow" system. She doesn't use the word "Kanban" directly. These are Scrum people, so she avoids raising their hackles while offering to alleviate their pain. Good coaching is humane. Good coaching has empathy for the humanity of the individuals involved. Sometimes this is referred to as "the Fight Club school of

Kanban" because "the first rule of Fight Club is that you never talk about Fight Club."[27] If mentioning Kanban risks raising resistance, then don't mention it. Address an emotional pain point directly with your proposal and proceed.

She had to limit the WIP in the whole system, not just for each individual. Her developers were ready to make this change. After several months of watching their board and seeing the cause and effect from limiting WIP, they now understood why it was necessary and the benefits it would bring. With the right WIP limits, Janice could create balance in which both developers and testers were equally busy, yet never overburdened. Work would flow better!

She sat down to discuss all her proposed changes with everyone involved, including business owners. She needed their buy-in and consensus to move forward. The changes felt counterintuitive to many, especially the more experienced ones. She was perhaps fortunate that this entire organization understood brain function, plasticity, and how humans cope with change. They were prepared to follow a path that felt wrong while understanding that it made logical sense: their limbic brain (their sensory perception and pattern matching capability) was objecting while their pre-frontal cortex (their logical inference capability) agreed with the analysis and logic of the proposal.

The next thing to address was the dysfunctional planning and prioritization. She needed to bring some organization and collegial collaboration to the process of selecting, sequencing, and scheduling work.

Contemporaneously to this, I was developing the manuscript for the Blue Book and attempting to codify classes of service, which had first emerged in the Corbis implementation in 2007, by identifying the nature of the cost of delay in a work item that in turn resulted in the selection of a class of service for that item. There were four empirically derived classes of service and I'd named them: Expedite, Fixed Date, Standard, and Intangible. Janice had asked me to advise her and help Posit with their transition plans. So, Posit had first access to new and, at the time, unpublished material and were the first organization to see the association of sketches of delay cost functions mapped to classes of service, as shown in Figure 8.1 on the next page.

The concept was simple: Ask business owners to describe the impact over time for a given function. This would enable a determination of urgency. The discussion would help facilitate scheduling as well as the class of service required after the work was selected and committed. Stakeholders were briefed on the concept and asked to select the delay cost function that best matched the business risks associated with the request. This worked incredibly well. It was perhaps the most easily adopted of any new technique Janice introduced at Posit. It quickly institutionalized and years later was still in use for assessing risk and selecting and scheduling work.

---

27. Based on the book of the same name by Chuck Palahniuk, *Fight Club* is an American film that has become a cult classic. According to one of its stars, Edward Norton, it examines the value conflicts of Generation X as the first generation raised on television. https://en.wikipedia.org/wiki/Fight_Club

The sketches show the *y*-axis labeled with the abstract concept of impact. This facilitated various ways of assessing "cost" related to time: opportunity cost of lost revenue, operational expense incurred, subscribers acquired over time, impact on intangibles such as customer satisfaction, brand equity, mindshare, investor confidence, and so forth.

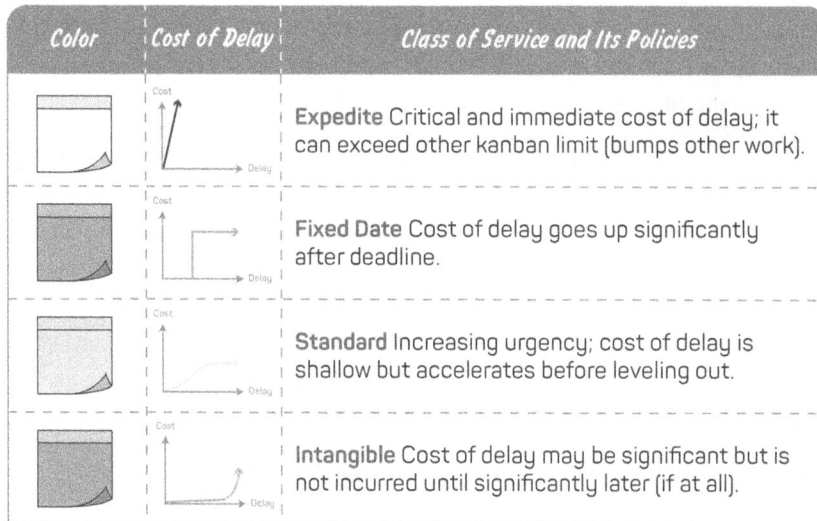

Color	Cost of Delay	Class of Service and Its Policies
		Expedite Critical and immediate cost of delay; it can exceed other kanban limit (bumps other work).
		Fixed Date Cost of delay goes up significantly after deadline.
		Standard Increasing urgency; cost of delay is shallow but accelerates before leveling out.
		Intangible Cost of delay may be significant but is not incurred until significantly later (if at all).

Figure 8.1 Sketches of Cost of Delay curves mapped to classes of service

While over the intervening years this set of sketches was extended, it remains the simplest, and possibly most powerful, way of qualitatively tying cost of delay to the class of service used for a ticket in a kanban system. Although quantitative techniques emerged later and are included in my Enterprise Services Planning training curricula available from Kanban University, they are much harder to understand and require difficult-to-acquire input data and the use of software to run a convolution algorithm in order to establish a "probable cost of delay in starting" function and, from its derivative, a quantitative value for urgency. Consequently, quantitative assessment of cost of delay remains an intellectual curiosity, while the simple qualitative approach using sketches showing impact over time has proven powerful and easy to adopt. The fact that this technique has prevailed for more than a decade is a strong indication of its effectiveness and robustness. Some mathematical analysis of quantitative data, conducted in 2018, has shown us that the original four curves in the sketches do, in fact, map to observed mathematical functions and accurately reflect the risk of delay. Hence, the robustness of the original four sketched curves isn't an accident; we now have a mathematical proof. Examining the detail of this mathematical proof is beyond the scope of this text but is taught in my Enterprise Services Planning curricula.

In addition to cost of delay, the executive team were also trained in another simple qualitative risk assessment taxonomy that describes the role played in the market by a given feature or function. These roles are:

- Table stakes (commodity features expected by customers; omission is unacceptable)
- Cost reducers (features that save [Posit] cost in development, production, or field service)
- Regulatory (required by a regulator, subject to regulatory changes; omission is unacceptable)
- Spoilers (also known as Catch Up, or Neutralizing features; these copy a competitor's differentiator)
- Differentiator (a new feature, unique to the market)

While this taxonomy made a great deal of sense to the business school–trained executive team at Posit, they rejected it. Their argument was that this taxonomy was clearly for more mature markets with an established set of competitors and well understood customer expectations. Their argument was that Posit was in a nascent and emerging market and, while other brain plasticity firms such as Lumosity existed, they weren't directly competitive. Hence, Posit would find little to no value in labeling features using this taxonomy. Knowing that something was either table stakes or differentiating wouldn't affect their decision making. So I challenged them to come up with something better, something more relevant and attuned to their business and their market. After a short huddle, perhaps fifteen minutes later, they returned with their own taxonomy. It was very simple:

- Existing Market
- New

They recognized that they needed to hedge risk by allocating capacity in their portfolio. They needed to enhance and develop existing products, broadening and deepening their market reach, while they also needed to continue to probe for new markets and market segments by commercializing more of their fundamental scientific research.

I challenged them a little further, and after another short conversation, perhaps only five minutes, there was a consensus that there should be a 60/40 split. Sixty percent of features flowing through their kanban system should be for existing market development, while forty percent should be for commercialization of research and introduction of new products.

So, two very simple methods were introduced to facilitate planning and prioritization: Requests would be triaged using cost of delay, and commitment would be deferred until the "last responsible moment" before an item was too urgent, with an appropriate class of service to facilitate flow and delivery; a capacity allocation would ensure a mix of work intended to manage risk exposure across their product portfolio.

Previously, business owners had anxiety about limiting WIP and deferring commitment. Now, with a better means to assess risk and a new language with which to discuss comparative business risks, they were comfortable with the introduction of a kanban system. Since 2010, methods of qualitative risk assessment have been recognized as essential to facilitate the successful implementation of Kanban, and such practices appear at the mid-levels of 3 and 4 in the Kanban Maturity Model.

There was one more obstacle: The developers objected to the naming of the classes of service, specifically the Intangible class of service. It turned out that almost all work likely to be classified as having a deferred cost of delay (and therefore assigned the Intangible class of service) was work proposed by the development organization. This was mostly work on system architecture, code main- tenance, and systems infrastructure. They objected to their work being labeled as having "intangible" value and feared it would never be selected.

Responding to their objections, Janice engaged in some negotiation: Two out of ten slots in the replenishment buffer, to be known as the Top Ten, would be reserved for Intangible class items; additionally, the classes would be renamed.

In 2009, I'd been persuaded by Julian Everett, at the time the super-smart chief architect for the BBC's websites, that cost of delay could be modeled as a linear function. Julian had shown that in discussions with business owners, he could get them to declare a business value for a feature, such as a new set of web pages for the forthcoming season of Dr. Who, and then determine a confidence level to adjust the number. The BBC's website made money from advertising; hence, the number of anticipated ad impressions was the metric for determining business value. If the business owner thought that a new set of pages would generate 1.2 million page views (and hence ad impressions) in a year, but they clearly had only around 75 percent confidence in this number, then Julian would adjust 1.2 million to 900,000 and calculate a monthly rate as an average—ef- fectively creating a linear regression for the value. Whether or not the rate of page views was truly flat and aggregated linearly was, in his experience, not important. When making a comparative selection between different opportunities for the same web development team, he found that linear functions were good enough. Given that Julian had real-world experience, my guidance was based on his reports and I initially provided Posit with a sketch of a linear rising line for the Standard class of service.

The Ph.D. neuroscientists were immediately smart enough to push back against this, arguing that typical delay cost functions were "accelerating" and ultimately would tail off as an S-curve. Ironically, my earlier guidance had stated this, but Julian's experience had suggested that linear lines were good enough and a lot simpler—the idea of cost of delay as a constant rate is attractive and alluring. Posit people weren't buying it and, in truth, their gut feeling is correct. Perhaps in Julian's constrained domain of comparative assessment of website features it did make sense, but time has convinced me that it was poor general guidance.

The Standard class of service was renamed Accelerating, and the sketch used was like the S-curve shown in Figure 8.2. This meant that the word "Standard" was not used for that class of service. Meanwhile, there was an emotional objection to "Intangible," and hence the lowest class of service came to be named "Standard" as a unique customization and enabler for Posit Science.

Color	Cost of Delay	Class of Service and Its Policies
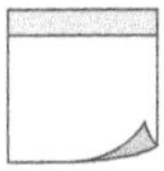		**Expedite** Critical and immediate cost of delay; it can exceed other kanban limit (bumps other work).
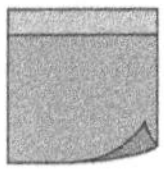	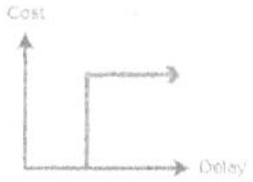	**Fixed Date** Cost of delay goes up significantly after deadline.
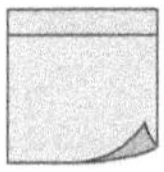		**Accelerating** Increasing urgency; cost of delay is shallow but accelerates before leveling out.
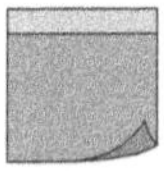	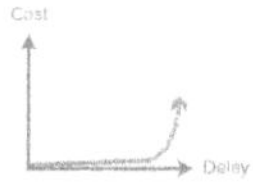	**Standard** Cost of delay may be significant but is not incurred until significantly later (if at all).

Figure 8.2 Classes of service at Posit Science

Every change agent—every Kanban coach—should expect some pushback on initial designs. Just as Janice was, they should be prepared to back off in the first instance and implement something shallow, something intended as a proto-kanban, and then be patient—wait for everyone involved to internalize the issues and for motivation to build to enable a full change. Equally, when getting pushback on minor elements such as the naming of a class of service, be prepared to negotiate and make changes. If there is a rock in your way, be prepared to negotiate around it. Texts such as this one are here to advise you and to provide illustrative guidance; they are not prescriptive. With Kanban you have the freedom to tailor and evolve your own unique workflow solutions. Embrace that freedom. Do not feel constrained by the words on these pages.

Takeaways

- Lumosity, a competitor of Posit Science, had a greater focus on the consumer market and developed a web-based platform for its games.

- The small print on Lumosity packaging, website, and advertising does not make any clinical claims for their products. Those are almost certainly not engineered to the scientific, medical-grade standards of Posit Science products. This compromise enabled Lumosity to offer lower prices and gain significant market share.

- As time passed, the business pressure rose and Posit Science became more and more reactionary. Although the proto-Kanban implementation helped them, there was a growing need for further improvement. People were increasingly overburdened and stressed.

- Given enough time, the heat from their "global warming" condition became sufficiently severe that the team pulled additional change. They were ready to implement Kanban properly.

- To gain acceptance of WIP limits and a kanban pull system, it was necessary to provide business owners with new means of assessing business risk and understanding how to select work, in what sequence to select it, and when to schedule it.

- Qualitative risk analysis methods are essential to successful enterprise adoption of Kanban.

- Associating delay cost function sketches (or curves) with classes of service was first introduced at Posit Science. It was highly effective and popular with business executives.

- Be prepared to negotiate on small details of a kanban system design in order to gain buy-in to proceed; for example, changing naming conventions for classes of service.

9

A Flow System

Design and Implementation of Kanban at Posit Science

"We just did our last iteration.[28] We have switched to flow." Janice announced on her Twitter feed that she had begun the adoption of the new "flow" system at Posit. The relief was tangible. Painful timeboxed sprints were now a thing of the past. Just like the company she had read about, it made no sense to timebox work in Posit's context. Three-week timeboxes weren't helpful to the business owners or to anyone on the service delivery side. Everyone was miserable. Switching to an on-demand flow system met everyone's needs much better.

Posit Science: The Kanban System

The table in Figure 9.1 summarizes the changes made from the proto-Kanban system of 2008 to the full Kanban system introduced in 2009. Sprints (iterations) were replaced with an on-demand flow system with a twenty-one-day service level agreement (SLA). The SLA was chosen to match the previous cadence of three-week sprints. The purpose was to encourage breakdown of work to be small enough to complete within three weeks and to allay fears that work would take longer without the pressure of a sprint boundary or specific delivery promise.

---

28. The Agile software development community often refers to timeboxed team activities as "iterations." This is a misnomer, as the activity is seldom iterative in the sense that work will be revisited and improved with greater fidelity as, say, an oil painting might be by its artist. Instead, Agile software development work is mostly incremental, and each "iteration" contains the completion of a small piece—part of a whole. "Iteration" is used synonymously with Sprint in the Scrum methodology, with "iteration" being considered more generic Agile terminology and not specific to Scrum.

	Before	After
Iterations	✓	✗ Flow & SLA
Scrum Master, PO	✓	✓
Sprint Planning	✓	✗ Triggered, per feature
Daily Standup Meeting	✓	✓
Product Owner Accepts	✓	✓
Demo	✓	✓ Calendar
Retrospective	✓	✓ Calendar
Estimation	By task	By feature per SLA
Other		More detailed workflow
Other		Workflow WIP limits

Figure 9.1 Summary of changes from 2008 proto-Kanban to 2009 full Kanban system

There is a commonly held myth that a lack of a time-bound delivery commitment, such as a sprint demonstration, will lead to a lack of focus, laziness, and increasingly long delivery times. There is, in fact, no such evidence from more than a decade of Kanban usage. The fear is one generated by those who sell Scrum training and coaching for a living and wish to dissuade adoption of Kanban or existing customers from switching.

Posit used, as coaches and advisors, consultants from a well-known Agile software development software vendor who had a long history of actively dissuading the adoption of Kanban at their clients' companies. Ironically, they used a kanban system for their own software development, but as their product was designed for Scrum, they didn't want their clients using it.

There was significant motivation for change at Posit. The consultants had already lost their argument suggesting that it was "a lack of discipline" and the fault of the people at Posit. They had lost their ability to provide leadership, and their contract would not be renewed. However, the fears they had laid had to be mitigated. Janice did this by including the three-week guarantee of delivery within the service level agreement.

In addition to the twenty-one-day SLA, there was a further change in how estimation was conducted. You will recall that they'd started with the very precise estimation method, of speculating how many person hours were needed for each task: This approach was prescribed by Ken Schwaber, one of the two founders of Scrum, in his original book. At the time, this approach to estimation was the preferred approach of the consulting firm assisting Posit. The precise estimates actually offered little information value, as they had a very low probability of being accurate. When they introduced the proto-Kanban changes, they moved away from precision to a t-shirt sizing approach for user stories. This moves up a level in the hierarchy, as stories usually consist of tasks. Hence, there was less need for analysis, and the story level approach was faster. They hoped it would also have greater accuracy and better information value.

Now, a year later, they would move away from estimation almost completely and move up another level of the hierarchy to the feature level. Hence, it was no longer necessary to break features down through analysis into user stories prior to making a commitment and deciding to proceed with the work. They would simply request a thumbs-up, thumbs-down vote after the requirements were read out and explained to the team, taking just a few minutes of discussion to establish a confidence level. If there was strong confidence that the feature could be finished within the SLA, it was marked as ready for selection. If not, its business owner was requested to rethink the requirement and submit the ticket again.

The roles of Scrummaster and Product Owner, key elements of Scrum, were unchanged. With Kanban, no one gets any new roles, responsibilities, or job titles—at least initially—and certainly none were imposed upon them.

Roles and job titles become key elements of an individual's professional identity. Changing a role, a job title, or significantly changing responsibilities tends to meet with resistance—and fear. There is a fear of being, at least initially, incompetent in the new role or with new responsibilities. Such a fear can be allayed through training, mentoring, and a failure-tolerant culture that provides personal safety for experimentation and learning. However, identity runs deeper than just the fear of initial incompetence. Identity provides the means of self-image and for determining self-esteem. Skills, competence, and the role played are also key to establishing status in a social group. A new role or job title directly attacks an individual's sense of self and their self-worth. New roles and job titles have both psychological and sociological effects. We might expect 70 to 80 percent of people to have misgivings and trepidation about a new job title or a new role with new responsibilities.

Kanban is the start-with-what-you-do-now method. Kanban also asks you to "go around the rock" and avoid obstacles to change (see Chapter 11). If you start by giving someone a new job title, then you are starting by throwing an obstacle in your way. Why do that? Let people keep their existing roles and job titles until they are ready to pull a new identity for themselves.

Each of the three Scrum teams at Posit would work on one feature at a time. A strict one feature per team WIP limit was imposed. Replenishment meetings would be triggered on demand when a team needed to pull a new feature to start. As the concept of three-week sprints was dropped, so too was the sprint planning every third week eliminated. These were the dreaded, stressful meetings with seventeen attendees, filled with emotion and anxiety. This brought great relief.

Replenishment meetings were facilitated using a small board, as shown in Figure 9.2. It has four regions: The Top Ten, In-Progress, Done, and Legend.

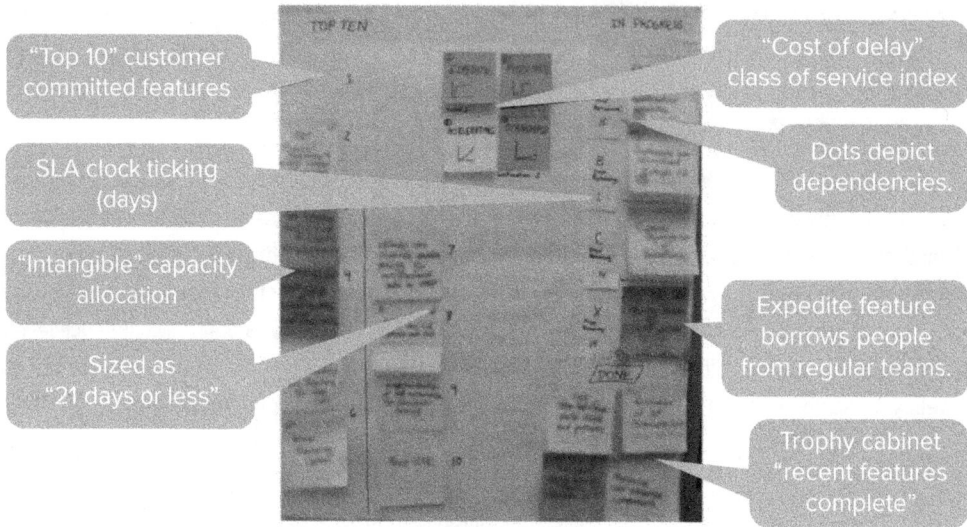

Figure 9.2 Posit Science replenishment meeting board

The Top Ten shows the input queue. In this case, it is a queue numbered 1 through 10. However, work wasn't necessarily pulled from the queue in strict prioritized order. Due to the nature of Posit's business, there was a lot of specialization and heterogeneity amongst their workforce and the work submitted. Consequently, their three Scrum teams were not homogeneous in skill sets. When a team finished a feature and was ready to pull another, the first item in the queue might not have been a good match for them. They would work their way down the queue until they found the first strong match for their skills. So, Posit implemented an almost-FIFO (first-in, first-out) input queue rather than the input buffer (sometimes called a "supermarket" in Lean literature) implemented at Microsoft and Corbis.

The Top Ten has a capacity allocation of two slots for Intangible class of service work.

In-Progress shows the features in progress for each of the three Scrum teams, shown only as A, B, and C. They didn't have names. This is an indication that the social cohesion was at the level of the whole department, and people didn't strongly identify with the smaller teams to which they were assigned. The teams were known as Scrum teams despite the Kanban implementation and the decoupling of cadences for planning, lead time, and delivery, together with the removal of timeboxed sprints.

The numbers below the team letter show the number of days elapsed on their twenty-one-day SLA. The picture shows what has triggered the replenishment meeting: The B team has completed a feature and pulled item 1 from the Top Ten. Items 2 through 10 should now shuffle up one place, and the current meeting will select a new item for slot number 10.

The features in progress are also annotated with decorations. The colored circles indicate peer dependencies—items that must be delivered together—same color, same delivery. The small fluorescent tabs indicate blocking issues and flag that the SLA may be in jeopardy.

Done is the trophy cabinet. Done provides a space for features completed in the recent past. Done provides time for reflection and feeling a sense of achievement. Done communicates to business owners "what we've done for you recently" and the value being delivered regularly.

The Legend shows the classes of service, the colors of the tickets, the delay cost function sketches associated with each, and any capacity allocation or other policies related to classes of service. In this case, Expedite items are limited to one, and the Intangibles have a minimum of two.

The board appears to show a fourth team, X. This actually represents the Expedite lane on the board. There wasn't a dedicated team for expedite requests. Instead, a feature with Expedite class of service was permitted to break the WIP limit. It didn't, however, completely pre-empt existing work. A cross-functional team from the entire pool of labor would form to complete the request. These individuals would come from any of the other three teams. Assuming that no one team was completely depleted, work would still continue on the current features in progress.

Not every element of Scrum was eliminated. As already mentioned, the Scrum roles of Scrum Master and Product Owner remained; so too did the daily "scrum," though effectively it became a daily Kanban meeting.

Demonstrations, retrospectives, and product owner acceptance would also stay. Demonstrations and retrospectives were scheduled every third week at exactly the same time and day as they had been with Scrum sprints. No change. Acceptance is fully explained later, in relation to the Kanban board implementation shown in Figure 9.5. Product owner acceptance continued. However, it became an on-demand activity, with work represented in a column on the board, as shown in Figure 9.3. The responsibilities of the product owner were unchanged.

Figure 9.3 on the next page shows the design for the new Kanban system and board. From a backlog of features, a top ten will be selected for delivery. The "Top Ten" queue had an interesting innovation—a two-phased, asynchronous commitment. In the Microsoft and Corbis examples, commitment is synchronous, in that both the customers and the delivery organization are represented at the meeting, and agreement is mutual. The customer says, "I want this done next," and the delivery service says, "In that case, we will do it next for you." The Posit design drops this synchronous commitment. Instead, at replenishment meetings, the business owners get to pick new items for the Top Ten, while the delivery organization doesn't have to commit to any of them. The commitment point occurs when one of the Scrum teams pulls a feature into the Design/Specification column of the board. Only then is there a two-sided commitment, and the clock starts ticking on the twenty-one-day service level agreement.

An asynchronous commitment has some advantages. It is especially useful when it is difficult to organize meetings involving all of the stakeholders. However, it is typically representative of a lower social capital culture, with lower trust and less collaboration. We've come to recognize that asynchronous commitment is typical of organizations maturing from Level 2 to Level 3 in the Kanban Maturity Model. Some of the Kanban Magic described in earlier chapters is unlikely to happen if you can't get both the upstream and downstream people together and have them agree together on specific commitments.

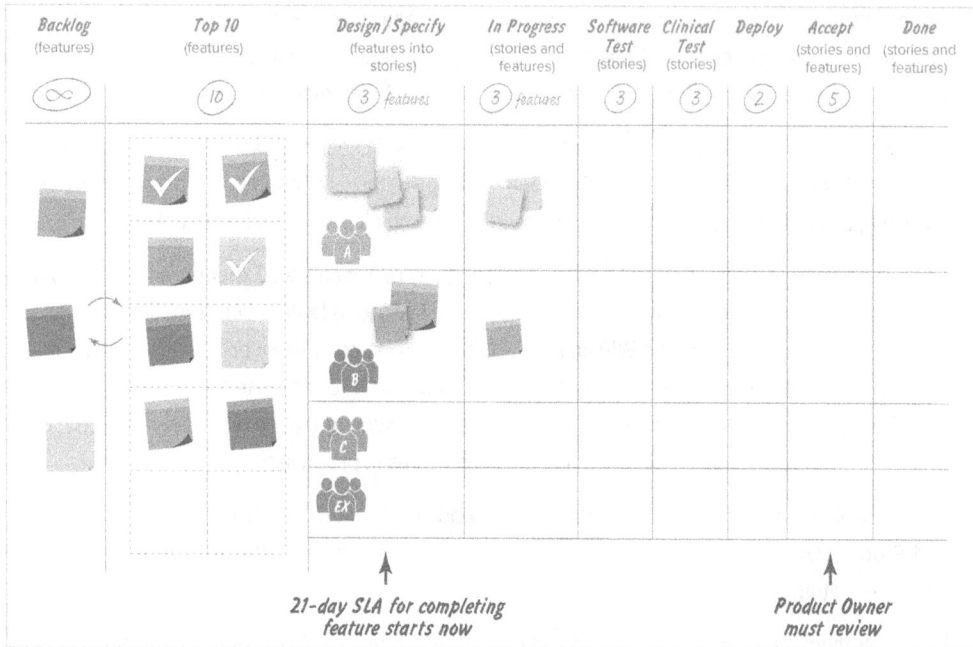

Figure 9.3 Design for Posit's new "flow system" kanban board

The delivery rate at Posit averaged approximately one feature per week. Consequently, the WIP plus the Top Ten represents around three months of work. Some items may wait ten weeks or more before being selected and pulled onto the kanban board. Something in the Top Ten is expected to be delivered, and hence, a forward signal for marketing, public relations, or even lead time to prepare delivery can happen as soon as an item enters the Top Ten. However, the items are ultimately uncommitted and have generated no impact downstream. Consequently, it was permitted for the owner of a Top Ten item to swap it during replenishment meetings for another feature they deemed of greater urgency and importance.

So, the Top Ten provides a means to forward-signal arrival while avoiding full commitment. It facilitates notice periods and deferred commitment together. The concept of an asynchronous commitment around the input buffer has appeared in other implementations subsequently. Sami Honkonen reported[29] a version that used a visual calendar to indicate tickets to be started on a specific week up to thirteen weeks in advance.

These asynchronous commitments around the input buffer are predecessors of the dynamic scheduling system now used for Enterprise Services Planning—the approach used for dependency management of enterprise-scale Kanban implementations.

The Posit Kanban board features a row for each of the Scrum teams, with an additional row for expedite requests. The board is two-tiered. A feature occupies a lane, but a feature is broken down

---

29. Unfortunately, Sami has removed the specific blog post, and there is no reliable alternative reference.

into stories—shown as the smaller tickets on the board. Stories are children of the "parent" feature. Stories flow across the board. Once completed through software test, typically the entire feature would then be pulled into clinical validation testing.

Recall that Posit suffered from a problem similar to Microsoft's: They had workers doing committed work also doing upstream analysis. The workers were multitasking across the commitment point in the workflow. This no longer happens. In the new design, analysis into stories is deferred until after commitment. This effectively means that Posit's teams were pursuing the "no estimates" approach that we first saw with Microsoft.

This, naturally, creates the danger that features are simply too big to fit within the twenty-one-day SLA. And again, we see that Posit utilized a strategy that we first saw at Microsoft, the "credit card fraud" solution. They would let things that might be too big into the system and hope to catch them quickly, within a day or two. However, unlike Microsoft, they put a small information request in front to reduce the likelihood of something too big entering the system. At Microsoft, the likelihood, historically, had been only 2 percent. This was already almost negligible. Hence, there was no need for such an upfront information request. At Posit, there was a perception that the likelihood of an item being too large to complete within three weeks was far greater than 2 percent. Hence, it was necessary to gather some more information prior to commitment.

Notice that some items in the Top Ten have check marks. This indicates that the software developers—the delivery service—believe that the feature can be completed within twenty-one days. Naturally, this approach won't be 100 percent foolproof, but the percentage that will slip through should be small, perhaps as small as the 2 percent too big in the Microsoft case study. Hence, just as in the Microsoft story, the development team were empowered to flag features that they believed were too big if they discovered this after starting work.

Unlike Microsoft, where an immovable governance rule meant that anything too big had to be rerouted to a capital-expenditure budget major project, Posit had three options:

- **Do it anyway.** We want it. We need it. It has some urgency attached to it. We don't care if it takes more than three weeks.
- **Trim it down.** Invite the business owners to inspect the analyzed stories and indicate which, if any of them, they deem to be excessive.
- **Throw it back.** Return it to the backlog and ask the business owners to think again about something simpler.

Figure 9.4 shows the 2009 revision of the feature request form business owners used to submit new features to the backlog. It introduces a compulsory request for new information regarding cost of delay and the required class of service, while relegating the older business case information as merely optional. The business owners are not being asked to drop their existing way of doing things. They are simply asked for some simple, additional information that is valuable while not being burdensome to provide. This approach represents evolutionary change in action: Cost of delay is the new species entering the environment, while return on investment assessment is the incumbent species; together they will compete to see which is the fittest solution. We can expect the fitter solution to survive and thrive, while the less fit alternative should wither away and fall out of use.

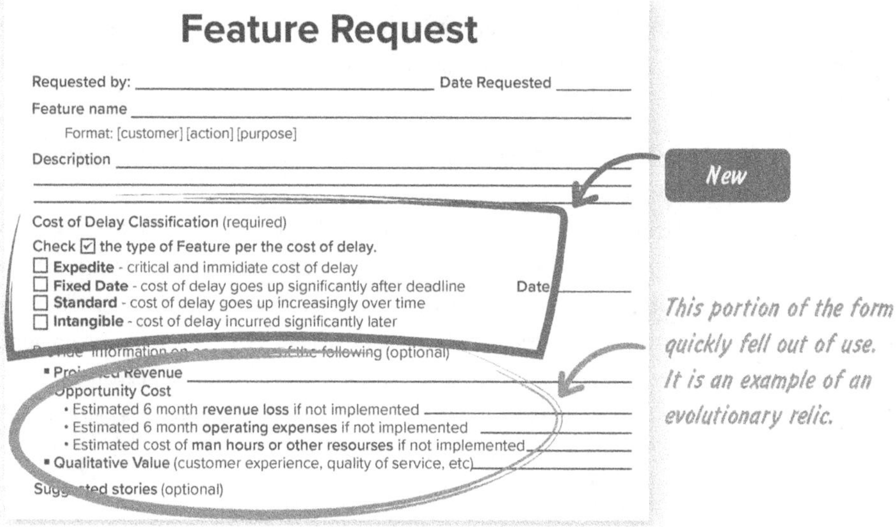

Feature Request

Requested by: ______ Date Requested ______

Feature name ______

Format: [customer] [action] [purpose]

Description ______

Cost of Delay Classification (required)

Check ☑ the type of Feature per the cost of delay.

- ☐ **Expedite** - critical and immidiate cost of delay
- ☐ **Fixed Date** - cost of delay goes up significantly after deadline Date ______
- ☐ **Standard** - cost of delay goes up increasingly over time
- ☐ **Intangible** - cost of delay incurred significantly later

... information ... following (optional)

- ... Revenue ______
- ...pportunity Cost
  - Estimated 6 month **revenue loss** if not implemented ______
  - Estimated 6 month **operating expenses** if not implemented ______
  - Estimated cost of **man hours or other resourses** if not implemented ______
- **Qualitative Value** (customer experience, quality of service, etc) ______

Su...ted stories (optional)

Figure 9.4 Feature request form at Posit Science, mid-2009

Within six weeks of introduction, none of the business owners were filling out the optional return on investment section of the form. Cost of delay and the discussions at the approximately weekly replenishment meetings were sufficient to make good quality selection, sequencing, and scheduling decisions. The lower section of the form had become an evolutionary relic, a vestigial organ of the Posit workflow! One year later, when we captured the form from a Microsoft Word document as part of evidence collection for this case study, the lower section was still there. Despite not being in use for a year, no one had removed it or even discussed removing it. Evolutionary change tends to leave evidence behind—things that have fallen out of use and can become hard to explain later.

Figure 9.5 is a photograph of the actual board, taken in 2009. The photograph is annotated to highlight some interesting elements of the design and implementation of the Kanban system and board.

The feature in the Expedite lane is an orange, fixed delivery date class of service ticket. Notably, it wasn't originally an expedite request. As the physical position of the ticket in the Expedite lane tells everyone that this feature must be expedited, the color isn't important to communicate that fact for operational purposes. Instead, leaving the original orange ticket, and not replacing it with a white[30] expedite ticket,

30. Posit actually used bright pink for Expedite, but this was unconventional. When using this case study for training purposes, we've changed it to white, reserving pink for blocking issues. While not historically accurate, this avoids confusing those new to the method.

actually communicates that "this feature had to be expedited because we were unable to start it early enough." This is an incredibly powerful educational message, and it is likely to catalyze improvement discussions. It is just the sort of gentle stressor that the Kanban Method thrives on.

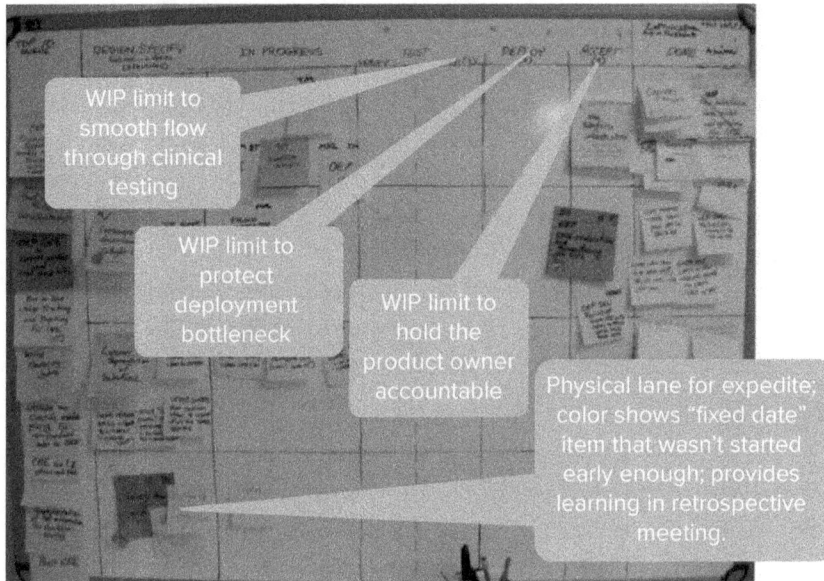

Figure 9.5 Annotated photograph of Posit Science kanban board mid-2009

Clinical testing, labeled "QA" on the board, has a column WIP limit. This tells us that clinical testing is a shared service that serves each of the three Scrum teams as well as an expedite team, if there is one. If the clinical testers were embedded within the Scrum teams in the cross-functional formation prescribed by Scrum, there would be no WIP limit on the column, just as we see on the previous column for software testing.

There is also a column WIP limit on Deployment. Packaging the code for production was a specialist role, and only one person in the company had permission to release code to production—for some younger readers, it may be hard to understand the concept of "Gold Code," which is released on a golden rewritable CD-ROM that was in turn passed off to a production facility that manufactured the CDs. The transaction costs of production were high, and it was important that the configuration on the disk was perfect before production. As such, this function at Posit was a potential bottleneck; the WIP limit was there to protect the bottleneck from overburdening.

There is also a column WIP limit on Acceptance. David Hoffman played the role of product owner in the Scrum process. The product owner is supposed to do many things, one of which is accept the delivered product, attending each sprint retrospective and demonstration. However, the global warming problem at Posit—that the money was running out—was consuming executive time. Consequently,

David was failing to attend the retrospectives and wasn't accepting the completed work. This was sending a very bad signal to the developers. It was demoralizing. It appeared that their leadership didn't care. These people were working hard, often heroic hours, and they were putting everything they had—often sacrificing their social and family lives, even their health—to keep promises and give the company a chance of success, only to find that the executive leadership didn't appear to care. At the same time, David was aware of this and knew it was poor behavior.

Metaphorically, David was a middle-aged man who comes to the realization that he isn't in the same physical shape he was in while in his twenties. He realizes he is overweight and in poor physical condition, so he buys a gym membership. At first this is great, but gradually his resolve to attend the gym wanes and he finds himself gaining weight again. So to counter this lack of self-discipline, he signs up for a personal trainer. It costs him $80 per session, two sessions per week. He schedules his gym appointments on his work calendar with a half hour prior and post for the transaction costs of walking to and from the gym and changing, showering, and so forth. He protects that time. He goes for every single session. Why? Because he'd lose $80 every time he misses!

So, David spoke with Janice and asked her to help him have better discipline to accept finished work. He understood how important it was to send the correct signals to the development team. Janice discussed with him whether or not acceptance was even necessary. Did he need to approve the finished work? This is another use of an important concept in Kanban: Acceptance was an explicit policy, and Janice was challenging its validity. We saw Dragos make similar challenges in the XIT Sustaining Engineering story. However, on reflection, it was agreed that acceptance was still important in a number of ways and that it should stay for governance, risk management, and staff morale reasons.

The solution was to give acceptance a WIP limit. Such a simple idea and yet incredibly powerful. There is power in simplicity!

If David failed to show up and accept finished work, then gradually the kanban board would fill up with work. The WIP limits would prevent the team from pulling new features, and gradually the team would become idle. Doomsday occurs when the entire team becomes idle and the board is stuffed full of blocked work. Imposing a WIP limit on an external dependency creates a potential Doomsday scenario. We call this a "Doomsday scenario" because of the awkward conversation that is likely to happen next and the possibility that the change agent, the Kanban advocate, will find that they are packing their office and looking for new employment. Imposing a WIP limit on an external dependency is a dangerous choice. What if the external party doesn't cooperate and Doomsday arrives? So WIP limits on dependencies are not for beginners! However, in this instance, Janice had the mitigating circumstance that David Hoffman, the external dependency, was collaborating. He didn't intend to let anyone down, and Doomsday should never happen. The WIP limit and its consequences were there to provide gentle pressure for David to act in a timely manner. What's more, David had to walk past the board from his office on his way to get a cup of coffee. He was going to see it multiple times per day. He wasn't going to be able to forget about pending feature acceptance. Of course, this worked as designed, and a considerable amount of social capital was restored.

Posit delivered new features to their business customers as each was completed, on average one every week. New work would be pulled when an existing feature was delivered, and everything flowed smoothly. It was a true victory for Janice and a major relief from three years of living in chaos and feeling guilty for the inability to make it all better. She always felt that the problems were not with the people—the scientists, developers, and clinical testers—rather, the problems were with the system in which they worked; it was simply not tuned to the nature of the environment in which they lived. She was also immensely relieved that the awful planning meetings every third week had been eliminated. Introducing Kanban enabled her to achieve a better balance in her life. She was relieved from a good deal of stress and anxiety.

Posit Science: Postscript

In the early summer of 2009, the long-awaited results of the Mayo Clinic study were published.[31] Encouragingly, the researchers found that the software boosted the brain in ways unrelated to the training. Rather than simply learning to parrot back what they had practiced, participants improved their test scores across a range of brain functions. What Posit had achieved was truly remarkable. Later that summer, they released *DriveSharp*. One of the games within it, Road Choice, later renamed DoubleDecision,[32] was especially beneficial. The accolade for it came at a time when there was a growing debate about whether brain games delivered the benefits their creators claimed.

Janice had great plans for many more improvements, but she ran out of time. Posit had failed to increase their cash flow fast enough, and a major retrenchment was necessary. While the Ph.D. neuroscientist researchers were retained, the entire product development group was let go. Janice moved on to work at another gaming startup in Berkeley, California.

Posit had resisted pursuing the consumer market. Their identity as scientists making medical grade products ruled their decision making, their strategy, and their investment choices. Meanwhile, their competitor Lumosity had embraced the consumer market and garnered a much bigger marketing budget, essential for selling something few consumers yet understood, and developed a web-based product available on an affordable subscription basis. They took the market by storm.

31. http://www.brainhq.com/world-class-science/published-research/impact-study
32. http://www.nature.com/news/a-little-brain-training-goes-a-long-way-1.12924

Lumosity's founders had, like Posit, assumed that much of their market would be aging baby boomers. But when they analyzed their user data, they found the games were appealing much more to twenty- and thirty-somethings, the millennial generation. Recognizing this early, they began targeting them. This resulted in millions of new users each year.[33]

Posit showed resilience. The decision to retrench had come early enough that they avoided collapse and remained afloat. They survived with a much-reduced cost base and recovered some years later with the release of their own web-based platform, *BrainHQ*.[34] Nowadays, it offers a broad range of games suitable for a broader audience at much more affordable prices, often brought to market as "white label" and sold under other brands, such as AARP.

While Janice had to leave the brain aerobics scene, she never left the Kanban scene. Kanban changed her life. In 2011, she moved to Seattle and founded Kanban University,[35] a licensed training organization, and soon afterward she took over the Kanban Conference and associated event-planning business.[36] Janice remains a highly respected figure in the Kanban community following her contribution over more than a decade from 2008 until 2018.

---

33. http://www.inc.com/magazine/201312/robin-schatz/from-research-lab-to-market-leader-in-no-time.html

34. http://www.brainhq.com/news/posit-science-launches-brainhq

35. Originally Lean Kanban University Incorporated

36. This went through several name changes, starting with Lean & Kanban Conference in 2009, then Lean Software & Systems Conference, and later Lean Kanban Conference.

Takeaways

- If the concept of Kanban meets with resistance, consider not calling it Kanban at all. This is referred to as the "Fight Club School of Kanban Coaching" because Kanban is not talked about.

- Due to the strong affinity with Scrum at Posit, the new process was introduced as the "flow system."

- The term "flow system" was chosen, as it directly addressed a pain point. A major source of dissatisfaction came from the constant interruptions and lack of flow in the development work. The new solution was positioned to attack this problem directly.

- Addressing emotional concerns is a means to move people and lead them to action.

- Replenishment was on-demand, without a regular cadence, and each feature was pulled individually.

- Capacity was set aside for Intangible class of service work to ensure it was done.

- A twenty-one-day SLA was chosen to match the existing three-week cadence for Scrum sprints.

- Replenishment used an asynchronous, two-phased commitment. This enabled developers to pull work from the input buffer without referring back to business owners.

- Asynchronous commitment as seen at Posit has come to be associated with organizations transitioning from Maturity Level 2 to 3 in the Kanban Maturity Model.

- The size of the input buffer, together with the asynchronous commitment, enabled forward signaling of "what is coming soon" while continuing to support deferred commitment until the "last responsible moment."

- The roles of Scrummaster and Product Owner were unchanged.

- Demonstrations and retrospectives were also retained and remained on the same three-week cadence.

- Product owner acceptance was retained, but it was explicitly introduced into the workflow, visualized on the board, and given a WIP limit.

- The Posit Science kanban board visualized two tiers of requirements hierarchy: features broken into user stories.

- There were three teams using one board, with each team using a specific lane (or row) on the board.

- There was an additional lane for Expedite class of service work. There wasn't a dedicated team for this work. People were taken from the three dedicated teams on an as-needed basis to work on expedite requests.
- Traditional business case information became an evolutionary relic as cost of delay replaced it as the means for selecting and scheduling work.
- The Posit Science kanban board also incorporated design elements for two shared services and a capacity-constrained resource (or bottleneck).

10

Lunch in Hibiya, Dinner at Anthony's

The Role of the Service Delivery Manager

My Kanban epiphany came as I exited the Imperial Palace Gardens, shortly before lunchtime on April 9, 2005. It was my birthday, and in honor of the occasion, my Japanese family (by marriage) would treat me to a sushi lunch. We proceeded through the East Gate and crossed the bridge over the moat toward Otemachi station, two blocks away. There, we took a train to Hibiya.

We exited Hibiya station on the northern Yurakucho side and proceeded past a block of office buildings until we found the tower we needed. It didn't look much different from any of the others in this central Tokyo business district, but within it lay a reputably reliable, good-quality sushi restaurant priced for the middle-class pocket. It was deemed suitable for the rightful birthday celebration of the honorable brother-in-law (me) without breaking the bank or embarrassing the credit card into a shy retreat. As we entered the atrium and descended the escalator, sinking underground, I recall that it seemed brighter than daylight. A water feature on the wall that covered several floors from the deepest basement level to the atrium at ground level was seemingly lit with daylight tubes. It gave off a warm, welcoming, happy glow. The sound of the water was relaxing. At the bottom, the second basement level ceiling was lower and the corridor not so well lit but adequate by the standard of any indoor mall or food court. Here lay all the restaurants: a long corridor about four metres wide in front of us. Spaced along it to either side were doors about ten metres apart. There was a variety of food on offer. The first window box to our right contained a selection of wax sushi replicas. A menu was fixed to a lectern at a 45° angle to the door. We had arrived. We entered, brushing the hanging curtains to one side.

"Irashaimase!" was the call to welcome us.

We were greeted by a bowing young woman. She bent upright, smiling and gesturing out the door with an open hand. She explained that they were currently full, but we were welcome to wait outside. Moments earlier, we'd walked past a row of dining chairs positioned along the wall away from the door back toward the escalator. She handed my brother-in-law a menu, and we all took a seat. I was glad to get the weight off my shoulders—literally—my younger daughter was still strapped to my chest. I passed her to her mother. My older daughter sat beside me repeating, "Are we going to have sushi now?" "Is this the restaurant?"

We waited a considerable time. Three young women joined us, sitting on the seats adjacent to me. My wife, her sister, and her brother-in-law spent considerable time looking over the sushi menu. It was little more than a scorecard against which the customer makes tally marks indicating how many pieces are desired. They considered the card in detail, as if studying the form and odds for a horse race. Every option was debated and potential winners selected. Fortunately, this form of amusement passed the time while we waited.

Perhaps twenty minutes went by, then a second woman appeared outside and advised us that we could be seated now. We followed her to a table in a corner. Each table was provided with privacy by a folding paper screen. Technically, our table wasn't a corner booth, but it felt that way. There were six of us altogether: four adults, a two-year-old toddler, and a baby. We had five chairs: two on each side and a fifth on one end. The other end butted against the wall. Our infant was in her mother's lap. We took our seats. My other daughter took a chair beside her mother in the corner. I took the end seat, in the aisle. I was, after all, the birthday boy, the center of attention. My in-laws presented me with a gift—a fine set of Japanese writing paper. Perhaps they were reminding me to take up painting again? It's a first-rate gift and typical of Tokyo. It's small, lightweight, easy to pack and store, and difficult to break whilst being of extremely good quality and probably very expensive. "Are we going to have sushi now?" asked the small voice from the corner.

No one had yet taken our order. The menu, it seemed, was just for our amusement. My brother-in-law was still holding it like a betting ticket for a horse race that's on hold because the starting gate misfired, leaving an animal wedged in the mechanism while race stewards frantically try to free the beast and reset the start. A young woman brought us water and towels. At least five more minutes went by before a young man about college age, tall and slender, fresh as sashimi, came over, bowed gently and offered to take our order. My brother-in-law handed it to him and spoke briefly, pointing to the miscellaneous section of the order into which he had written in katakana (Japanese characters for foreign words) California roll. The waiter nodded and walked away. The lady who brought the water returned with beer: two large bottles of Sapporo and four small glasses.

"Kanpai!" Clink, clink, clink, clink.

Time passed.

Beer disappeared. The small glasses were refreshed several times from the large bottles.

More time passed.

"Is the sushi ready yet?" "I want my sushi!"

"I want my sushi!"

Someone was getting hungry. It seems a long time since the mid-morning picnic in the Imperial Palace Gardens. We chatted away. As a family, we had plenty to catch up on. Anticipation was growing. "Is my sushi coming soon? I want my sushi."

Ah-ha! A large, square white plate of sushi arrived, carried by yet another member of staff. A space was cleared. Our waiter lowered it over my shoulder. As he did so, I observed that there was no California roll on the plate.

As he turned away, the family looked at the plate; something was wrong. My sister-in-law turned to her husband and said, "Han-bun, ne?" (Rather feminine Japanese, meaning "half measure, is it not?")

For the uninitiated, Japanese is a very hard language to learn—not least is the grammar, and the three alphabets, but equally difficult are all the different ways of talking. There is the polite form. There is the very polite form. There are forms reserved for speaking to members of the royal household and yet another for the Emperor. And then there are the casual forms and the form used to talk to children. In the casual forms, men and women speak differently. Hence, the age-old traditional way for a man to learn a foreign language—to find a girlfriend who is a native speaker and copy her—isn't to be advised for the Japanese language. Otherwise, guys end up talking like girls, which the natives find highly amusing!

"Mmm. So!" my brother-in-law replied. (Man talk for "Yes, precisely!")

Only half of our order had been fulfilled. There was considerable surprise. The waiter was summoned. A very polite waitress arrived, bowing deeply and frantically. She explained that all the sushi chefs were fully loaded. They hadn't expected to be so busy today, a Saturday, and were not adequately staffed. As a result, they recognized that people were hungry and, to keep them happy and make their lunch as enjoyable as possible, they were fulfilling half of each order first. They were doing this with everyone.

Now, this was clearly a good tactic. They understood that value delivery in a restaurant comes, at least partly, from delivering food. By delivering half, they were putting some value in the hands of the customer more quickly.

Actually, this was a multitasking tactic, which in most professional services circumstances is a bad idea: It means that there is more work-in-progress. If we think of a lunch as a customer project, then each individual project takes longer to complete because staff are task-switching from one project to another. Generally speaking, ordering projects or project tasks to be done as a single-piece flow in a strictly prioritized or dependent order is better. The time to complete any one task or project is shorter.

If, for example, the sushi chefs had concentrated solely on our order, they would have completed it quickly while others waited. The next table along would have waited a little longer before receiving their whole order. The next longer still. No one would want to be the last table to be served. The overall wait time may not have been within customer tolerance levels: It wouldn't have been fit-for-purpose.

With the tactic of fulfilling half the order, the time to initial delivery of any one order is cut in half. So, a table that might have waited fifty minutes for its full order gets half of its order in twenty-five minutes. In this circumstance, the tactic works, because the restaurant understands its customer and their tolerance levels. The customer doesn't need the whole order all at once: It takes some time to eat and enjoy the first part of the meal. The half-serving tactic will work so long as the other half arrives in a timely fashion as the customer is ready to consume it. This tactic of working on small batches and transferring them to the customer on demand or just-in-time is very effective and minimizes the amount of inventory waiting for processing at any given time: Two smaller batches provide fresher sushi for consumption when it is needed.

Now, imagine that we issued kanban cards equivalent to, say, the number of sushi chefs in the kitchen. To be worked on, an order must be associated with a card. Other orders simply queue in a first in–first out (FIFO) stack. As a chef finishes an order, he would pick up the next one, assigning the kanban card from the order he'd just completed to the new order taken from the FIFO queue. A kanban card approach would avoid multitasking and the possibility that too many meals were being prepared simultaneously. A kanban system would shorten the time to prepare any one order by avoiding too much multitasking. Systems like this are common in short-order cooking. A short-order chef can prepare only so many burgers or breakfast sandwiches at a time, while other orders queue, often pegged to a string or wire pulley, in a first in–first out fashion. This provides for single-tasking by the cook, short lead times through the kitchen, and fresh food delivered to the customer. The whole restaurant is paced at the speed the chef can flip burgers, fry eggs, or slice sushi.

"I want my sushi!" proclaimed my two-year-old. To her, at that age, all sushi was a California roll. There was no other type of sushi in her universe. She could plainly see that it wasn't on the plate. Hence, there was no sushi. Just a plate of fish on rice.

She was annoyed and frustrated. She started to chant—thankfully in English—I WANT SUSHI! I WANT SUSHI! Gently, she banged her clenched fists on the table. The background noise of the restaurant and the paper screens prevented anyone from really noticing that there was a pending meltdown from the smallest client hidden in the corner.

I'm sure every parent reading this empathizes. You recognize the scene. Reading it made you cringe in anticipation of what was to come next.

Meanwhile, this was a serious sushi restaurant. You could tell, because the sushi was served with ginger—but no wasabi. This prevented the uncouth from insulting the chef by adding more. The chef lovingly prepares each piece for your delight. It has just the right amount of wasabi. Equally, it is uncouth to dip the sushi in too much soy sauce, but this is a skill that takes years to master. Hence, the uncouth still have an outlet—bathing nigiri in soy before eating.

We offered the vocal toddler the tamago (egg) nigiri. Tamago sushi does not contain wasabi. She mistook the square-cut piece of omelet as a piece of cheese. "I don't want cheese." She peeled the "cheese" off the top and passed it to Daddy. "You eat my cheese. I don't want cheese." Very well. The rice kept her happy for a short while.

The plate we had was filled with nigiri of different varieties: There was eel (unago) and grilled eel (unagi); there was a special 3-piece eel all for me—a birthday treat; there was salmon (sake), tuna (maguro), and fatty tuna (toro); octopus (tako) and mackerel (saba). Although that sounds like a lot, it didn't go far among four of us.

The beer ran out. As it was lunchtime, we didn't order more. Green tea arrived instead.

We emptied the plate: Our stomachs weren't yet full. We chatted away, passing the time. It seemed to take at least as long as we'd waited for the first order before the second one turned up. If you stop to think about the queuing mechanism in use at the sushi bar, this is completely explainable. Meanwhile, my little girl was eager with anticipation. She'd been talking about this sushi outing during a whole week of vacation. Like most kids, she lived to eat, and the food was always the highlight of any trip. "How was the zoo?" "We had lovely salad in the cafe." "How was your flight?" "I got chocolates from the flight attendant." "How was Japan?" "We went to a sushi restaurant but they didn't make my sushi!"

The wait was too long because there weren't enough sushi chefs to meet demand. To make sushi for all the tables in the restaurant, even half-orders, was taking longer than the tolerance of the guests' stomachs. The restaurant management had completely failed to anticipate demand. Yet, it could be argued that the popularity of the restaurant was anticipatable given its proximity to the Imperial Palace and abundant blooms on the trees in the vicinity. Despite it being a Saturday, the management could have arranged for the same staffing level as for a typically busy weekday. But they hadn't! Because the staffing level for sushi chefs was lower than required to meet demand, the chefs couldn't supply the completely full restaurant quickly enough.

There were really two management choices in this situation: The restaurant could choose to fill all the seats, maximizing demand, or they could choose to seat only as many tables as the chefs could handle. In other words, seat a table only when a (theoretical) kanban card was available. The latter makes for better customer service once guests are seated, but there might be a longer wait outside. This may cause some guests to take their business somewhere else that had a shorter wait. By seating everyone they can, the management avoids the fear of losing customers who would otherwise walk away, but they risk a reputation for poor service. They put short-term profit before customer service.

Finally, another waiter turned up with a similar-looking plate as before: white, square, and similarly sized. How many members of staff had we met by now? Four? Five? I'd lost count. How many staff worked there? It wasn't clear to me. I couldn't see the whole space. There doesn't seem to be any set rule about who serves whom. It felt like we were meeting the entire team.

Our new waiter lowered the plate.

My daughter held her breath.

Before the plate hit the table, she exclaimed, "Where's my sushi?" and burst into tears uncontrollably and inconsolably. The waiter was dumbstruck. He was far too young to have children of his own. He had no idea what had just happened. My brother-in-law explained to him through the background of screaming. He ran off. Our table was now the center of attention across the whole restaurant.

Another waiter returned. I was sure it was the one who first took our order. There was much bowing, apology, and some explanation given. My brother-in-law translated for me. They couldn't, or more likely wouldn't, make us the California roll. Japanese snobbery! It really was a serious sushi restaurant. Our sushi chef was too proud to make California maki.

Some negotiations ensued and off he went. They would make us an alternative, nori maki derivative. So now, the chefs were expediting an order for us to make up for their mistake. As we already knew that they were fully loaded, and our long wait was testimony to the truth of this, our expedited request meant that others would have to wait yet longer. Customer service suffered yet again.

Our little girl, calmer now—we asked her to wait once more—sushi, we assured her, was coming. Honestly, it was!

We continued to eat.

The Japanese eat their sushi in a set order—nigiri (individual pieces) first, maki (rolls) later. Miso soup is used to wash down the maki. As this was a serious sushi restaurant, they knew that we'd want to eat in that order, so the second plate was mostly filled with rolls ranging from simple stuff like cucumber (kappamaki) to more adventurous raw fish such as tuna (tekkamaki).

A small plate turned up with something approximating a California roll. It had avocado and fish. As if in protest, the chef had piped a trail of mayonnaise across the top of the pieces in a serpentine pattern—his final statement of protest to the uncouth!

We scraped it off. It looked alien to my daughter. She had never seen sushi with yellow sauce on it before. Skeptical at first, finally, she munched away, maki in hand, with a big, broad smile on her face.

◆　◆　◆　◆

Self-Organizing

So, what had happened at that serious sushi restaurant in Hibiya? Who was managing our lunch?

The answer was simple—no one! This restaurant was self-organizing!

The sushi chefs were left to self-organize. They managed a queue of orders on score cards. They didn't take direction from anyone; they just made sushi to order using a few basic rules like nigiri first, maki last. They were a sushi-making function.

Someone else seated the customers, someone else took the drinks orders, someone else took the food orders, someone else delivered the orders to the table, someone else bussed the dishes from the table. The restaurant was a set of perfectly defined functions, each self-organizing and each triggered by certain signals—such as guests queuing outside waiting to be seated, or sushi orders on a score card clipped to a carousel by the sushi bar. There was a clear division of labor among all the tasks: seating, waiting, bussing, sushi making, and drinks. What had been lost was the context of the customer's order. No one really cared about delivering value to the customer. No one took the trouble to understand why there was a special order for a California roll. Even if they had, that context would almost certainly have been lost in the handoffs between functions. There was no means to communicate customer purpose or any business risks associated with an order. California roll wasn't on the menu. It was a special order. They didn't get too many two-year-olds who only ate California rolls. No one anticipated its importance. And hence, no one understood when eventually that child had a meltdown.

The real problem was that no one was responsible or accountable for our lunch project. No one was responsible for service delivery. The concept of service delivery was missing from the organization.

Someone needed to advocate for the customer. Someone needed to own the delivery of value to the customer. Someone needed to own the context for the customer's requirements. In Kanban, we've come to call that role the service delivery manager.

◆　◆　◆　◆

My second Kanban-related epiphany arrived as unexpectedly as the first. This time on a beautiful, warm, sunny evening at Anthony's Pier 66 restaurant on Seattle's waterfront in August of the same year. Contrasting the service at Anthony's with that which I'd experienced in Tokyo revealed the need for an explicit role in Kanban implementations: the role of service delivery manager.

Service Delivery Manager

I had visitors in town: Brian O'Byrne and Martin Hogan of a Dublin-based startup, Statesoft, were visiting me at Microsoft; while Robert Holler and Michael Leeds of Version One, a company with a popular tool for tracking work done using the Agile methodology Scrum, were making sales calls in the area. I knew Brian from my time working in Dublin in 1999, while I knew Robert from online discussion forums for Agile software development and got to know him better, in 2005, when together we famously gate-crashed the Rally Software party at the Agile conference in Denver. Rally being Version One's main rival for Scrum tracking, Robert hadn't been on their party invite list. That 2005 late-summer evening, I had agreed to meet them all for dinner, thinking that two sets of founders from two small companies selling developer tools would have a lot in common. Anthony's was a favorite choice for me when I had guests in town. On such a summer evening, it has spectacular views over Elliott Bay with the to-and-fro of the ferry boats and cruise ships. If the weather is clear, there is a spectacular view of Mount Rainier, 14,000 feet high and still snow-capped even in summer, against the foreground of the downtown skyscrapers and the sports stadiums that offer homes to the Seattle Seahawks and the Seattle Mariners, while the sun sets, the sky glowing red to the west over the Puget Sound and the Olympic Mountains in silhouette. So, Anthony's is a great location, but its view alone doesn't make it fit-for-purpose. I wouldn't keep going back unless the service and the food were also good.

At 11:00 a.m. on a sunny, clear day in August, I called the restaurant from my office desk. I asked to book a table for dinner that evening. The young lady on the other end asked me what time. I tell her 6:00 p.m. She replies, "We can't do 6:00 p.m., but I can offer you 5:45 p.m. or 6:15 p.m." I opt for the later time and say that I have five people in the party. I emailed my friends to confirm the appointment; they should meet me in the bar of the restaurant around 6:00 p.m.

That evening, I arrive first. I walk up the stairs from the main entrance to the restaurant desk on the upper level. I'm greeted by three smiling faces. I state my name and they confirm my booking. I know I'm early, so I take a seat in the bar. I look across at the restaurant tables. The room isn't full. The greeters aren't busy. They are mostly just hanging out by the lectern. Why couldn't they have seated us at 6:00 p.m? I order a gin and tonic and sit at the bar. The Version One guys arrive after ten minutes. I'm just about to order them a drink when the Irish boys arrive, too, so we proceed immediately back to the desk. We are walked to our table, a fine, large, round table in a corner window with spectacular 180-degree views.

"How are you gentlemen this evening? My name is Andy, I'll be your waiter this evening." He looks at me. "Where are you from?" he asks, clearly detecting an accent. I tease him with "Ballard!" (a neighborhood in Seattle about five miles north of the restaurant). Smiling, he asks where I'm really from. He goes around the table and is rightly impressed by the geographic diversity assembled before him: one from California, another from the state of Georgia, and two more from Ireland.

"And what brings you folks in this evening? Business dinner?"

"They are all in town for business, but tonight we're just catching up and hanging out."

"Very good then! Lovely evening for it. And you have the best table, so enjoy."

He talked us through all the specials for that day, from memory. We ordered some wine. A few minutes later, a wine steward arrived and served us a local, Washington State Chardonnay. Andy was back moments later to check that it was to our liking and that we were happy with our choice. He took our food order. I had agreed to split the Thai mussels with Michael as an appetizer. The Thai mussels were a house specialty at Anthony's. Lovely!

As time passed, we saw just a few tables seated every fifteen minutes or so. There were always empty tables. Almost everyone in the restaurant was at a different stage in their meal. What was happening? The restaurant management understood their constraining function—the kitchen and the chefs. So, they staggered arrival of guests in fifteen-minute intervals. They seated only two or three tables every fifteen minutes, and as a result, they limited the work-in-progress in the kitchen to a manageable level for the chefs. They were balancing demand, at any given moment, against their capability to supply. They had scheduled arrivals and guest seating to smooth flow. They used the front-desk staff as the regulating function; like the drummer on a longboat, the front desk beat the drum one, two, or three times every fifteen minutes, and the whole of the restaurant system took their beat from that.

Anthony's avoided all the mistakes that I experienced in Tokyo. Our waiter, Andy, was our waiter for our entire visit. Andy understood our context. He took the time to get to know us a little. Knowing where we were from and why we were visiting Seattle and Anthony's, he derived a strategy for our service. Andy understood the purpose for our visit, and he guessed from that our fitness criteria for a successful meal. He took our orders and understood subtleties such as that I would share the mussels with Michael as an appetizer because a half-portion each would be sufficient as a starter. Andy ensured that our dinner was successful, and we rewarded him with a fine tip. The service was always speedy, and each course seemed to appear almost as soon as our plates from the previous course were whipped away.

Anthony's is a lean, slick operation. The waiters advocate for the customer, while the functions in the back are never overloaded. Andy was our service delivery manager for the evening. The flow of new customers was restricted at the input point with a scheduling system that seats guests in fifteen-minute slots and never overloads the system with too many guests arriving at once. The result is a restaurant that operates as an integrated system with sufficient capability and capacity to ensure good end-to-end customer service. Anthony's is organized to deliver good quality meals quickly. This allows them to turn the table and cover it again and again throughout the evening. Smooth flow, stemming off demand at the input point, and enabling fast, efficient, accurate service makes Anthony's a popular restaurant with a stellar reputation. It continues as a robust and profitable business as I write this in 2023, eighteen years after the evening in question.

◆ ◆ ◆ ◆

We can learn from this tale of two restaurants that self-organization of functional responsibilities isn't enough: There needs to be context—an understanding of who the customer is and what their purpose is for patronizing our service. Context helps scheduling, prioritization, and accurate delivery of the customer's real needs. The Agile software development community has been obsessed with self-organization for more than twenty years. However, it can't stand on its own in isolation. Self-organization is useful for moving with agility when it is framed by a context, providing a shared purpose, an understanding of the customer's needs, desires, expectations, fitness criteria, and tolerance for variation and errors. Without context and customer advocacy, self-organization can be self-serving.

Understanding the customer's purpose helps us understand their tolerance for delivery time and other aspects of the service—do they want a chatty waiter, or do they want discreet, silent service? By understanding the customer's purpose for their visit, the waiter can decide the appropriate batch size: Does the client want everything together, or do they want each course served separately? Are they in a hurry? Or, will they appreciate a more leisurely pace, time to talk, enjoy their wine, perhaps a second bottle and dessert to follow?

Someone needs to own the delivery of customer value and take responsibility for the flow in the value chain. We saw that Anthony's clearly valued flow and balanced demand against capability to supply by pacing the arrival of new guests and seating only a maximum of three tables every fifteen minutes.

In Kanban, understanding customer value and taking responsibility for flow and delivery against expectations is the role of the service delivery manager. Without someone playing that role, Kanban implementations tend to be shallow and small scale and limited to individual teams or functions; they rarely visualize an end-to-end flow. When the service delivery manager role is present, the customer is understood, and the customer's purpose and the risks associated with that purpose become core considerations in the design of the kanban system and board. With customer context, we see deep implementations with a pull system, replenishment meetings involving the customer, WIP limits across the whole board, and utilization of advanced ideas such as risk-hedging capacity allocation, risk profiling, and classes of service.

In *Kanban*, I didn't describe any roles. Kanban was the "start with what you do now" method, and no new roles, positions, or job titles were required. However, I was blind to the need for the service delivery manager. Blind to it because that role existed in all our reference implementations: Dragos played that role at Microsoft XIT Sustaining Engineering; Darren Davis, Diana Kolomiyets, and Daniel Vacanti played that role at Corbis; Janice Linden-Reed played that role at Posit Science; Eric Landes played that role at Robert Bosch; and Rob Hathaway played that role at IPC Media. It wasn't until later, much later, after we'd seen many shallow, team-level implementations that we began to look for what was missing. Eventually, hard evidence emerged with case studies such as that of Christoph Achouiantz at Sandvik, where he'd kicked off more than fifty team-level kanban implementations without any end-to-end flow. Eventually, Christoph realized that Sandvik was so siloed that simply identifying the customer and communicating their context on kanban tickets wasn't enough: He had to create the position and job title of delivery manager to focus attention on flow and service delivery. Hence, this book has new guidance; where there is an existing person who carries responsibility and accountability for taking the customer's order and ensuring its smooth flow and timely delivery, the old guidance stands—no new roles are needed when Kanban is introduced. If, on the other hand, there isn't a single person responsible and accountable for ensuring the end-to-end coordination from customer order to delivery, then that role is needed for a deep, meaningful, fully functional kanban system to emerge, and the name for that role is service delivery manager.

In the Agile software development community, and to a lesser extent in the DevOps community, the immediate response to the dysfunction described in the Hibiya restaurant example is to suggest a reorganization into cross-functional teams. Were they to follow this advice, the restaurant would be organized into "lunch project teams": Each team would consist of a seater, a waiter, a busser, and a sushi chef. Perhaps we'd cross-train our waiters as seaters and bussers and reduce each team to a simple pair—front of house (customer facing: seating, order taking, and bussing) and back of house (the chef). We'd allocate fixed tables to each sushi team pair to avoid resource contention and fighting over tables as guests were seated. The team would stay together and either work only one lunch project at a time or multitask over several tables but within their capacity limit.

First of all, when you describe it this way, it is self-evident that this advice of "form cross-functional teams" is ridiculous and nonsensical in some contexts. We don't see restaurants organized that way. It therefore isn't general-purpose guidance.

Secondly, it quite simply isn't the Kanban way at all. Kanban is about using visualization and promoting cooperation among individuals and across functions to deliver customer value. A team can form around a purpose—a shared goal—but that formation can be dynamic, virtual, and ephemeral and does not require any formal reorganization or restructuring. Kanban is the "start with what you do now" method; it isn't the "first, reorganize into cross-functional teams" method. Kanban does not share the Agile software development agenda of formation of cross-functional teams. Kanban is based on the belief that you can evoke collaboration by communicating purpose and creating an environment that encourages cooperative working toward a shared goal. There is no need for reorganization. The role of service delivery manager is a key element in making it work. So long as there is an "Andy"—the customer advocate, the service delivery manager for our dinner project—there can be effective collaborative working, there can be flow, there can be satisfied customers, and there can be fit-for-purpose service delivery.

Stop reorganizing! Start collaborating with a shared purpose. Make the service delivery manager the steward of that purpose!

Takeaways

- The Kanban Method views reorganization as a last-resort approach to change and improvement, preferring to promote service-oriented collaboration among existing organizational units.

- Understanding the customer's purpose or goals and communicating it transparently with a customer-requested work item are core to the Kanban Method.

- An understanding of customer purpose enables unity and alignment across and throughout a workflow involving multiple functions.

- In circumstances where someone is not already responsible and accountable for taking a customer's order and ensuring that the order progresses and is delivered to the customer within their expectations and fitness-for-purpose thresholds, the role of service delivery manager should be introduced.

- Service delivery manager is ideally a role played by an existing staff member.

- In extreme circumstances, service delivery manager may be a new position carrying that title or a variation of it such as "delivery lead," "delivery manager," or "delivery director."

- Self-organization at the team or department level is not sufficient to ensure good customer service and adequately satisfied customers.

- The Kanban Method does not share the Agile software development methodologies' agenda of forming cross-functional teams, preferring instead promotion of inter-functional collaboration and cooperation toward a common or shared goal.

11

Be Like Water

The Philosophy behind the Kanban Method

In May 2009, Joe Campbell published a short blog[37] that had a profound impact on the direction of the Kanban Method and its community: He suggested that "Kanban should be like water." This was a reference to the philosophy and teachings of the late Bruce Lee, the famous martial artist and movie star who studied philosophy at the University of Washington, in Seattle. He was buried in Seattle, and it is a curious coincidence that Lee's work with Chinese martial arts contains some interesting parallels to my own work with Kanban, with both sets of ideas originating in Seattle.

Chinese Martial Arts

Traditionally, Chinese martial arts are taught as a set of moves, known as kata, each one practiced individually. A collection of kata is known as a patterned style, and this collection usually has a name. The name is effectively a brand, or a handle, with which to describe the collection of moves and the fighting style associated with the originator—the grandmaster, or "shifu." Wikipedia lists well over 100 patterned styles of Chinese martial arts, divided into traditional (often two to three thousand years old) and modern (mostly from the last 150 years) styles. They have names such as Southern Praying Mantis, Snake Fist, Black Tiger Fist, and Monkey Fist. Analogously, a patterned style, a collection of

---

37. Originally titled "Kanban should be like water;" the post appears to have been edited later to simplify the title to "Be like water." https://joecampbell.wordpress.com/2009/05/13/be-like-water/

kata, can be compared to a defined process or methodology, a collection of practices, roles, responsibilities, and workflows.

Lee used water metaphorically to suggest that it could take any form, that it could adapt to its circumstances. If you pour water into a cup, it becomes the cup. It is fluid: It can take any shape. He wanted his followers to have a fluid, adaptive style, to approach martial arts without a fixed mindset, without a desire to conform to following a set patterned style, but instead to adapt and evolve their own unique style. In this sense, Lee's philosophy precisely matches that of the Kanban Method. Rather than following a prescriptive process or methodology, instead, start with what you do now and adapt and evolve the process to achieve a particular goal or serve a specific purpose.

With Kanban, I wanted people to free their minds of the idea that processes and software development methodologies should be installed in an organization and that the organization should adapt to follow it. Instead, organizations should develop their own unique processes and workflows such that they adapt the fittest available solution to their own circumstances, the risks they are managing, and the outcomes expected of them. Instead of following a prescribed style, evolve a way of working that is fit-for-purpose and enables you to meet customer expectations and the expectations of other stakeholders such as business owners, regulatory authorities, and so forth.

The epiphany that I'd had while working as a manager at Sprint in 2002, that each department in our business unit had its own unique set of customers and was managing a unique set of risks, meant that it was nonsensical that all four customer-facing development groups should have to follow the same processes. That they were all using similar technology and similar development tools was irrelevant; the nature of the work, the urgency, the cost of delay, and other business risks were all different. It was clear that the concept of a "standard process" followed by each department was inappropriate. Tools and technologies shouldn't dictate the process followed; business risks should! Hence, while Lee's guidance on martial arts stood in the face of approximately 3,000 years of convention and established "best practice," my advice was facing down forty-plus years of convention and established "best practice" in software engineering and perhaps ninety-plus years of established thinking in industrial engineering and quality-assurance processes.

Go Around the Rock

Writing in *Striking Thoughts*, his collection of philosophical thinking, published posthumously by his wife Linda, Bruce Lee dedicates a whole section to water. Water, he observed, flows around the rock. The rock is an obstacle in its way, but rather than beat against it and try to push the rock away, water simply flows around it. The rock is a metaphor for resistance: In Lee's case, the resistance is from the opponent in combat. Instead of hitting the opponent head-on using excessive force, Lee's advice was to go around the rock, to avoid the resistance: to be fluid and adapt to the opponent's attacks, or their defenses, to use an oblique rather than direct approach. Former military officers reading this may recognize similarities to their doctrine of processes and methods used for large-scale combat based in the teachings of *Auftragstaktik*, Maneuver Warfare, or Mission Command.

For us, the rock is the resistance to change that happens when individual professionals feel a threat to their identity, their social status, their competence, their dignity, or the level of respect they command amongst their peers and professional community when changes are proposed to processes and ways of working. The traditional approach of applying a defined process or methodology is always going to raise hackles, to stir up the natural emotional defenses, resulting in stubborn resistance and inertia. Instead, a philosophy of "start where you are now" and evolve your processes to be fitter for their circumstance, fitter for their purpose, is an approach designed to lower resistance, to avoid the rock of emotional resistance so easily provoked.

Lee broke down martial arts to first principles. There were four ranges of combat:

- Kicking
- Punching
- Trapping
- Grappling

And (initially) Five Ways of Attack:[38]
- Single Direct Attack (SDA)
- Attack by Combination (ABC)
- Progressive Indirect Attack (PIA)
- (Hand) Immobilization Attack (HIA)
- Attack by Drawing (ABD)
- Single Angle Attack (SAA)

Lee encouraged his followers to borrow practices from wherever they saw fit, and he led by example by adopting parrying maneuvers from epee fencing. In this case, Lee deliberately chose a European sport and added these foreign practices into Chinese martial arts—deliberately pushing the boundaries, exhibiting liberal behavior in a very traditional, conservative community.

Lee continued to use water as inspiration, with a glass half-full. He would pour away some of the water and tell people to "absorb that which is useful" and discard the remainder. In other words, if there are practices that you find useful, that you like, that are working for you, keep them; and if there are others that fail to produce the results you expect, that

---

38. Lee later added a sixth way of attack by splitting Single Attack into Single Direct Attack and Single Angle Attack. However, the Five Ways of Attack had been established as a proper noun, and hence, the name stuck. That the Five Ways of Attack have six ways is an example of evolutionary change in action. "Five Ways of Attack" as a proper noun is an evolutionary relic.

you find challenging to execute, that you find difficult, or expensive, or unreliable, discard them. Each martial artist should adapt their own unique style, their own way of fighting. They should not feel constrained by patterned styles or any need to conform to a set of defined practices.

Lee's friends and disciples around Seattle demanded that his approach be given a name. At first, Lee rejected this; it was, he said, "the way without way." In other words, it was a method of developing a fighting style that did not follow any patterned style and had "no limitation as its limitation"—that adopting novel practice or any existing practice from other approaches to martial arts from anywhere in the world was also appropriate. Hence, it couldn't have a name. He was afraid that giving it a name would result in practitioners approaching it with the fixed mindset of a patterned style and trying to copy it. Instead, he wanted people to think for themselves, to make their own choices, and to adapt their own unique style. Around Seattle, his approach was often referred to as "street fighting," but this wasn't a suitable brand on which to build businesses teaching it. Lee elected to call his approach Jeet Kune Do, "the way of the intercepting fist"—after a trapping (or parrying) maneuver that was a particular favorite of his. He then played with people's minds by suggesting that followers could drop the intercepting fist from their practice and still be following Jeet Kune Do—the way without way, having no limitation as its limitation.

The similarities to the Kanban Method are uncanny. Kanban suggests that you start with what you do now, but do not remain married to any specific practices. You can discard those that are not working for you and adopt others from elsewhere that might work better. Kanban asks you to break down what you do into these fundamental elements:

- Think in terms of services.
- See your organization as a network of interdependent services.
- Identify the types of work: the requests made of each service, representing the customer-deliverable items of work—the work item types
- Map the workflow to identify the series or sequence of activities used to discover new information or new knowledge that represents the value-adding workflow for each service.
- Identify the decision points: Recognize that knowledge workflows primarily consist of a series of decisions, and making decisions requires information. Hence, a workflow consists of a sequence, or series, of information-gathering steps that enable decision making. A point of diminishing returns occurs where more time and energy spent gathering information does not significantly improve the decision making or change the result of a decision.
- Understand the capacity of each service to process work: Understand your capability to deliver in terms of volume, lead times, quality, and predictability and to match (or balance) demand against your capability to supply.

- Identify policies: Understand the policies used to guide and make decisions, including selection decisions about items of work based on the risks associated with each request, such as its cost of delay. It is these decisions that control the flow.
- Develop a triage discipline: a capability to decide what to work on now (or immediately), what should wait until later (and if later, when), and what not to do at all—to develop a capability to say no based on value and risk.

Your emergent process, evolved and adapted to your unique circumstances, should consist of practices, both previously existing and recently adopted, that represent one or more of these fundamental elements. For example, a testing practice produces information. This information can be used to make a decision as to whether the work item is of sufficient quality to flow to the next step in the workflow.

By 2009, this method of developing uniquely evolved processes and workflows for improved service delivery, using a framework consisting of virtual kanban systems, visualization, metrics, and feedback mechanisms, needed a name. If the method was to be communicated, to be taught, to be learned, adopted, and implemented with consistency, it needed a brand name, or a handle with which it could be referenced and described. While writing the Blue Book, I decided that the unique and unusual element, the "sticky" element in what we were doing, the thing people remembered, the remarkable thing that was often surprising and eye-opening, was the use of virtual kanban systems. In general conversation, people had taken to simply referring to the concepts and approach as "kanban." In a sentence that might more accurately have been spoken as "So, to improve our IT service delivery, we've adopted the use of virtual kanban systems"; instead, a more succinct shorthand had been adopted: "We're using Kanban for IT services." It seemed only natural, then, to officially name what we were doing the Kanban Method.

Takeaways

- Both the Kanban Method and Bruce Lee's martial arts philosophy originated in Seattle, Washington.

- "Be like water" applies to both: Instead of pushing against an obstacle, go around it, as water does with rocks.

- In IT, the "rock" is resistance to change.

- Continuing the water metaphor, Lee would tell people to "absorb that which is useful" and discard the rest.

- In martial arts or in software development, rather than following a prescriptive process or methodology, start with what you do now and adapt and evolve the process to achieve a particular goal or serve a specific purpose.

- The Kanban Method asks you to break down your work into fundamental elements: See your organization as a network of interdependent services; identify the types of work; map the workflow; identify the decision points; understand the capacity of each service to process work; identify policies; and develop a triage discipline.

- By 2009, the method of developing uniquely evolved processes and workflows for improved service delivery, using a framework consisting of virtual kanban systems, visualization, metrics, and feedback mechanisms, needed a name. As virtual kanban systems were the unifying factor, I called it the Kanban Method.

12

Codifying the Method
A Short Definition of Kanban

We've reached a point in this story where it is now possible to codify a method such that others may copy it and produce similar results. The story so far brings us to 2009, and the point at which I sat down to write the Blue Book. The point when I had to ask myself, what exactly is the Kanban Method?

The Meaning of "Kanban"

Kan-ban is both a Chinese and a Japanese word. It can have several meanings depending on how it is written in Japanese. The Japanese have three systems of alphabet: *kanji*, adapted from Chinese characters; *hiragana*, the original Japanese handwriting; and *katakana*, a more modern and angular form of hiragana used to express words adopted from foreign languages into Japanese. When written in kanji, Kan-ban, 看板, means sign or board (in American English, literally, "shingle"[39]). It is typically used to refer to the signs that would hang outside medieval shops or artisans' workshops. In Chinese, only the pictogram (kanji) form exists. It is generally interpreted as a verb, and hence, would be translated as "looking at the board (or sign)." In this sense, the cartoon by Pujan Roka, shown in Figure 12.1, made complete and perfect sense to a Chinese audience, though they may have pondered why the people are looking away from the board rather than toward it.

---

39. The expression "to hang out your shingle" is still in common usage in American English and is understood to mean "to be open for business." This usage is arcane in British English.

When written in hiragana (かんばん), kan-ban refers to a small, handheld token (in American English the word "tally" is the best equivalent and remains in common usage, particularly with respect to queuing systems, for example, in a car ferry's waiting area). Using these tokens, or signal cards, was pioneered by Taiichi Ohno and adopted by the Toyota manufacturing company in the late 1940s to limit inventory within a factory and to signal production based on customer demand. This technique creates what is known as a kanban system. The term "kanban" was not adopted until the early 1960s, when Toyota was being audited for the Deming Prize.[40] When we talk about kan-ban in this text, it is this latter, hiragana-expressed meaning from which we draw inspiration.

Figure 12.1 Manga-style cartoon by Pujan Roka developed for the cover of the Blue Book

What we are doing in the Kanban Method should rightfully be called "virtual kan-ban," as the mechanism to limit WIP and signal upstream activities for knowledge development work or information discovery is usually implemented indirectly through the display of so-called kanban limits or through the use of virtual implementations in software where the code is aware of a kanban limit for a given step in a workflow.

While the number of different meanings of the word has often caused confusion over these past fifteen years, such confusion seems needless. A kanban board evolved to become a core part of the Method as early as 2007, and although virtual kanban signal cards or tokens in a kanban system may have preceded that, both tools—the board and the signal cards—have proven useful and are now considered core to the whole Method, as both significant meanings of "kanban" are relevant. It seems pointless to argue which meaning has greater importance.

40. Kōichi Shimokawa et al., *The Birth of Lean: Conversations with Taiichi Ohno, Eiji Toyoda and Other Figures Who Shaped Toyota Management* (Cambridge, MA: Lean Enterprise Institute, 2009).

What is a Kanban System?

A number of kanban (or cards) equivalent to the (agreed) capacity of a system are placed in circulation. One card represents one piece of work. Each card acts as a signaling mechanism. A new piece of work can be started only when a card is available. This free card is assigned to a new piece of work and remains with it as the work flows through the system. When there are no more free cards, no additional work can be started. Any new work must wait in a queue until a card becomes available. When some work is completed, its card is detached and recycled. With a card now free, a new piece of work in the queue can be started.

This mechanism is known as a pull system because new work is pulled into the system only when there is capacity to handle it, rather than being pushed into the system based on demand. A pull system cannot be overloaded if the capacity, as determined by the number of signal cards in circulation, has been set appropriately.

In the Imperial Palace Gardens, discussed in Chapter 1, the gardens themselves are the system: The visitors are the work-in-progress, and the capacity is limited by the number of admission cards in circulation. Newly arriving visitors gain admission only when there are available tickets to hand out. On a normal day, this is never an issue. However, on busy days, such as a holiday or a Saturday during cherry-blossom season, the park is popular. When all the admission tickets have been given out, new visitors must queue outside, across the bridge, and wait for cards to be recycled from visitors as they leave. The kanban system provides a simple, cheap, and easily implemented method for controlling the size of the crowd by limiting the number of people inside the park. This allows the park wardens to maintain the gardens in good condition and avoid damage caused by too much foot traffic and overcrowding.

What is the Kanban Method?

The Kanban Method is both a codified management approach for professional services—designed to improve customer service and satisfaction—and an evolutionary approach to improvement intended to deliver institutionalized change: improvements in culture, organizational maturity, and business and economic outcomes that stick and are capable of surviving changes in personnel, managers, leaders, and customers.

We've come to recognize three agendas that are typically held as a motivation for adopting Kanban. These are:

- Sustainability
- Service Orientation
- Survivability

Sustainability

The desire is to avoid overburdening both the people and the organization and to enable a sustainable pace. The focus tends to be internal, and the goals are related to alleviating problems such as staff burnout, staff turnover, poor quality, lack of employee engagement, and a stressful working environment while improving pride of workmanship.

Service Orientation

The focus is outward, more altruistic and purpose-driven. The goal when adopting Kanban is a desire to satisfy currently unhappy customers—to meet their expectations and achieve fit-for-purpose service delivery. You realize that you lead a services business and that it is essential to think in terms of services, to view your organization as a network of inter-dependent services and recognize that for each service in this network, you can deploy a kanban system to improve service delivery.

Survivability

We often find this motivation amongst the leaders of multi-generational family businesses and privately held enterprises in which professional managers are tasked with preserving the wealth of the business for future generations. The desire is to create a more innovative business, with a more liberal culture, that is willing to take risks and recognizes that change and modernization are essential to survival. Knowing that wholesale changes carry signifi-cant risks to short- and medium-term survival, leadership recognizes that the organization needs to be wired with the DNA to help it evolve and remain relevant in a fast-changing world. Therefore, there is enthusiasm for incremental, evolutionary change rather than dramatic, designed-and-managed change—humane change that is respectful of the past and the people who are part of the business now.

Change That Is Humane

Kanban delivers change that is humane. An organization adopts Kanban because it values its customers and wishes to satisfy their needs while also valuing its workforce and treat-ing them with respect. Organizations adopting Kanban believe it is possible to create a three-sided win-win-win: happy customers; workers who are fulfilled through autonomy, mastery, and a sense of purpose; and superior economic results that delight investors or other stakeholders such as donors or taxpayers, with a built-in mechanism to evolve, adapt, maintain competitiveness, and stay relevant in an ever-changing world of fickle markets and economic uncertainty.

Kanban Systems Are at the Core of Evolutionary Change

The Kanban Method uses kanban systems as its core driver for, or the catalyst of, change. Kanban systems enable predictable service delivery; at the same time, they also create some stress and tension, which motivates change. They, together with a collection of feedback mechanisms for reflection and action, called Kanban Cadences, are key to the Kanban

Method, which enables a repeatable system for business agility in a wide variety of professional services and knowledge worker industries.

Kanban Applied to Professional Services Work

How to implement Kanban is examined in greater detail in volume 2, *Implementing Kanban*; a brief overview is appropriate now.

Using "kanban boards," as they are known (an example is shown in Figure 12.2), is a technique adopted by the Extreme Programming Agile software development community around the turn of the century. The "extreme programmers" had taken to writing their software requirements, known as "user stories," on index cards and then pinning them to a board or a wall, displayed for all to see. The boards displaying these "story cards" were known as "card walls." As discussed in Chapter 4, card walls from Extreme Programming were adopted and adapted into Kanban starting in 2007. A kanban board enabled greater insight into workflow and how a process was functioning. What immediately differentiates a Kanban board from an Extreme Programming card wall is workflow. Extreme Programming only ever had simple states such as Backlog, In-Progress, and Done. Kanban boards typically have more than one activity in a series of knowledge or information discovery steps that make up an entire service delivery workflow.

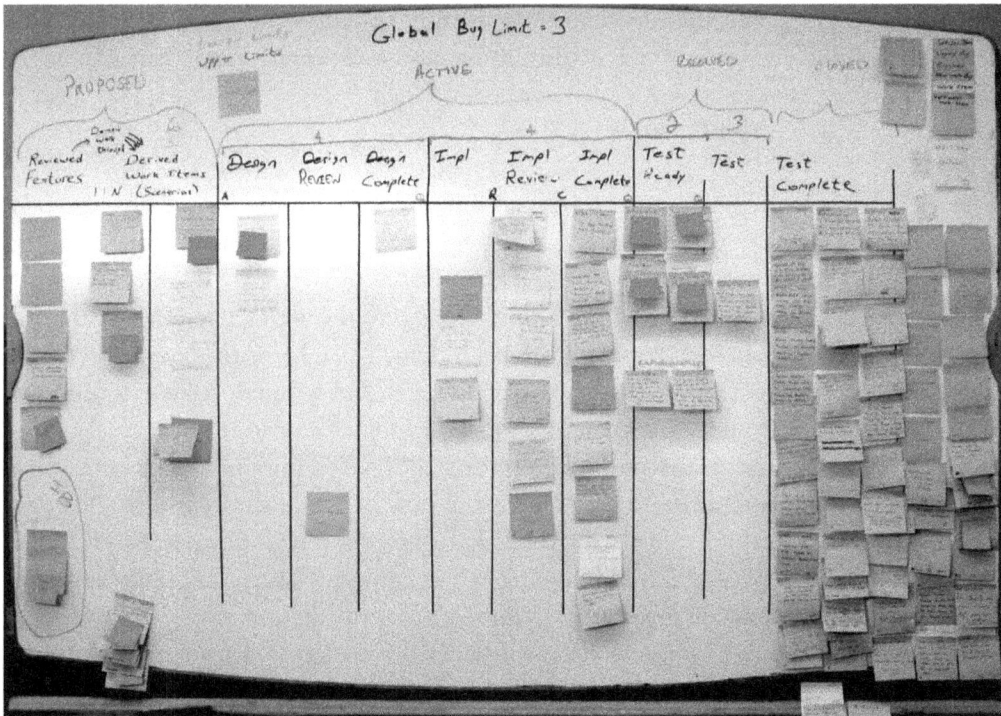

Figure 12.2 A kanban card wall (courtesy of SEP)

Given that one of the meanings of kanban in Japanese is sign, or board, it is easy to see why the term "card wall" has largely dropped out of usage. Some software tools for tracking knowledge work activities, such as Azure Devops from Microsoft, simply refer to them as "boards" with the sub-product Azure Boards. Each ticket on the board represents a single item of work.

Benefits of Kanban

There are several reasons to adopt a kanban system. Each has a simple, explainable cause and effect.

Prevention of Overburdening

First, to prevent overburdening workers, we use a kanban system to set a limit for work-in-progress that reflects a reasonable capacity. By effectively preventing growth of work-in-progress—preventing the starting of new work without either completing or abandoning existing unfinished work—demand on the workflow is stemmed off and balanced with the rate of completion. This enables a sustainable pace of work. Demand is balanced against capability (to deliver finished work).

By enabling workers to focus on only one or just a few service requests at a time, stress is reduced, and the quality of work often improves. Individuals can achieve a work versus personal life balance, and this should enable them to continue working indefinitely at a steady pace producing work of high quality. Kanban systems enable the sustainable pace I was looking for in the early 2000s (as described in Chapter 1).

Deferred Commitment

A kanban system also enables us to defer commitment. By limiting the quantity of work-in-progress, a kanban system encourages us to start work when we are confident that the customer really wants to take delivery, and the scarcity created by a WIP limit encourages us to start work only shortly before we know we need to deliver it. The effect is that we defer commitment as late as is reasonably possible, which enables us to choose other work that may be more urgent. Kanban systems encourage the adoption of what in Lean literature is referred to as "the last responsible moment." Deferred commitment means that proposed work remains optional and uncommitted until pulled into the system when there is a signal that there is capacity to start something new.

Deferred commitment is game changing in knowledge worker industries. All too often, workers complain not only of overburdening but of constantly changing priorities while new work being introduced is apparently more important than existing work, only for priorities to change again later and yet more new work is started. Kanban systems force this behavior to stop. Deferred commitment means that business stakeholders are asked to think very carefully about whether or not they really want something. The implication is that once committed and pulled into the kanban system, work should not be discarded or returned to the pool of optional work requests awaiting selection. This shift causes a significant change in how risk is managed in technology businesses and focuses debate on how to select items of work for development and delivery.

Visibility of Problems

As you will see, kanban systems also quickly flush out issues that impede the flow of work and impair the economic performance of a service. Kanban systems challenge an organization to focus on resolving those issues in order to maintain a steady flow of work. By providing visibility onto quality and process problems, it makes obvious the impact of defects, bottlenecks, variability, and transaction and coordination costs of batch transfers. The simple act of limiting work-in-progress with kanban encourages higher quality and greater performance. The combination of improved flow and better quality helps to shorten lead times and improve predictability and due-date performance. By establishing a regular release frequency and delivering against it consistently, kanban systems help to build trust with customers and trust along an entire workflow, including other departments, external suppliers, and dependent downstream partners.

Cultural Growth

By doing all of this, kanban systems contribute to the cultural evolution of organizations. By exposing problems, focusing the organization on resolving them, and eliminating their future effects, the full Kanban Method facilitates the emergence of a highly collaborative, high-trust, highly empowered, continuously improving organization.

Improved Customer Satisfaction

Kanban has been shown to improve customer satisfaction through regular, dependable, high-quality service delivery of intangible goods such as software, architectural plans, advertising campaigns, design collateral, photography, blueprints, website code, editorial copy, and so forth. It also has been shown to improve productivity and quality, while doing so with shorter lead times and improved timeliness. In addition, there is evidence that Kanban is a pivotal catalyst for the emergence of a more agile, flexible business, as it installs an evolutionary capability that, as it matures, enables a business to move quickly, pivot, and maneuver as markets change and economic conditions ebb and flow.

Continuous Improvement

Kanban systems are compelling for their ability to eliminate overburdening, control the effects of variability in the flow of work, and manage risk through the benefits from deferred commitment and the changes it forces on how work is selected, capital allocated, and cash spent. Kanban systems change the way a business operates for the better. This alone creates a compelling argument for adoption. However, I was not aware of kanban systems' reputation as being instrumental in driving incremental process improvement. I did not, in 2007, know that Taiichi Ohno, one of the creators of the Toyota Production System, had said, "The two pillars of the Toyota production system are just-in-time and automation with a human touch, or autonomation. The tool used to operate the system is kanban." In other words, kanban is fundamental to the *kaizen* (continuous improvement) culture at Toyota. It is the mechanism that drives continuous improvement. I have come to recognize that this is also true with virtual kanban systems applied to professional services, knowledge worker activities.

The Six General Practices of Kanban

The Kanban Method defines a set of high-level or abstract practices necessary to create a mechanism for evolutionary change and improved service delivery within organizations. These six general practices were extracted from observation of successful Kanban implementations at a number of organizations between 2007 and 2009. It became evident that six general practices were common, necessary, and sufficient to create positive results with some confidence and predictability. These are:

- Visualize
- Limit Work-in-Progress
- Manage Flow
- Make Policies Explicit
- Implement Feedback Mechanisms
- Improve Collaboratively, Evolve Experimentally (using models and the scientific method)

Specific implementations will have their own distinct practices for visualization, limiting WIP, and managing flow. They will also have their own unique set of explicit policies and a selection of feedback mechanisms inspired by the canonical set of generic examples known as the Kanban Cadences, and their own methods to identify and implement improvement opportunities based upon the default set of models and example approaches described in volume 2, *Implementing Kanban*.

Operational versus Management Practices

Some early work by other authors, largely appearing between 2008 and 2010, focused only on the first three general practices: visualize, limit WIP, and manage flow. This led to a lot of rather shallow implementations and a focus on service delivery. Evolutionary change and a culture of continuous improvement (kaizen) tended not to emerge in these implementations.

One of the goals of a Kanban system, and something that is necessary to enable business agility, is the empowerment of the workforce to act on their own initiative and to make their own decisions. Empowerment is a necessary element if an organization is to move quickly and to act with agility. It is therefore necessary to train managers to think in terms of systems and as leaders to design systems of work that enable workers to make many of their own decisions. What was missing from those shallow implementations following only the first three general practices was the systems thinking required to create empowerment—a change in management behavior did not occur. Consequently, I have grouped the original set of six general practices into two sets of three: the Operational Practices, designed to be enacted by the workforce, on their own initiative; and the Management Practices, providing guidance for and answering the question, "What do managers do?"

The Operational Practices:

* Visualize
* Limit Work-in-Progress
* Manage Flow

The Management Practices:

* Make Policies Explicit
* Implement Feedback Mechanisms
* Improve Collaboratively, Evolve Experimentally (using models and the scientific method)

The latter set is required to drive evolutionary change. The job of managers is to create a system that is capable of emergent behavior to adapt and evolve until it consistently achieves fit-for-purpose service delivery.

Kanban Principles

Before I came to Kanban, as described in Chapter 1, I'd been working on synthesizing some ideas combining the software development methodology Feature-Driven Development with the Theory of Constraints and Lean Product Development. Or put another way, synthesizing the work of Peter Coad, Jeff de Luca, Eli Goldratt, and Donald Reinertsen. My initial attempt at this appeared in my book *Agile Management for Software Engineering* in 2003. I continued to evolve this thinking, introducing the work of W. Edwards Deming (and others from the Statistical Process Control community, such as Donald Wheeler) during the following year, publishing these newer integrations via my blog or in conference presentations. It was this slightly more developed version that Donald Reinertsen first encountered when, as he mentions in the Foreword to *Kanban*, he suggested that I focus on batch size and reducing, or indeed limiting, work-in-progress, and that kanban systems were an interesting way to control undesirable variability.

I began to develop a set of principles that underpinned my thinking, my philosophy of management. I taught these principles in my training curricula for some years without explicitly naming them. Likewise, it did not occur to me to codify them in *Kanban* in 2010.

Now, writing in 2023, this seems like a good time to correct that failure. These principles provide a fundamental underpinning to everything that followed with Kanban. I call these the Flow Principles and the Service Delivery Principles.

The Flow Principles

The Flow Principles underpin my work in management theory and practices for over 20 years. They are so fundamental that I always assumed them to be present and did not until recently attempt to write them down or codify them. These principles are at the root of my ideas published in my first book, *Agile Management for Software Engineering*, where I synthesized ideas from Donald Reinertsen's *Managing the Design Factory*, Eli Goldratt's Theory of Constraints, particularly from his book *The Goal*, and Feature-Driven Development, a lightweight software development lifecycle process considered to be one of the original "Agile" methodologies. Seeing flow in intangible goods, professional services, and knowledge work activities opened the door to a new way of managing that has changed the world of modern work, well beyond adoption of the Kanban Method.

The Flow Principles are:

- Intangible goods (professional services) businesses can be managed in a somewhat similar fashion to physical, tangible goods businesses.
- Represent intangible goods with tangible artifacts: Make invisible work and work-flows visible.
- Control and limit the "inventory" of intangible goods.

The Service Delivery Principles

The Kanban Method was driven by core principles and the goal of improving service delivery and enabling institutionalized changes that stick and survive beyond periods of deliberate management attention and intervention as well as personnel changes at both the individual contributor and managerial levels. When managers move on or change their focus, the changes they've made should stick around. This is the concept of "institution-alization." In addition, there were principles I used when developing the method and its guidance and driving its adoption across the world.

Improved service delivery (at Microsoft's IT division) was the original motivator for adopting kanban systems. If delivery is erratic, unpredictable, of poor quality, or simply taking too long, and the workflow has poor flow efficiency, then Kanban should help.

The **Service Delivery Principles** are:

- Understand and focus on your customers' needs and expectations.
- Manage the work; let people self-organize around it.
- Evolve your management policies to improve customer and business outcomes.

The Change Management Principles

Beginning in 2002, I was looking for an evolutionary approach to change. Evolutionary change needs a stimulus or stressor to provoke discussion and motivate change. It needs a feedback mechanism to evaluate issues and propose changes, and it needs acts of leadership to take the risk to enact changes and stick with them long enough to ensure their success.

We now call this the **Evolutionary Change Model**:

- Stressor
- Feedback mechanism
- Act of leadership

Although there are many practices that can act as stressors, limiting work-in-progress with a kanban system is an excellent means with which to introduce such stress. Metrics such as cumulative flow diagrams and lead time histograms, together with the Kanban Cadences such as the Service Delivery Review, provide the feedback mechanisms. Hence, the Kanban Method codifies and prescribes two of the three required elements for evolutionary change and creates the opportunities—the meetings and reviews—to encourage the acts of leadership needed to invoke action that creates improvement. It is the Management Practices of the Kanban Method that drive evolutionary improvement.

We can see this illustrated in the cartoon on the cover: Clearly the group are under some stress; work is not flowing and, from their conversation, all is not well with their service delivery. They use the Kanban Meeting in front of the board to reflect on how things are going—their feedback mechanism—and then it takes an act of leadership from the fourth character, who says, "Let's do something about it!" to provide the Kanban Magic, to catalyze change, take the initiative, and make it happen. It was an oversight and omission in *Kanban*: I failed to recognize the importance of leadership to drive evolutionary change and consequently omitted the topic from the text. If there is a single failure in that book, it was the failure to recognize the necessity of leadership and to dedicate part of the narrative to enabling it.

"People do not resist change, they resist being changed." — Peter Senge

"All politics is local." — Tip O'Neill

"If all politics is local, then all change is personal." — David Anderson

---

Recognizing that organization, collaboration, and leadership are sociological phenomena, and that getting things done in business requires groups of people cooperating together, it is possible to overlook the fact that all change, even when happening to groups of people—to organizations—is perceived and interpreted personally, by the individuals. The study of how individuals cope with change is part of social psychology.

Individuals can be in one of four states in relation to change:

- **Stability:** happy, no motivation to change
- **Inertia:** unhappy, but fearful and resistant to change
- **Incremental:** (might better be called Evolutionary) willing to accept normative changes to practices and ways of doing things, providing these changes do not affect the social structure and hierarchy
- **Dramatic (or Structural):** changes to identity, role, social status, level of dignity, respect, or recognition; invokes psychological crisis, leading to resistance and inertia

Almost all traditional change management—and particularly that of software engineering process methodologies and Agile methods that prescribe new processes, roles, responsibilities, and cooperation—disrupt the social structure, invoking psychological crisis in response to a perceived identity threat. Our goal with the Kanban Method is to overcome inertia and lead incremental, evolutionary change through the use of small changes perceived as normative in nature: Our goal is to avoid the "rock" of identity threat and dramatic structural social change. If we can achieve this, we can make progress. As any elite athlete, such as Dragos Dumitriu in his earlier years, might tell you, "Every small improvement is still an improvement."

Knowing that Kanban should "be like water," recognizing that "water flows around the rock," and knowing that the rock is emotional resistance to change invoked by identity threats and dramatic structural social change, I developed the change management principles of the Kanban Method.

The **Change Management Principles** are:

- Start with what you do now:
  - Understanding current processes, as actually practiced
  - Respecting existing roles, responsibilities, and job titles
- Gain agreement to pursue improvement through evolutionary change.
- Encourage acts of leadership at all levels.

The Essence of Effective Change Leadership

I also recognized that none of this was worth anything if people were unable to replicate my results with Kanban and lead change effectively. Inspired by my boss in the late 1990s, the creator of Feature-Driven Development and a great leader of significant IT projects, Jeff De Luca, I created the brand essence for my business, Kanban University.

Pragmatic, Actionable, Evidence-Based Guidance

- **Pragmatic:** It is possible to get it done.
- **Actionable:** You know what to do.
- **Evidence-based:** We never teach anything or offer guidance unless we have already observed that it works.

These core values have guided the development of the Kanban Method since the beginning. I attribute, in large part, the robustness of the Kanban Method, and its effectiveness in the marketplace, to these underlying values. Kanban works because we've always focused on promoting pragmatic, actionable, evidence-based guidance. It's harder to do: It takes time to collect the evidence. Guidance is extracted and abstracted from real-world experience. Larger-scale guidance, such as the Kanban Maturity Model, required around fifteen years of development and a lot of time and energy from many people to run the experiments, gather the evidence, report the findings, tell the stories, write the case studies, and present the experience reports, and then for others to analyze these, look for recurring patterns, find the common elements, and codify them. Changing the world of change management has been a long and expensive process that has needed a great deal of patience.

The Kanban Values

In January 2013, Mike Burrows published his observation that Kanban was a method underpinned by a collection of values—a credo. These values define the organizational culture in which Kanban can thrive. Mike's work changed Kanban and changed his career, as he focused his thinking on outcome-driven change and driving cultural change through values. This led to his own body of work and approach to organizational change leadership known as Agendashift. Mike identified and defined nine values specifically associated with the Kanban Method. More recently, through work with the Kanban Maturity Model, Teodora Bozheva and I augmented the list to reflect the corporate culture that we determined was required to deliver each of the outcomes defined at the seven levels in our organizational maturity model. The full list of values now associated with Kanban is:

- Achievement
- Collaboration*[41]
- Transparency*
- Taking Initiative
- Acts of Leadership
- Customer Awareness
- Evolutionary Change
- Flow*
- Narrative
- Respect*
- Understanding (internal)*[42]

---

41. *Denotes one of the original nine Kanban Values defined by Mike Burrows in 2013 and described in his 2014 book *Kanban From the Inside*

42. Originally documented as "Understanding" and later divided into the subcategories of "internal" and "external," reflecting the level of empathy observed at organizations of differing maturity levels

- Agreement*
- Balance*
- Customer Service*[43]
- Fitness for Purpose
- Leadership at All Levels[44]*
- Short-term Results
- Understanding (external)
- Unity and Alignment
- Business Focus
- Competition
- Customer Intimacy
- Data-driven Decision Making
- Deeper Balance
- Fairness
- Leadership Development
- Regulatory Compliance
- Equality of Opportunity
- Experimentation (tolerance of failure)
- Perfectionism
- Social Mobility
- Congruence
- Long-term Survivability
- Tolerance and Diversity

This extended list reflects the organizational values we believe are needed to deliver the desirable business outcomes associated with increasing levels of organizational maturity, enterprise scale, and longevity of an organization. This long list goes beyond what is needed simply to embrace Kanban.

See Appendix A for a brief explanation of the original nine organizational values that arose from Mike's work with Kanban.

Mike distilled his list of Kanban Values retrospectively from the observation and practice of Kanban. They represent observed reality rather than a thought experiment. They offer not only insight into the purpose and meaning of Kanban, but also a means to determine its appropriateness for adoption in an organization. Do you, your team, your

---

43. Originally documented as "Customer Focus"

44. Originally documented simply as "Leadership"

department, your business unit, and your wider organization share these values? If not all of them, how many? Alignment of values shared between Kanban and the adopting organization is a predictor of success and a leading indicator of the depth of implementation that might be achieved. The more values you share with Kanban, the easier it should be to adopt, and the greater the benefit you might expect.

This observation led to the mantra for the Kanban Maturity Model:

Outcomes follow practices.
Practices follow culture.
Culture follows values.
Therefore, lead with values.

Leadership is the Secret Ingredient

The cartoon commissioned for the cover of this book, shown in Figure 12.1, was designed to capture the essence of the method in full. It clearly shows visualization. Perhaps it could show limiting work-in-progress more clearly? This was omitted as a simplification by Pujan Roka, the cartoonist. In retrospect, it created an interesting outcome. The cartoon depicts a proto-Kanban implementation. It reflects what we might now call an organization in transition from Maturity Level 2 to Maturity Level 3. While the original Kanban book was designed to teach organizations how to implement fit-for-purpose, reliable, predictable service delivery at what we now call Maturity Level 3, in reality the industry was much shallower. The cartoon more accurately reflected the typical workplace in 2010.

We see a small team discussing the flow of work with the implication that workflow is being managed. There are clearly some policies in place controlling the work. Some of these policies may be explicit; for example, the use of colors must indicate something about the work and how it should be treated. However, there is also an implication that some policies are implicit and perhaps could be improved. The tester in the cartoon is idle, and this suggests a lack of flexible working policies, while the analyst appears to have too much work-in-progress and perhaps some policies are not being adhered to, or adequately enforced. The entire cartoon and the meeting taking place illustrate a feedback loop. And the work displayed on the board, together with the speech bubbles, gives an indication that development is a bottleneck, and hence, we are compelled to introduce the use of a model into our understanding of the workflow and the issues that beset it.

The cartoon captures the six general practices of the Kanban Method very neatly, but the character on the right-hand side of the picture shows us the most important aspect required to make the Kanban Method work. By suggesting, "Let's do something about it," he illustrates a small act of leadership. He is not content to hear the reports from his colleagues. Perhaps these reports show a repeating pattern over several days or weeks? At today's meeting, he has heard enough; it is time to act. It is what happens next that is truly interesting. This is called an "after meeting," which will be described in full in volume 2, *Implementing Kanban*. In formal Lean literature, such a spontaneous meeting resulting in action to improve flow is known as a "spontaneous quality circle," or a "kaizen event."

A group of interested people, perhaps from several functions, will meet and discuss what they see. They might question why the tester is idle. They might confirm that the developer is constantly loaded and has no slack. They might observe the build-up of analysis completed tickets waiting on development and they may conclude that the development function is a bottleneck. They may then question existing policies. They may ask the developer if there is work that she feels could be done by others. Perhaps she would trust a tester to do lower-risk, less novel, more repetitive work? It may then be agreed that it would be acceptable for idle testers to assist by performing development work on, say, blue tickets, as these tickets represent work that is sufficiently low-risk that the professional developers do not object to someone from another function completing it. In other words, this is a change that does not threaten their identity or their place in the social hierarchy; nor does it affect the status, respect, or recognition accorded to developers or undermine the dignity of the testers being asked to do the lower-risk development tasks. And thus, policy is changed and, little-by-little, barriers between job functions and demarcation lines between roles are eroded. The workforce becomes a little more flexible through multi-skilling, and the level of social capital (or trust) increases amongst the workers in this system.

What happens at after-meetings shows the complex nature of knowledge work service delivery and the emergent effects that are commonplace when the Kanban Method is implemented fully.

Takeaways

- Kanban recognizes three common agendas for people adopting the method: sustainability, service-orientation, and survivability.

- The Kanban Method is named for its use of kanban systems, which limit work-in-progress and create a positive tension that catalyzes change.

- Kanban systems are a specific example of systems known generically as pull systems.

- A kanban system consists of kanban (or signal cards), with one kanban representing one unit of capacity within the system.

- Kanban is both a Chinese and Japanese word and has different meanings in different contexts and whether it is written in Japanese using the kanji system of Chinese characters or the hiragana Japanese alphabet. All the possible meanings have relevance to the Kanban Method: "sign," or "visual board," or "shingle," "looking at the board" (the Chinese meaning), and "signal card" or "tally" all represent aspects of the Kanban Method.

- Kanban systems are used to prevent overburdening of workers, and as a process or system of working that spans an entire workflow or value chain.

- Relief from overburdening has a secondary effect of improving quality.

- Kanban systems are also used to defer commitment and avoid starting too many pieces of work.

- Deferred commitment encompasses the Lean concept of "last responsible moment."

- Deferred commitment causes a change of focus, pushes risk management upstream, and catalyzes demand for better means to assess and manage business risks associated with work requests.

- Kanban systems provoke a focus on flow of work.

- Kanban systems contribute to the cultural evolution of organizations and facilitate the emergence of collaboration, high levels of trust, worker empowerment, and continuous improvement.

- Kanban improves customer satisfaction through faster, more predictable, more timely delivery with improved quality.

- The Kanban Method has six general practices: operational practices of visualize, limit WIP, and manage flow; and management practices of make policies explicit; implement feedback mechanisms; and improve collaboratively, evolve experimentally.

- The Kanban Method is based on three sets of principles:

- The Flow Principles: Intangible goods businesses can be managed similarly to physical goods businesses; make invisible work and workflows visible; and control and limit the "inventory" of intangible goods.

- The Service Delivery Principles: Understand and focus on your customers' needs and expectations; manage the work, let people self-organize around it; evolve your management policies to improve customer and business outcomes.

- The Change Management Principles: Start with what you do now, understanding current processes as actually practiced and respecting existing roles, responsibilities, and job titles; gain agreement to pursue improvement through evolutionary change; and encourage acts of leadership at all levels.

- The Evolutionary Change Model consists of a stressor, a reflection mechanism, and an act of leadership.

- To make a difference in the world and create change that sticks, Kanban guidance must be pragmatic, actionable, and evidence-based.

- Retrospectively, Mike Burrows observed that Kanban encapsulated a value system, a credo. Initially, he defined nine values:
  - Collaboration
  - Transparency
  - Flow
  - Respect
  - Understanding
  - Agreement
  - Balance
  - Customer Focus
  - Leadership

- More recently, during work on the Kanban Maturity Model, this set of values was augmented to cover motivations for very shallow, or personal, adoptions of Kanban as well as very deep implementations in highly mature organizations.

- Values-driven change has become a core part of Kanban coaching guidance and is best illustrated in the mantra of the Kanban Maturity Model:
  - Outcomes follow practices.
  - Practices follow culture.
  - Culture follows values.
  - Therefore, lead with values.

- Leadership is required to drive improvements.

- Leadership is the secret ingredient of the Kanban Method.

- Leadership was not given sufficient attention in *Kanban*—an unfortunate omission.

13

Kanban Maturity Model

Mapping Patterns of Kanban Implementation to
Levels of Organizational Maturity[45]

Working with Teodora Bozheva, we recognized that there were many different patterns of Kanban implementation and, from case study evidence, experience reports, community anecdotes, and observations made when visiting clients, there appeared to be a correlation between the complexity of a Kanban implementation and the maturity of the organization. These patterns are fully explained in volume 2, *Implementing Kanban*.

The Three Pillars of the Kanban Maturity Model

Figure 13.1 illustrates the 3 pillars of the model, focused on outcomes, that are achieved through practices, in turn enabled by culture, with all of it driven by a managed approach to evolutionary change. The organizational maturity model is built around observable outcomes, illustrated in the next section through customer experience.

---

45. A version of this chapter first appeared as an appendix in Anderson, David J, and Alexei Zheglov. *Fit for Purpose: Synthesizing Customer Experience and Strategy for Accelerated Business Results*, 3rd ed. Seattle: Blue Hole Press, 2023.

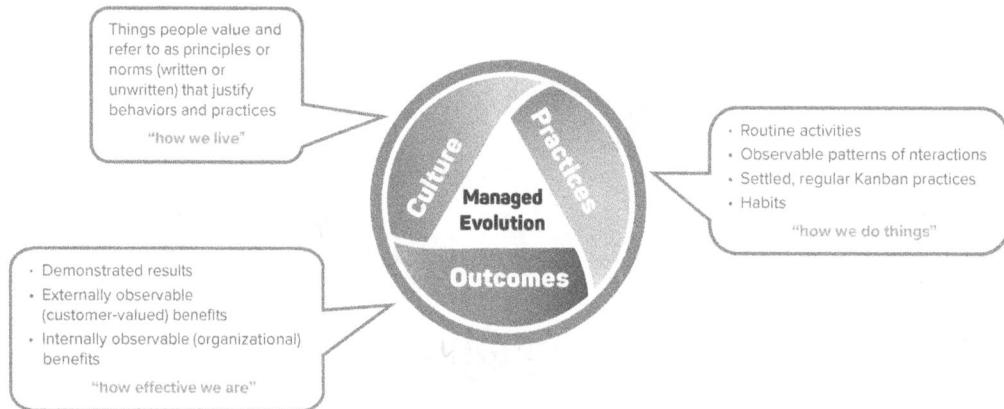

Figure 13.1 Three Pillars of the KMM

The Organizational Maturity Model

We built a model of organizational maturity and demonstrated that Kanban implementations are driven by organizational maturity. The design of Kanban systems, boards, and tickets are all driven by the needs of the organization, and those needs vary as the organization matures. As organizational maturity improves, changes emerge related to business behavior, leadership, risk management, organizational culture, and ultimately the business outcomes that result from and correlate to differing levels of maturity in the business. The Kanban implementation always reflects the maturity of the organization implementing it. If the organization cares a lot about risk management, then the design of the Kanban board and its tickets reflect the need to visualize risk information and hedge risks.

Our organizational maturity model is an updated, evolutionary adaptation of work from several earlier sources including Philip Crosby, Gerald R. Weinberg, and the Capability Maturity Model (and its successor, the Capability Maturity Model Integration) of the Software Engineering Institute at Carnegie Mellon University. The model has seven levels of maturity numbered 0 through 6, with 0 being the lowest, or shallowest, and 6 being the highest, or deepest, level. Generally, we prefer shallow to deep as opposed to low to high. Previous literature tended to use low to high. Hence, both sets of labels are in common usage. We tend to draw the model from top to bottom, shallow to deep; a low to high visualization would be best drawn bottom to top.

As the model shows, most businesses must aspire to Maturity Level 4 in order to exhibit resilience, robustness, and risk-management capability to give themselves a strong chance of long-term survival.

What follows is the briefest overview of the seven levels in the model illustrated by a description of how it might manifest in a pizza restaurant. This example is deliberately chosen as a service industry example, but equally deliberately, something very different from IT services typically associated with Kanban. Also included are graphics of typical Kanban boards at Levels 0 through 5 to illustrate patterns of kanban implementation. There are many more examples of kanban board implementations provided in volume 2, *Implementing Kanban*, and in my book with Teodora Bozheva, *Kanban Maturity Model: A Map to Organizational Agility, Resilience, and Reinvention*[46] or online at kmm.plus.

It is important to recognize that it is the organization that matures; their Kanban implementation merely reflects the maturity of the organization. The Kanban implementation reflects what they value, the risks they manage, and the nature of their decision making. At lower maturity levels this tends to be simple and homogeneous, while at higher maturity levels it tends to be sophisticated, embracing significant variety.

Maturity Level 0—Oblivious

Maturity Level 0	Oblivious
Characterization	My way, or, every customer has their pet.
Leadership	Abdicated
Leader's Character Traits	Authenticity
Cultural Values	(Individual) Achievement
Service	Staff of individuals who know how to make pizza
Process	Staff members compete to take customer orders and for resources such as countertop space, ingredients, and access to ovens.
Customer Experience	Depends entirely on the individual taking the order and making the pizza. No trust in the business as a system.

The restaurant staff all act independently. Each knows how to make pizza. Staff members compete to take a customer's order, then compete for resources such as countertop space, ingredients, and access to the ovens so they can fulfill the order. The customer experience depends entirely on who is serving them, and customers often develop a preference for a specific team member, effectively choosing them as their pet pizza producer. Customers wait to place their order with their pet chef, as they have no trust in the restaurant's systems. See Figure 13.2 on the next page for an example of an individual kanban board.

---

46. Anderson, David J, and Teodora Bozheva. *Kanban Maturity Model: A Map to Organizational Agility, Resilience, and Reinvention*, 2nd ed. Seattle: Kanban University Press, 2020.

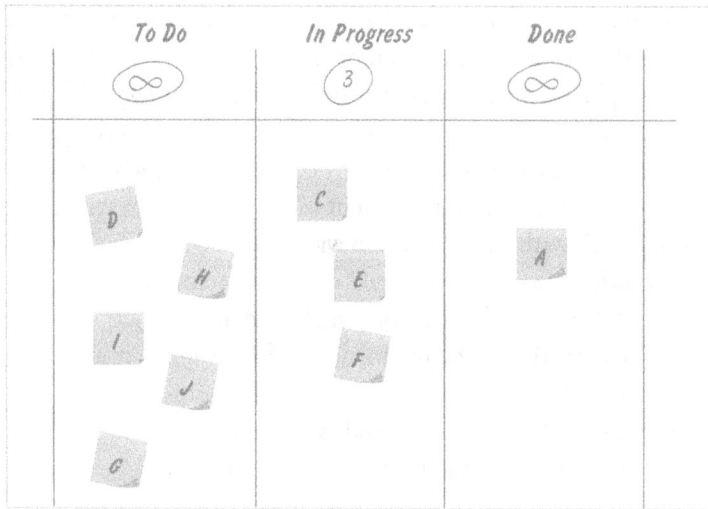

Figure 13.2 Example of an individual kanban board (Maturity Level 0)

Maturity Level 1—Team-Focused

Maturity Level 1	Team-Focused
Characterization	Never the same way twice
Leadership	Selfish
Leader's Character Traits	Confident
Cultural Values	Collaboration, taking initiative, transparency
Service	Depends highly on the individuals involved: There is variance in the method of preparing, baking, and delivery; problems with order accuracy; and issues with taste and quality.
Process	Is emerging but is inconsistent: Pizzas are frequently of the wrong type, or are missing ingredients; or they are of poor quality upon delivery or delivery times vary dramatically to an unacceptable level.
Customer Experience	The vendor is unreliable and untrustworthy.

Working at this restaurant feels like being part of a team. However, the method of preparing, baking, and delivering pizza, the accuracy of order fulfillment, and the quality and taste of the pizza depend highly on the individual making it. Our processes are emerging but are still inconsistent. Often, the pizza is the wrong type, is missing ingredients, is of poor quality upon delivery, or the delivery time depends dramatically on the person who delivers it. The customers' experience leads them to conclude that this restaurant is extremely unreliable.

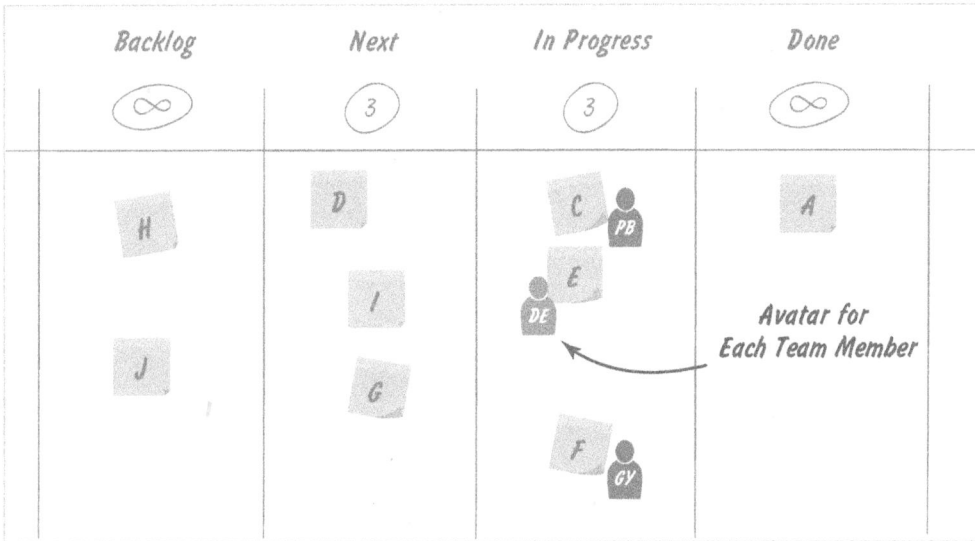

Figure 13.3 Typical team kanban board (Maturity Level 1)

Maturity Level 2—Customer-Driven

Maturity Level 2	Customer-Driven
Characterization	Never the same result twice
Leadership	Tribal
Leader's Character Traits	Charisma
Cultural Values	Customer awareness, evolutionary change, flow, leadership, narrative, respect, understanding of internal processes
Service	Depends on the supervisor, manager, or owner on duty: Pizzas delivered may have slight quality issues, are occasionally of the wrong type, slightly burnt, or missing ingredients.
Process	Defined procedures are now followed consistently.
Customer Experience	Depends entirely on the supervisor on duty

This is a maturing pizza delivery business with a focus on its customers. The method of preparing, baking, and delivering pizza is now consistent, and defined procedures are now followed consistently. However, the pizza delivered depends highly on either the main cook or the manager being involved in the process. If she or he is not there, the pizza delivered might be the wrong type, be missing some ingredients, or be slightly burnt. Therefore, the customer's perception is that the restaurant's reliability depends on the supervisor on duty. Customers adjust their behavior accordingly.

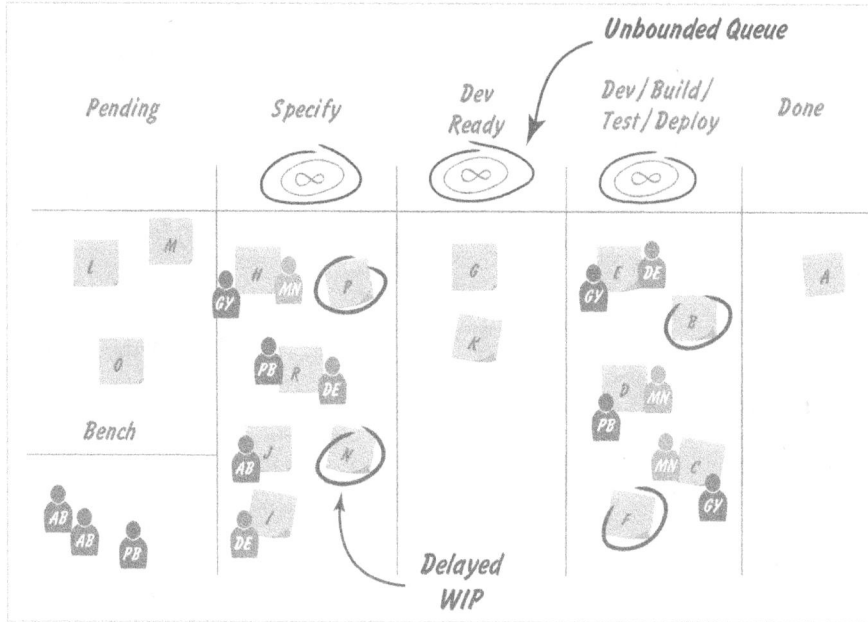

Figure 13.4 Service workflow kanban board (Maturity Level 2)

Maturity Level 3—Fit-for-Purpose

Maturity Level 3	Fit-for-Purpose
Characterization	Always happy customers; "no more heroes anymore."
Leadership	Purpose-driven
Leader's Character Traits	Altruism
Cultural Values	Agreement, balance, customer service, fitness for purpose, leadership at all levels, short-term business results, understanding external supply chain and customer demand, unity and alignment
Service	Consistent: pizzas delivered match expectations, are of the right type with the right ingredients and are almost always warm, tasty and of good quality upon delivery. Time for Improvement: time and space to think about changes to the menu, special dietary needs, opening new locations, and developing special offers
Process	Defined procedures are followed consistently regardless of which staff or supervisors are working on any given day or shift.
Customer Experience	Vendor is reliable and trustworthy but doesn't yet have a deep empathy with their customers or understand why they visit.

This sophisticated city-center pizza restaurant has a home or office delivery service. Their method of preparing, baking, and delivering pizza is consistent, and defined procedures are followed consistently, regardless of which night of the week it is, who is working that evening, or whether the manager is there.

Consistently, the pizza delivered matches the order, is of high quality, and is within service delivery expectations. The customer's perception is that the restaurant is reliable and trustworthy. Because the process and the outcomes are consistent, the restaurant owner has time to think about growing his business—open restaurants in other locations, or offer pizzas for people with dietary restrictions, or develop special menus that differentiate this restaurant from its competitors.

However, although this Maturity Level 3 organization can fulfill orders within expectations, they aren't yet good at understanding why customers choose them or what additional expectations customers might have. They sell a lot of basic Margherita pizzas for delivery to business premises after 5:00 p.m. on Thursday evenings, but no one has bothered to think about it, or to ask why. They haven't yet achieved customer intimacy, and their ability to anticipate demand and expectations hasn't yet evolved.

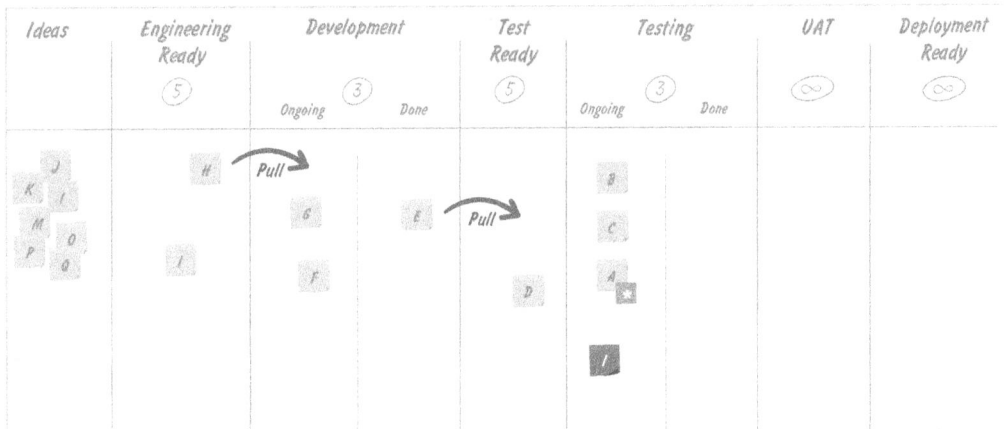

Figure 13.5 Service workflow board featuring an end-to-end virtual kanban system (Maturity Level 3)

Maturity Level 4—Risk-Hedged

Maturity Level 4	Risk-Hedged
Characterization	Everyone is happy; "cope gracefully with unexpected events."
Leadership	Risk Manager
Leader's Character Traits	Empathy, pragmatism, integrity
Cultural Values	Business focus, competition, customer intimacy, data-driven decision making, deep balance, fairness, leadership development, regulatory compliance
Service	Several different classes of service catering to customers with different needs and risks • Optimally staffed • Economically successful • Anticipatory
Process	Gracefully copes with ebb and flow in demand. Costs are tightly controlled without affecting delivery capability or customer satisfaction. Solidly predictable economic performance.
Customer Experience	Customer satisfaction is invisible—it is always there, and customers have come to take it for granted. Business anticipates customer needs and demand; they understand customers'"why" and purpose for visiting. Well-respected brand.

This is a mature pizza restaurant and delivery service. It has successfully scaled beyond a single location. The owner is running an economically successful business offering several different classes of service, such as an express delivery menu. His locations successfully cope with ebb and flow in demand and understand the cyclical nature of their business. They are optimally staffed most of the time and their costs are tightly controlled without affecting their delivery capability or impacting customer satisfaction. They have a well-respected brand and solidly predictable profitability.

They sell a lot of basic Margherita pizzas for delivery to business premises after 5:00 p.m. on Thursday evenings, and they know why: Thursday is the night that colleagues hang out together after work. On Fridays, people have plans for the weekend, but on Thursday nights they can afford to stay late for an hour or two. A Margherita pizza is the perfect accompaniment for a glass of beer or soda, just enough to take the edge off hunger at the end of a day's work. Because they know why their customers order, they can anticipate this demand—it's not luck! They can also anticipate when the demand will ease off, drop completely, or shift to a different evening of the week. If they have to introduce a new type of cheese because the one used so far is no longer produced, they study their customers' preferences, offering them pizzas with several alternative types of cheese to find out which they like best.

At Maturity Level 4, customer satisfaction is invisible—it is always there. Customers learn simply to take it for granted.

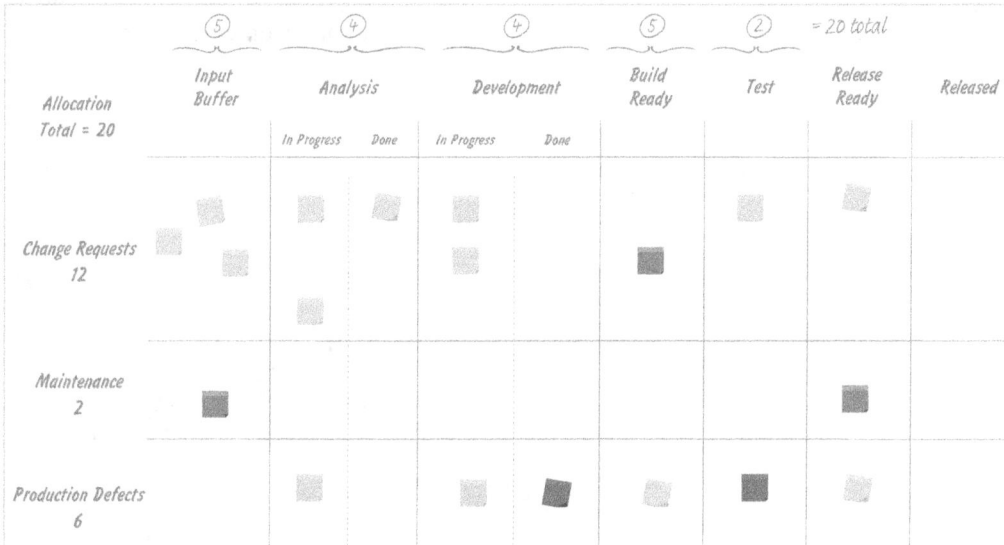

Figure 13.6 Multi-Service workflow board with risk-hedging capacity allocation strategy implemented by work item type (Maturity Level 4)

Maturity Level 5—Market Leader

Maturity Level 5	Market Leader
Characterization	Simply the best
Leadership	Relentless perfectionist
Leader's Character Traits	Humility
Cultural Values	Equality of opportunity, experimentation, perfectionism, social mobility
Service	The best in the market by geographic region or language or ethnic/cultural region or by business sector, vertical industry, or technology
Process	The best design. The best implementation. The best service delivery and customer experience.
Customer Experience	Customers boast about the products and services and advocate for them, proactively introducing others.

This restaurant is now widely viewed as the best in the entire metropolitan area. Residents boast about it to visitors. They insist that experiencing their dine-in or home delivered gourmet pizza is a necessary rite of passage. Their pizzas excel in design—they have the best menu; implementation—their dough and crust are legendary and always are baked to perfection; and their delivery service is second to none—effective, with polite, well-trained, uniformed riders who ensure their pizza arrives in perfect condition every time.

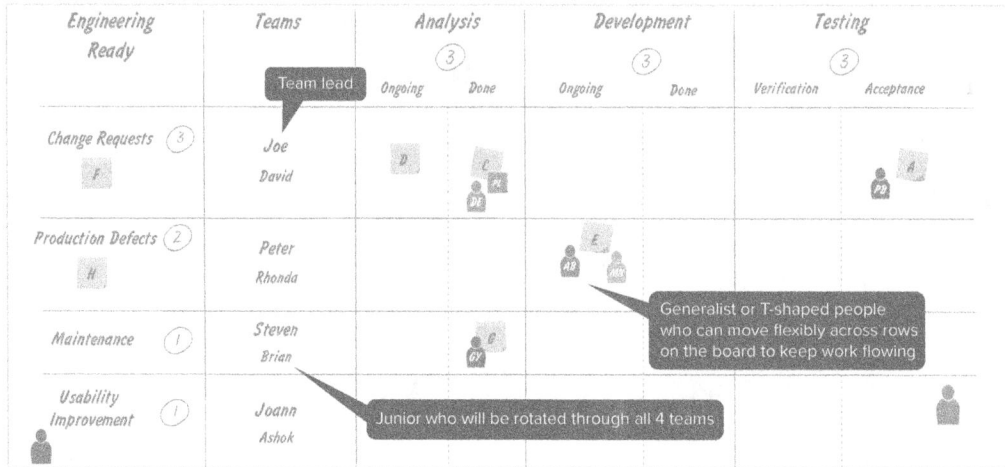

Figure 13.7 Board implementing a sophisticated labor pool liquidity strategy in addition to a risk-hedged, multi-service workflow (Maturity Level 5)

Maturity Level 6—Built for Survival

Maturity Level 6	Built for Survival
Characterization	Managed Reinvention
Leadership	Culture hacker and identity manager
Leader's Character Traits	Sense of duty
Cultural Values	Congruence, long-term survival, tolerance, and diversity
Service	Facing an extinction-level event, or disruption from new technology, the leadership think deeply about the identity and purpose of the business and the core motivation for its continued existence.
Process	Reinvention by making lateral or adjacent moves, amplifying existing capabilities, adopting a new identity, or a change in purpose. Requires a solid understanding of who they are as a business, why they exist, and what makes them happy and provides fulfilment.
Customer Experience	It's the same brand with similar values, the same high levels of service, but it's new, with different products and services; recognizable, familiar, and yet new and different. Customer loyalty remains.

The restaurant chain has been closed due to the Covid-19 pandemic. Consequently, facing an extinction-level event, the owner thinks deeply about the identity and purpose of the business and his core motivation for starting it. He concludes that it exists to deliver exotic gourmet pizzas with the highest quality fresh, local, organic ingredients atop the finest pie with crust thrown from fresh, live-fermenting dough. However, he realizes that the delivery model can change.

As many other restaurants around the greater metropolitan area reinvent themselves as gourmet markets and delicatessens, he decides that he simply cannot follow their lead. However, perhaps they provide him with a new distribution channel. Perhaps he can partner with them to distribute pizza?

He decides to reinvent the business, making gourmet pizza kits. Each kit contains the fresh dough and ingredients for a lovely, tasty, home-baked gourmet pizza experience.

It isn't a whole new business, rather a reinvention of who they already are. They switch to supplying their take-home pizza kits to these new markets. They shoot video of the sous chef demonstrating how to throw the dough to make the crust, how to spread the toppings, and how to set the oven to bake the pizza to perfection. Their highly perishable, totally fresh-ingredient pizza kits aren't to be stored; they're to be used within two days of purchase.

With a solid understanding of who they are, why they exist, and what makes them happy and delivers satisfaction from doing business, the chain successfully pivots and reinvents itself as the nation's favorite premium brand of gourmet, bake-at-home pizza.

Kanban Maturity Model Architecture

The KMM architecture defines the foundational relationships among the three pillars of the model. Figure 13.8 on the next page provides an overview of the KMM architecture. For the most part, the architecture forms a two-dimensional matrix with organizational culture and general practices mapped across the columns, and the seven organizational maturity levels mapped on the rows. Each cell in the table then contains either specific cultural values for a given level, or specific kanban practices, mapped to a general practice and a maturity level.

The three key components—Culture, Kanban Practices, and Outcomes—are shown in three adjacent areas. The vertical axis of the architecture plots the organizational maturity levels.

Specific Practices

Each of the general Kanban practices can be implemented with one or more specific practices. These practices may have varying levels of fidelity, which is generally related to the depth of organizational maturity. Therefore, the name and number of a specific practice reflects both its fidelity and the depth of maturity of the organization implementing the practice.

KANBAN MATURITY MODEL

CULTURE				Organizational Maturity Level	SP	GP	PRACTICES						OUTCOMES	
Leadership	Values	Focus	Scope				Visualize	Limit WIP	Manage Flow	Make Policies Explicit	Feedback Loops	Improve & Evolve	Actions	F4P

Leadership (SELF): HEROIC — IDENTITY DRIVEN; HOLISTIC THINKING | ALIGNMENT | UNITY | SHARED PURPOSE — ALTRUISTIC / PURPOSE-DRIVEN / HUMBLE / DUTY-DRIVEN

Organizational Maturity Levels:
- 0. Oblivious — Focus: Who I am — Scope: Tasks
- 1. Team-Focused — Focus: Who we are — Scope: Deliverables
- 2. Customer-Driven — Scope: Products/Services
- 3. Fit-for-Purpose — Focus: Why we exist — Scope: Services; Product Lines and Services in a Business Unit
- 4. Risk-Hedged — Focus: What we do
- 5. Market Leader — Focus: How we do it — Scope: Multiple Business Units
- 6. Built for Survival — Focus: Challenge How, What, Why, & Who

SP / GP: Transition, Consolidation

OUTCOMES — Actions: REACTIONARY (CHAOTIC, UNALIGNED); ANTICIPATORY (EXPLAINABLE, CONGRUENT)

OUTCOMES — F4P: UNFIT, UNSUSTAINABLE, SUSTAINABLE

Figure 13.8 KMM Architecture

For example, **Implement Feedback Loops** has the following specific practices:

- FL2.1 Conduct internal workflow replenishment meeting.
- FL3.1 Conduct replenishment meeting.

These are effectively just two versions of the same practice with differing fidelity.

The focus of FL2.1 is internal, and the attendees tend to be the workers involved in the service delivery workflow or process. The selection of new work is determined by the workers, who pull from some predefined backlog. This is typical of organizations operating at Maturity Level 2.

With FL3.1, the meeting now includes customers, and selection is generally made by the customers or by a consensus of all present stakeholders. The purpose of the meeting is the same regardless of implementation, but at the deeper maturity level there is a recognition that there are customers, there are risks that have to be managed, and customers' expectations must be met. By including customers in the system replenishment meeting and enabling them to affect the sequencing and scheduling of work through the system, risk is pushed upstream to people better informed to manage it appropriately. Hence, risk management is improved, and we recognize that the replenishment meeting (FL3.1) is a deeper, more mature variation of an internal team replenishment meeting (FL2.1). This reflects an organization operating at Maturity Level 3.

The specific practices defined at each maturity level are derived from patterns observed in the field and are associated with organizations exhibiting the behaviors and outcomes associated with the corresponding maturity level.

Transition and Consolidation Practices

To ensure a smooth evolution for an organization, the specific practices at Maturity Levels 1 through 6 are organized into two broad groupings:

- Transition practices
- Consolidation practices

When an organization aspires to achieve the outcomes that characterize the next level of maturity, it can add transition practices. These typically inject a little stress into the operation and act to catalyze the evolutionary change process as defined in the evolutionary change model. So long as there is motivation to achieve the outcomes defined at the next level, adopting and implementing these practices should meet with little or no resistance.

Consolidation practices are practices that are necessary to achieve the outcomes that define a maturity level; however, an organization at a lower level tends to resist or repel them unless some preparatory work is done first.

Avoiding the Two Known Failure Modes with Kanban

With around fifteen years of observations and experience from around the world and across a broad spectrum of industries, two patterns of failure, or failure modes, have been observed with the implementation of the Kanban Method: the false summit plateau and overreaching.

A predecessor of the Kanban Maturity Model (KMM) was known as the Depth of Kanban Assessment Framework. It emerged in 2012, and its purpose was to assess the appropriateness of Kanban practice adoption mapped to organizational readiness. There was broad recognition that each of the six general practices could be implemented with differing degrees of fidelity. When adoption failures occurred, these were generally because inappropriate practices had been chosen—either too simplistic, failing to push the organization to a higher level of performance, or too challenging, resulting in resistance leading to a failure to adopt.

The coaching or consulting skill required was that of a sports coach: knowing the playbook of practices and being able to map them to the existing skill level and capability. The goal was to stress the organization just enough to provoke it to a higher level of performance, but not stretch it so much as to break it, causing a regression to a lower level of performance. The KMM represents a considerable advance over its predecessor, codifying over 150 specific practices and mapping them against maturity levels. Consequently, it provides extensive guidance on appropriate practice adoption, but it goes much further in terms of understanding organizational readiness with a much more thorough map of organizational culture, leadership, and observable business outcomes.

As a coaching tool, when used correctly, the KMM eliminates both of these known failure modes. Using the KMM to understand organizational maturity and how it affects Kanban implementation has become a vital part of Kanban coaching practice.

False Summit Plateau

The false summit plateau comes from the arrogance of believing that since an organization has adopted Kanban already, they've already experienced all of its benefits. Typically, we hear a reaction such as, "We've done Kanban! It helped us [. . .]." Usually from a shop-floor, bottom-up initiative, they list some practices such as using boards and some benefits they've enjoyed that map to Maturity Level 1, such as:

- Relief from overburdening and a stressful, abusive working environment
- Improved transparency
- Improved collaboration
- "Gave us what we needed"

In part, the Kanban Maturity Model exists to show that these shallow adoptions have left a lot of additional benefits on the table and that the organization can take Kanban a lot further.

Overreaching

Overreaching usually results in aborted adoption. The problem is rooted in an overly ambitious transition plan, often to a design intended to achieve Maturity Level 4 or even 5 in an organization currently at Maturity Level 0 or 1. The problem often manifests because of "the smartest guy in the room." This person is a consultant or a coach who feels psychological or social pressure to show off their knowledge and expertise or is simply too optimistic and overly ambitious. Or there may be a sponsor or senior executive who suffers from a magpie-like adoration of a new, shiny object—that metaphorical shiny object promises a nirvana of magical business transformation. Maturity Level 4 sounds very attractive to executives, and they may be impatient to get there.

With either of these patterns, "the smartest guy in the room" consultant or the "obsessed with the shiny object" executive, there is pressure to abandon evolutionary change and instead design an elaborate, often large-scale, Maturity Level 4 solution and lead a traditional managed-change initiative to install the final solution as quickly as possible—to accelerate achieving Maturity Level 4. Ironically, this is the behavior of a Maturity Level 2 leader. Organizational maturity is always bounded by the maturity of the leadership. Hence, a whip-cracking, heroic managerial effort to drive quickly to Maturity Level 4 is doomed to failure. The initiative stresses the organization with too much, too fast. What is needed is first to develop the leadership maturity. With it should come recognition that change must be led incrementally in an evolutionary fashion if it is to succeed—to survive and to thrive.

When the practices are too advanced for novices or for organizations with immature culture, existing behaviors, or supporting practices, the result is that the new practices simply don't stick. Often, the people are incapable of understanding the benefit. For example, if every work item is a task, what would be the point of risk hedging using capacity allocation of WIP limits across work items of different types? In a world where everything is homogeneous, the concept of hedging risk is incomprehensible. Speaking Maturity Level 4 language in a Maturity Level 1 organization is, quite literally, speaking with an alien tongue.

It is said that when the first European settlers arrived on the shores of North America, the native Americans "could not see the ships."[47] Instead, they saw the rowboats with which an away party had come ashore. They understood the concept of small boats, canoes, kayaks, and the like. They had no concept of how big the ocean was, or that it might be navigated in large ocean-going vessels. While their eyes could see these vessels on the horizon, perhaps at anchor, they could not process what they were seeing—they could not

---

47. A short search of the World Wide Web produces no definitive academic research or proof that this claim is true. However, Joseph Banks, documenting Captain Cook's voyage to Australia in 1770, does record the lack of reaction from Aboriginal tribespeople to Cook's ship *Endeavour*. Hence, the story may have been adapted or become accepted "common knowledge" amongst explorers and emigrants to "The New World."

see the ships. A ship was incomprehensible to them. Their brains could not make sense of what their eyes were seeing. When you use advanced concepts from deep in the model in an environment with a shallow level of maturity, you speak in an alien tongue. They cannot see the work item types, they cannot see the risks, they have no concept of these things—and hence no need to visualize them or tokenize the concepts.

The Kanban Maturity Model also exists, in part, to provide a road map and a means to interpret and appraise organizational maturity and readiness for any specific Kanban practice. A competent coach can use the model as a guide to suggest the right next steps and avoid overreaching. The objective is to move incrementally, making progress that sticks, and with each little improvement, to create a new base on which to build the next improvement.

Takeaways

- The Kanban Maturity Model (KMM) exists to illustrate how patterns of Kanban implementation and specific practices commonly used with the method map to different levels of organizational maturity.
- The KMM uses a seven-level model of organizational maturity. The seven levels are:
  - Oblivious
  - Team-Focused
  - Customer-Driven
  - Fit-for-Purpose
  - Risk-Hedged
  - Market Leader
  - Built for Survival
- It is important to recognize that it is the organization that matures. The Kanban implementation merely reflects the maturity of the organization, what its people value, what they care about, and the information they need to make decisions.
- The KMM architecture consists of mapping organizational cultural values and general practices against the seven maturity levels.
- Kanban practices are grouped into sub-levels within a maturity level. They are classified as either transition practices or consolidation practices.
  - Transition practices help to create momentum away from a comfortable equilibrium at an existing maturity level, while introducing just enough stress to catalyze an evolutionary improvement.
  - Consolidation practices are needed to consolidate behavior and deliver the outcomes for the next level of maturity. These often meet with resistance and require some preparation and coaching before their adoption institutionalizes.
- There have been two commonly observed failure modes when implementing Kanban:
  - False summit plateau
  - Overreaching
- The Kanban Maturity Model provides a clear road map illustrating how Kanban practices map to specific levels of organizational maturity. Consequently, the KMM can be used as a coaching tool to avoid both failure modes.

14

Recipe for Success

A Leadership Road Map for Maturing Your Organization

Accountability: The Magic Ingredient

From our work developing the Kanban Maturity Model, we studied the challenges of why and how organizations struggled to adopt practices that lead to improvements. Culture is often cited as the top reason why practices were resisted in organizations. Culture is the product of behaviors and actions, and these are driven by values. To change the culture, you need to lead with values. To drive adoption of new values, you need leadership. Lack of leadership is at the core of why organizations struggle to improve their capabilities and outcomes.

Lack of leadership is explained away with excuses such as "Leadership is rare," "Leadership requires courage and risk, and therefore, a culture of psychological safety. As we don't have psychological safety in our culture . . . ," "Leadership doesn't grow on trees," or "You can't just snap your fingers and invent leadership." There is resigned complacency to the effect that "Things can never get better—we don't have the leadership."

While leadership development is a deep and challenging topic—and one that most organizations ignore—you can go a long way toward catalyzing acts of leadership at all levels in an organization by holding people accountable. Accountability is the secret to unleashing the latent leadership in your organization, driving cultural change, and ultimately, to adoption of practices that improve agility, resilience, customer experience, and economic performance.

Leading a Maturing Organization[48]

This leadership guidance is intended to drive accountability in your organization, improve trust and social capital, increase cooperation across organizational units, and produce the improvements in agility, customer satisfaction, resilience, and innovation that you've been looking for.

- Lead with purpose.
- Create customer-centric metrics.
- Implement feedback loops.
- Hold people accountable.

Let's look at these in turn . . .

Lead with Purpose

Define goals that are meaningful to the success of your business. What is the mission of your business, your business unit, your project? Why do you exist as a business? What is your purpose? Why do your customers come to you? What are their reasons for selecting you? What is their purpose? What expectations do they have? And what outcomes do they expect? You need an outcome-driven organization. Define the outcomes you expect and measure your performance against those expected outcomes.

Everyone should understand the purpose of their work and the outcome that they are contributing toward. Those outcomes should have meaning to the mission of your business and be meaningful to your customers—a customer should recognize that outcome you are striving for as something that is valuable to them.

Create Customer-Centric Metrics

Given your customers' purpose and expectations, what do they care about? Timely delivery? Fast delivery? High quality? Affordability? Convenience? Ease of use? Choice, optionality, adaptability, or reconfigurability? These are the common things customers care about. What do *your* customers care about? Define your anticipated outcomes based on what your customers care about. Create metrics that reflect these customer concerns. Aim to meet your customers' expectations.

Together with Alexei Zheglov, our book, now in its third edition, *Fit for Purpose: Synthesizing Customer Experience and Strategy for Accelerated Business Results*[49] teaches how to define the right objectives and create the right metrics to drive desirable evolutionary

48. I'd like to acknowledge Travis Birch, whose article, "You don't need to reorg, you just need service-oriented managers," inspired and influenced the leadership guidance at the beginning of this chapter. https://medium.com/@travisbirch/you-dont-need-a-reorg-you-just-need-service-oriented-managers-9710b31c9772

49. Anderson, David J, and Alexei Zheglov. *Fit for Purpose: Synthesizing Customer Experience and Strategy for Accelerated Business Results*, 3rd ed. Seattle: Blue Hole Press, 2023.

change in your organization—objectives and metrics that align people across organizational units and drive the cooperation you need to fulfill customer expectations.

Implement Feedback Loops

Metrics are useless unless you take the time to reflect on them—to compare your goals and your customers' expectations with your current capability and performance. The Kanban Method prescribes several of these reviews that are designed to hold people at different levels in an organization accountable for achieving expectations. These are:

- Flow Review/Service Delivery Review
- Operations Review
- Strategy Review

Some other feedback mechanisms exist in Kanban that have a secondary but still important role to play in accountability:

- Replenishment Meeting
- Kanban Meeting
- Delivery Planning Meeting
- Risk Review

Many of the failings I see in organizations can be fixed by measuring the right things, implementing feedback loops to reflect on the measurements and metrics, and holding people accountable. So often I hear, "We've been doing Agile for years, but our customers continue to complain that we are too slow and unpredictable."

So I ask them,

"Are you tracking lead time from customer commitment to delivery?"

"No, we don't do that!"

"Do you have a feedback loop—a review or retrospective where you compare customer expectations with your delivery times?"

"No, we don't have that either!"

"Are managers being held accountable for meeting customer expectations?"

"What do you mean by that, exactly?"

This simple formula of measure and report things that customers care about, implement a feedback mechanism to reflect upon your current capability, and hold managers accountable will fix most problems—you don't need to reorganize, and you almost certainly don't need an Agile framework or methodology to achieve it. Simply start with what you do now and make a few augmentations to your existing processes.

Hold People Accountable

My colleagues in our European office in Bilbao tell me that "accountability" cannot be translated into Spanish, as the translation means "the person that is responsible for." Hence, responsibility and accountability are the same thing in Spanish, which also is true in Portuguese and, more generally, in Latin culture. Similar comments have been reported from other parts of the world. The same linguistic problem exists in German and Slavic languages such as Russian and Ukrainian. Accountability, it seems, is rather difficult to communicate in many languages and many cultures. This problem requires just the briefest of thoughts to resolve. Someone who is responsible for doing the work, responsible for the activity—even the output—isn't the same as someone who is responsible for the outcome. This is the essence of accountability—accountability is responsibility for an outcome. To hold someone accountable, first, define the desirable outcome or objective and then make someone responsible for achieving it.

To use a sports metaphor or analogy: The players on the team are responsible for playing the match and scoring the goals, but the team manager or head coach is held accountable for whether they win or lose.

Your organization needs to be outcome driven. Lead through defining outcomes that are aligned with customer needs and the mission of your business. Define outcomes, measure and report metrics that align with the outcome, implement feedback loops to reflect on actual versus desired outcomes, and hold people, at all levels in your organization, accountable for those outcomes.

Management Action to Mature Your Organization

So, you've inherited a team, a department, a product unit, a business unit, some enterprise organization tasked with a function, or perhaps a higher calling, a purpose or mission. It's dysfunctional and, you've learned, of low organizational maturity. You'd like to make a difference quickly and produce tangible results that allow everyone to believe that not only are things getting better, but those improvements can be sustained. Have you, like me, found yourself in this position in your career?

You may recognize that the leadership recipe above will take time—evolutionary change takes time; giving your metrics and your feedback loops time to work requires patience, and not everyone shares your patience and your belief that newfound accountability is the secret sauce that will enable magic to happen and the right solutions to emerge. You want to make progress quickly, to show some quick wins, to show tangible progress that will build trust and bolster belief that you are going in the right direction.

In 2010, *Kanban* included the following six steps:[50]

---

50. I'd like to acknowledge Donald Reinertsen, who gave me the first two and the last steps in the recipe, and how his advice from 2005, alluded to in his Foreword to *Kanban*, has stood the test of time.

- Focus on Quality
- Reduce Work-in-Progress
- Deliver Often
- Balance Demand Against Capability
- Prioritize
- Attack Sources of Variability to Improve Predictability

These were offered in sequence of execution. This guidance predated the KMM by many years, and yet, it is uncanny how the sequence of steps, or management interventions, reflects the maturity model. With the benefit of the KMM, we might modify this guidance, but first let's consider what I wrote in 2010 . . .

Implementing the Original Recipe

Focus on Quality is first, as it is under the sole control and influence of a function manager such as a software development or test manager, or the manager's supervisor, with a title like Director of Engineering. Working down the list, there is gradually less control and more collaboration required with other downstream and upstream groups until the Prioritize step. Prioritization is rightly the job of the business owners, marketing function, or the customer, not the service delivery organization. Prioritization typically should not be within a technical or service delivery manager's remit. Unfortunately, it is commonplace for business management to abdicate their responsibility and leave downstream delivery managers to prioritize the work—and then blame them for making poor choices.

As discussed previously, kanban systems, WIP limits, and deferred commitment push risk-management decisions upstream to the businesspeople, where they belong. Attack Sources of Variability to Improve Predictability is last on the list because behavioral changes are required to reduce some types of variability. Asking people to change their behavior is difficult! So, attacking variability is better left until a climate change results from some success with the earlier steps. It is sometimes necessary to address sources of variability to enable some of those earlier steps. The trick is to pick sources of variability that require little behavioral change and can be readily accepted.

Focusing on quality is easiest because it is a technical discipline that can be directed by a function manager. The other steps are more of a challenge because they depend on agreement and collaboration from other teams. They require skills in articulation, negotiation, psychology, sociology, and emotional intelligence. Building consensus around the need to Balance Demand against Capability is crucial. It makes sense to go after things that are directly under your control and that you know will have a positive effect on both your organization's performance and the business outcomes you deliver. "Clean up your own yard before you complain about your neighbor's" is a commonly used expression in American English. Before you complain about problems with others, or problems with cooperation and collaboration, ensure that you've tidied up your own affairs, and that things under your own direct control are in good order.

Developing an increased level of trust with other parts of the organization is necessary to enable the harder things. Building and demonstrating high-quality software with few defects improves trust. Releasing high-quality products with regularity builds yet more trust. As the level of trust increases, you as a manager gain more political capital. This enables a move to the next step in the recipe. Ultimately, your team will gain sufficient respect that you are able to influence product owners, your marketing team, and business sponsors to change their behavior and collaborate to prioritize the most valuable work for development. We saw this demonstrated in the Corbis case study described in Chapters 4 and 5.

Attacking sources of variability to improve predictability is hard. It should not be undertaken until a team is already performing at a more mature and greatly improved level. The first four steps in the recipe will have a significant impact. They will deliver success for you as a new manager. However, to truly create a culture of innovation and continuous improvement, it is necessary to attack the sources of variability in your processes and workflows. So, the final step in the recipe is for extra credit: It's the step that separates the truly great technical leaders from the merely competent managers.

A Retrospective on the 2010 Recipe

Revisiting the *Kanban* manuscript thirteen years after its publication, I had fully expected there to be no need for the Recipe for Success chapter. Some reviewers of the original book had commented that it "didn't seem to fit" with the rest of the text and it wasn't really about Kanban. It felt like I'd included it simply because there wasn't another better place for it to go. Either it was bundled into Kanban or it wouldn't see the light of day. Hence, it felt like a natural candidate to leave out of this book. Instead, it got a promotion—rewritten, extended, and updated. To understand why, we need to review the recipe against the maturity model.

Relief from overburdening—overburdening of individuals, teams, and entire workflows—is the theme for Maturity Levels 0, 1, and 2. Reducing work-in-progress to relieve overburdening also has a magical effect on quality—it is possible to focus on quality precisely because there is no overburdening. Hence, the first two steps in the recipe map directly to the lower maturity levels.

"Deliver Often" is intended to build trust. Trust and social capital improve with improving maturity, and the social capital earned can be exchanged for the political capital needed to change behavior beyond the service delivery organization. Achieving the changes required to arrive at Maturity Level 3 requires that you build trust—improving quality and delivering often will both contribute to that. These provide the building blocks that will enable the difficult discussions needed to balance demand against capability.

To create balance, you need an ability to refute demand, to say "no"—your organization needs to develop a triage discipline. You need to be able to divide demand into three categories: what you will do now; what will wait until later, and if later, when; and what you will not do at all. To negotiate these changes, you need the trust that comes from delivering frequently with high quality. If you can get this done and achieve this balance, that completely relieves your delivery organization from overburdening, and you will have achieved Maturity Level 3. You should now be capable of delivering with predictability precisely because your capability isn't overburdened.

Once you have a reliable, predictable delivery capability, the focus can switch to optimizing the value delivered by that capability. It becomes important to make good choices about what to work on now, what should wait until later, and what should not be done at all. Selection, sequencing, and scheduling work to start becomes important once your delivery capability is stable and predictable. The priority given to flowing work that is started—its class of service—is also important. To do these things—to triage—to select, sequence and/or schedule work and allocate its class of service requires that you understand cost of delay and are able to use it effectively to make decisions that optimize delivery capability. All four of these disciplines together are referred to in plain language as "prioritization." We see these practices emerge at Maturity Level 3 and consolidate at Maturity Level 4 together with other risk-management and risk-hedging strategies.

"Attack Sources of Variability to Improve Predictability" is probably more important than I recognized in 2010. The 2010 version of the recipe associated reduction in variation with the ideas of statistical process control and the teachings of W. Edwards Deming. It was an optimization strategy. We might typically associate such strategies with market-leading organizations such as Walmart or Toyota. It's for organizations aspiring to Maturity Level 5.

The 2010 version used the language of Walter Shewhart, separating variation into assignable causes and chance causes. Optimization is rightly the reduction of chance-cause variation, what Deming called common-cause variation. It requires changes in working practices, improvements in skill levels, new tooling, or automation. It is difficult to do and often expensive. It is rightly the domain of high-maturity organizations. However, elimination of assignable-cause variation is essential to achieve predictable delivery and Maturity Level 3. Hence, attacking sources of variability, if those sources are impediments, blockers, dependencies, and other assignable causes, actually needs to start earlier. It needs to start before we can balance demand against capability. We must also recognize that reducing work-in-progress is also a means to attack variation, as batch size, inventory, and batch transfers are all sources of chance-cause variation. Hence, the 2010 recipe was simplistic about variability, and the guidance could have been more nuanced.

So, how might we rewrite the Recipe for Success in 2023?

The New Recipe for Success

We can let the maturity model guide us. The management interventions and changes in behavior introduced should be directed at improving organizational maturity:

- Focus on Quality
- Reduce Work-in-Progress
- Focus on Flow
- Deliver Often
- Improve Predictability (trim the tail!)
- Develop a Triage Discipline
- Focus on Cost of Delay

This new version of the recipe maps directly to the maturity model and will take you most of the way to Maturity Level 4. The specific Kanban practices to enable each of these six steps are described in volume 2, *Implementing Kanban* and in the *Kanban Maturity Model*, second edition, also available online from kmm.plus.

To complete the journey to Maturity Level 4, we must also understand how to scale and why existing approaches to enterprise-scale business agility have been failing.

Takeaways

- Accountability is the "magic ingredient" that leads to successful implementations of Kanban.
- Lack of leadership is at the core of why organizations struggle to improve their capabilities and outcomes.
- To drive accountability, improve trust and social capital, increase cooperation across organizational units, and produce improvements in agility, customer satisfaction, resilience, and innovation:
  - Lead with purpose.
  - Create customer-centric metrics.
  - Implement feedback loops.
  - Hold people accountable.
- The Kanban Method prescribes feedback loops that are designed to hold people at different levels accountable for achieving expectations:
  - Flow Review/Service Delivery Review
  - Operations Review
  - Strategy Review
  - Replenishment Meeting
  - Kanban Meeting
  - Delivery Planning Meeting
  - Risk Review
- Guided by the Kanban Maturity Model, management interventions should be directed at improving organizational maturity. For a good shot at reaching Maturity Level 4:
  - Focus on Quality
  - Reduce Work-in-Progress
  - Focus on Flow
  - Deliver Often
  - Improve Predictability (trim the tail!)
  - Develop a Triage Discipline
  - Focus on Cost of Delay

15

The Tyranny of the
Ever-Decreasing Timebox

Why Flow Systems Are Essential for
Enterprise-Scale Business Agility

The continuous flow of work delivered through the use of a kanban system has significant advantages for enabling enterprise-scale business agility compared with original Agile methods such as Scrum. I call this the decoupled cadences of Kanban: The cadence of replenishment can be different from typical service delivery lead times, which in turn can be unrelated to the cadence of the delivery of finished work. With Agile methods such as Scrum, these three concepts of replenishment, development lead time, and delivery are all bound together into a single cadence, a single block of time known as a sprint.

Timeboxes

Agile software development methods, with the odd, long-since-forgotten exception,[51] use fixed-time increments, often wrongly called "iterations."[52] In Scrum, a sprint is a fixed period of time with a defined scope

---

51. Feature-Driven Development, from Peter Coad and Jeff De Luca

52. Iteration implies that something should be reworked. Iterative methods in software engineering, such as Barry Boehm's Spiral Method, already existed in the literature long before Agile methodologies. Agile methods use incremental development, with each piece of scope building on the last rather than reworking that which has gone before, and although reworking to improve the fidelity of functionality is both possible and feasible with Agile methods, it is unusual, particularly with Scrum.

of work and a commitment[53] to complete that scope within that time window. Originally, Scrum defined four-week sprints. This was changed later, circa 2004, to a recommendation for two-week sprints as the default. In general, agility is related to the frequency of interaction with customers or business owners and the frequency of deliveries. Hence, smaller timeboxes enable greater agility.

Batches

Software quality is often related to batch size and the time taken to complete a piece of work. The relationship is known to be non-linear—the defect rate rises faster and accelerates away as the batch size or length of time extends. Hence, smaller batches, completed in shorter periods of time, lead to dramatically fewer defects. So, in theory, small batches of work are desirable.

Two Ways to Constrain Small Batches of Work: Timeboxes or WIP Constraints

There are two ways to constrain the batch size of work: Constraining the amount of time available to do the work, resulting in scoping to small numbers of requests that can be completed in the given time; or simply constraining the number of work items, constraining the size of the batch of requests, also known as WIP constraints. All mainstream Agile methods use timeboxes to constrain batch size by scoping work to fit in the available time. Instead, the Kanban Method adopts WIP constraints to constrain batch size directly.

At a small scale and with lower maturity organizations, it doesn't much matter which of these two strategies you pick—they are both effective. Scrum is a perfectly good methodology to take a team from Maturity Level 0 to 1. However, as you scale both your ambition and the size of the organization, the timebox strategy breaks down. With the goal of consistently delivering against customer demand within those same customers' expectations at larger scales, such as a product unit of 150 people, or greater, to a business unit of 300 to 1,200 people or more, you will need to mature the organization to manage risk, manage dependencies, and coordinate at scale. You simply cannot scale agility and organizational maturity with team-level timeboxes. The remainder of this chapter explains why not.

The Pressure for Shorter Timeboxes

As a result of all the advantages of smaller batches—higher quality, more frequent interaction between customers and the delivery organization, and potential gains from earlier delivery of valuable work (also known as the avoidance of opportunity cost of delay), organizations have been under pressure to pursue shorter and shorter sprint lengths. I was invited to give a keynote speech at the internal conference of a well-known credit

---

53. The Scrum Guide has been modified to remove "commitment" and replace it with "forecast." While most organizations still use the term "Sprint Commitment," and customers interpret it as a promise, the official guide has modified it to what we might consider a "soft commitment," an indicator rather than a hard promise.

card company in the UK. The vice president of the business unit gave a short speech to introduce the event before I took the stage. During this speech, he commended the business unit of around 400 people for achieving the goal of weekly delivery of new software. While weekly releases of new functionality was good, he stated that his goal was for them to move to daily releases. This organization followed the Scrum framework. According to the Scrum Guide, Scrum is immutable. If you drop the use of a practice, then it isn't Scrum. So, if they were to stick with Scrum at the scale of a 400-person business unit while pursuing the goal of daily delivery, what challenges would they face?

The Challenges of Shorter Timeboxes

On the face of it, smaller timeboxes, and hence, smaller batch sizes for the sprint backlog, are a good thing. However, smaller timeboxes create three types of pressure that are often difficult to cope with and adjust to: First, smaller batches require an ever more detailed approach to requirements analysis and development—the need to write ever more fine-grained user stories that can be completed within the smaller time window. Second, an ever more accurate approach to estimation is needed so that a realistic commitment can be made; with smaller time windows, greater precision is required in estimation. Finally, if a piece of work will be affected by dependencies, such dependencies need to be tracked and managed between teams and multiple sprint backlogs and potentially across sprint boundaries. Failure at any of these three things causes the timebox approach to break down and fail spectacularly. The timebox approach is inherently fragile on a large scale. Let's examine why . . .

Requirements Analysis

Developing capability with a new and (you hope) better requirements analysis technique designed to provide the granularity to ensure work items are sufficiently small to fit neatly into a short timebox is hard, even when you are confident of which technique you should adopt. The challenge with very short sprints is that there is still, after twenty-plus years of Agile, little or no solid guidance on writing fine-grained, consistently small user stories. Even if there is a good method that your team is comfortable using, then (a) you now have a lot of up-front analysis before sprint planning, and (b) you have introduced a peer-to-peer or parent-child dependency management problem because small-scale requirements may not be meaningful to the customer—they may not enable value. This means that if one small requirement has a peer relationship to others, they all must be delivered together in order to release value. Or if that one small requirement is one of several siblings belonging to a parent or container requirement, only the delivery of the whole will release value. This challenge becomes especially acute as soon as you are unable, due to capacity constraints, to select all of the peers for the same sprint with the same team.

> Fine-grained requirements analysis coupled to short timeboxed sprints introduces a dependency management problem to Agile methodologies.

Alternatively, in the absence of strong guidance on requirements analysis, anxiety over short sprints leads to undesirable effects such as breaking up stories into functional units based on information discovery activities such as "architecture story," "design story," "development story," "test story," where the real customer value may now span across multiple sprints, and peer-to-peer dependencies between stories across sprints is now a tracking requirement. This type of breakdown defeats the purpose of the ever-smaller timeboxes and creates a false sense of agility when, in fact, customer value and quality are not improving; perhaps even the opposite is true. A failure to instrument for and track customer lead time disguises the problem, and Agile teams focused locally and only on themselves merrily ignore that they are not delivering customer value.

The concept of a "Design Sprint" (or other similar, upstream, pre-commitment information discovery) is now recognized, and there are classes teaching the unique elements needed in a design sprint. Have no illusions, however; design sprints are an anti-pattern; they are an indicator that timeboxed increments in Agile methods are a dead end—they do not scale! To be Agile, strictly following Agile software development methods, you need to be small—small teams, small products, small codebase. To scale with this same approach, you need to abandon agility and use much larger timeboxes. This is precisely what we observe with the Scaled Agile Framework (SAFe)—larger timeboxes, typically three months, known as product increments (or PIs).

Estimation

As sprints become shorter and shorter, the challenge of knowing whether a work item can be completed within the time limit becomes more and more important. Consequently, over the last fifteen to twenty years, I have watched on the sidelines as the Agile community has pursued ever more elaborate means of estimation. The shorter the timebox, the more upfront effort is required to estimate whether the work will fit into the available time. Big estimation up front is an anti-pattern that destroys the concept of agility—you need to estimate everything in your backlog first to play some magical game of Tetris trying to fit odd-shaped, fine-grained requirements into the sprint backlog. As we shrink the timebox, we increase the economic costs (the transaction costs of sprint planning) and decrease the efficiency of sprints. It is neither Agile nor Lean.

Dependencies

What if a story in our sprint backlog gets blocked because of a dependency? That might prevent it from completing on time. Hence, the shorter the sprint timebox, the greater the need to identify dependencies up front. This requires yet more analysis of as yet uncommitted items in the product backlog. And what if there are dependencies? Agile methodologies resort to organization design to solve this—using the magical cross-functional team. The idea is simply that everyone on a team can do everything that might be required to produce a top-quality product and, as a consequence, there will never be external dependencies. For any firm that aspires to market leadership, this has never been true—you don't win at anything with generalists; winning requires specialists. A small band of elite generalists can and does happen, but again, it doesn't scale. You don't staff a 500-person IT department, or a 600-person business unit, with elite generalists. It isn't pragmatic. There simply isn't a suitable pool of labor available, and even if there were, you probably couldn't afford all of them.

All too often, I see organizations like one from a case study I use regularly in my training classes—they had five development teams, three database administrators, and two user-experience designers. What might be possible with these constraints? You could put the two UX guys in each of two teams and the three database guys in the other three teams. As a result, you have two front-end teams and three back-end teams. Now, try to plan the sprints such that those teams pick only front-end or back-end stories, but oh, whoops, you are now disconnected from the customer-requested functionality and have created dependencies between your front-end and your back-end stories. Alternatively, you accept the truth and you use the DBAs and the UX people as shared services and, once again, you have dependencies.

Dependencies are a fact of life in all but very small-scale software development or mediocre development done by largely dilettante generalists. If you are doing anything at scale, or anything that aspires to market leadership, you will have specialists and you will have dependencies. The Agile movement has been in denial of this basic truth—to be Agile you either have to aspire to be mediocre or accept that you cannot scale!

Scaling, Business Agility, and Timeboxes

As mentioned previously, the Scaled Agile Framework (SAFe) approach to dependencies is to reverse agility and instead use three-month timeboxes called product increments. Effectively rolling the clock back to 1994, a big planning up-front approach, involving big analysis and big estimation up front—and lots of red string[54]—produces incredibly brittle plans that are unlikely to survive the first few of the intended thirteen weeks. One famous brand from Germany was in the habit of hiring a sports arena in Frankfurt, pre-pandemic, and inviting around 1,500 people from offices around Europe to attend a three- to five-day jamboree of red string once per quarter, at a cost of several million euros each time. Scaled Agile Framework and its product increments and PI planning quite simply aren't Agile. To cope with the challenges and anxieties of agilists everywhere, it gives them permission to

---

54. Scaled Agile Framework recommends visualizing dependencies by using red string to link the cards for separate stories or features together on a visual board, illustrating the scheduling of those stories or features across the sprints with the longer timebox of the product increment.

stop being Agile and instead do everything in quarterly timeboxes. Increasing the timebox to three months is a simple, elegant solution, but it isn't Agile; rather, it is the antithesis of Agile and the antithesis of the motivation for the lightweight methods movement of the late 1990s that evolved into the Agile movement.

Dependency Management Anxiety is Rooted in the Sprint Constraint

If you want to be Agile beyond the team level, beyond Maturity Level 1, you have to remove the constraint of timeboxes to control batch size. A time constraint is a fantastic way to take a chaotic organization from the anarchy of Maturity Level 0 to the control and predictability of Maturity Level 1, but that is where it ends. Time-constrained sprints are an evolutionary cul-de-sac, a dead end. You cannot scale Agile using timeboxed sprints!

The answer is to focus on quality and short delivery times by using a WIP constraint rather than a time constraint. Of established, well-documented, and well-supported approaches with a global network of trainers, consultants, and coaches, only the Kanban Method offers this recipe. For organizations struggling to scale Agile and deliver on a vision of enterprise-scale business agility, the Kanban Method provides an approach focused on quality and frequent, fast delivery using WIP constraints rather than time constraints.

Leaving Scrum Behind: The First Step on a Journey to Large-Scale Business Agility

I am now convinced that the pattern shown in Figure 15.1 (taken from *Kanban Maturity Model*, second edition, page 133) is a necessary step to large-scale agility.

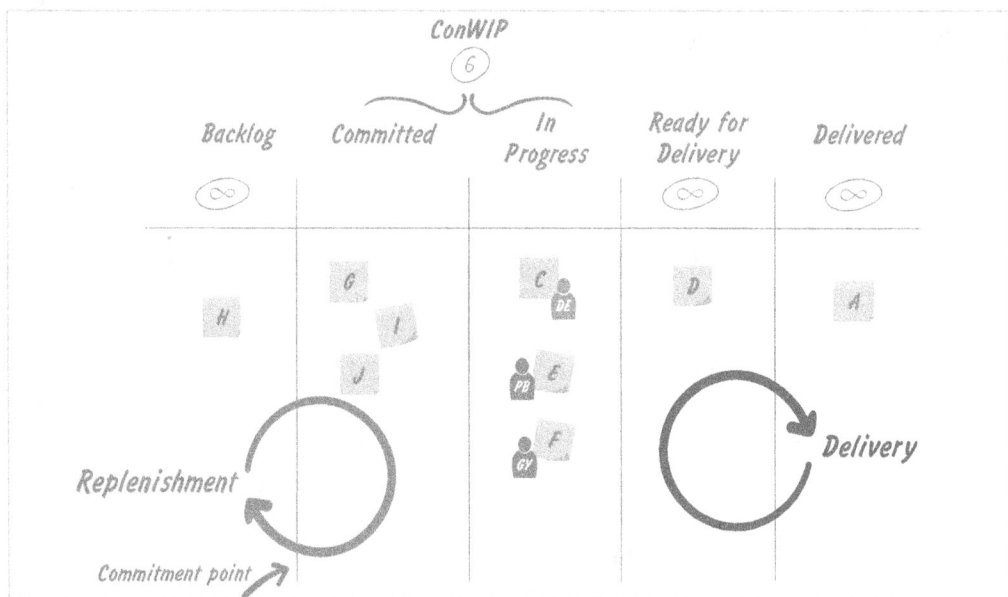

Figure 15.1 Delivery kanban board with defined commitment point and constant WIP

For each Scrum team, leave everything else alone, but remove the sprint timebox—stories, once started, simply don't have to finish within two weeks. Instead of limiting the time, limit the WIP; use a constant work-in-progress (CONWIP) limit. Initially, replenishment and delivery cadences can remain synchronized with the former sprint cadence. Eventually, you are likely to tune these to the needs of the business domain, adjusting to suit the transaction and coordination costs of holding the meetings and the arrival rate of new information that affects selection, sequencing, scheduling, and priority. This is your first step on a journey of evolutionary change away from Scrum and your first step on the road to large-scale business agility.

Relief from the Tyranny of the Timebox

This switch from a time constraint to a WIP constraint frees you from the tyranny of the timebox and its three dysfunctions of upfront analysis, excessive and costly estimation, and heavy-weight dependency management.

Avoid: Will It Fit within the Timebox?

If work items are to take, however long it takes to complete them, there is no need for upfront analysis to break items into smaller items, no need to track complicated dependencies between sprints or across teams. Instead, let the work breakdown happen naturally once the work is committed for delivery. Track that work with a two-tiered kanban board that uses parking lots and avatars to show the involvement of shared services.

There is no need for awkward, elaborate, big upfront analysis estimation efforts. Just track historical lead time through your workflow and use the lead time distribution chart to determine probabilistically how long something might take to complete.

Avoid: Will It Get Delayed by a Dependency?

If work items are to take, however long it takes to complete them, there also is no need for upfront analysis to determine the need for specialists or expertise, nor do you need to constantly reorganize, pursuing the nirvana of the perfect cross-functional team that never needs assistance from outside. Let dependencies happen as you discover them, create visibility onto them, and actively track them. Use a service-oriented approach and define workflow kanban boards (and systems) that encourage cooperation across functions. Don't reorganize into cross-functional teams or attempt to design out dependencies from your product architecture; instead, start where you are and learn to be proficient at coordinating shared services.

A General Solution for Dependency Management

To pursue large-scale business agility, drop the use of time constraints to control batch size and improve quality and time-to-market. Instead, use WIP constraints and embrace specialist-shared services within the organization. Stop reorganizing! Start flowing work across a network of interdependent services!

To have a truly effective general solution for dependency management,[55] we need to understand the opportunity cost of delay. We need to understand the urgency of a piece of work and how dependency delays will affect it. We need to understand my Mile Five Epiphanies.

---

55. Kanban University released its general solution for dependency management as an infographic poster in print-ready PDF format available from http://kmm.plus (https://www.mauvisoft.com/posters_download/). You can also find it in Appendix F of the *Kanban Maturity Model*, 2nd edition.

Takeaways

- Separating replenishment, development lead time, and delivery from a timeboxed sprint by using a kanban system has significant advantages for enabling enterprise-scale business agility compared with original Agile methods such as Scrum.

- Traditionally, Scrum used fixed-time increments (initially four weeks, now usually two) for completing a defined scope of work.

- Constraining batch size by way of WIP limits is more effective than doing so with time limits.

- Generally, software development using small batches completed in short periods of time leads to higher quality than timeboxed larger batches.

- Shorter timeboxes require detailed requirements analysis, greater precision in estimation, and if there are dependencies, it can be difficult to manage them between teams and across sprint boundaries.

- The Scaled Agile Framework (SAFe) approach to managing depedencies uses three-month timeboxes called product increments. This entails big analysis and big estimation up front and produces brittle plans that don't often survive the first few of the intended thirteen weeks.

- To attain enterprise-scale business agility, the Kanban Method enables high quality and frequent, fast delivery using WIP constraints rather than time constraints and embraces a network of interdependent services.

16

Mile Five Epiphanies

Autonomous, Agile Dependency Management

I coasted out of my driveway and clipped into my pedals. As I turned to head north on the arterial road, my shadow raced ahead of me. "Tell us how to manage dependencies" was echoing in my head. It was 2015, and I'd recently returned home from Barcelona, Spain, to Clallam County, the most northwesterly county in the lower-forty-eight states of the United States. I'd been visiting eDreams Odigeo, the European online travel business that rivals Seattle's Expedia. I'd been teaching workshops in Enterprise Services Planning, two of them, twenty-five people each time for five full days. Working with eDreams Odigeo's internal change agents Peter Kerschbaumer and Ivan Font, each evening we'd solicit feedback after class; the next morning we'd analyze what we'd learned, then adjust the schedule, agenda, and curriculum if necessary. Every morning the story was the same: "Tell us how to manage dependencies."

This frustrated me.

I'd always felt that Kanban was designed for, and capable of, scaling. Certainly, it scaled to a product unit consisting of approximately 150 people—we'd shown that in 2007 at Corbis. The concepts could be taken to the size of a business unit of between 300 to 1,200 people—we'd seen that in implementations that had taken place since, and by 2010 we had some notable examples such as at Petrobras in Rio de Janeiro. In an initiative led by Amanda Varella, a business unit making five software products for oil exploration and seismic survey data analysis, consisting of five product teams and five shared services, such as user interface design, used a total of ten interdependent kanban systems serving around 450 people.

How to Scale Kanban: Do More of It!

The solution was always simple. The way you scale Kanban is to do more of it: Scale it out in a service-oriented fashion. Think in terms of services; see your organization as a network of interdependent services. For each node in that network—each service—"kanbanize" it, starting with principles using STATIK (the systems thinking approach to implementing Kanban), a workshop that we'd formalized based on emergent real-world experience dating back to that first encounter with Dragos Dumitriu in 2004.

To manage dependencies, use parking lots to visualize tickets waiting for dependent requests to be delivered back. Each kanban system would consider others that sent it requests "customers," and design the kanban system to cope with that "customer's" demand—their requests, the arrival rate, and the pattern of demand over time. Hence, a network of interdependent kanban systems can be naturally designed to gracefully cope with dependencies, and each kanban system can act autonomously. If the design of individual kanban systems needs adjustments, and it most certainly will, network-level feedback mechanisms—risk review and, most importantly, operations review—provide the evolutionary wiring to adapt and evolve the nodes in the network such that customer requests (from outside) can gracefully flow, cascading through a network of interdependent service nodes, each utilizing its own kanban system. It is an elegant, simple solution.

Scaling Frameworks—Organizational Insanity?

It frustrated me that the market felt the need for scaling frameworks—complicated, cumbersome sets of process definitions. It seemed that the human ego couldn't cope with the idea that complicated and complex problems are best solved with simple, elegant solutions. "If it is so simple, then we must be stupid, because we have been struggling with this challenge for many years already." The human ego seemed to demand a big, complicated, cumbersome, heavyweight solution to the problem—a crutch for the fragile ego: "Ah, it's so difficult that it needs such a big, heavyweight framework in order to overcome the challenges; no wonder humble little me couldn't possibly solve it alone."

There is another possible explanation: Kanban has always required people to take responsibility, and for at least some of them to be held accountable for outcomes. In a network of autonomous service nodes, acting with empowerment, people at every node in the network need to take responsibility, assume accountability, and show acts of leadership. With a large-scale framework, it is easy enough to blame failure on the framework: Either it didn't deliver on its promises or our organization didn't have the leadership and culture to implement it properly. Either way, it isn't our fault. Framework adoption and subsequent failure to produce the anticipated outcomes is the misdirection of victims of circumstance.

It's the world of wishful thinking: "If only . . ." our circumstances were different, then [this framework] should have worked for us. Rotate out the consultants, the Agile coaches, and the senior management until the institutional memory is lost, then try again.

Albert Einstein is erroneously[56] credited with saying, "The definition of insanity is doing the same thing over and over again and expecting a different result." Regardless of who said it, it makes sense. Over the past twenty years, we've seen institutionalized organizational insanity at many large companies that have tried to scale Agile, largely failed, and then a few short years later tried again. One well known American credit card business and bank tried five times over fifteen years to scale Agile; finally, in 2023, they eliminated 1,100 positions with Agile-related job titles such as Scrummaster, Product Owner, Release Train Engineer, and the like. This retrenchment represented 2 percent of their total workforce. It seemed that someone at the helm of this hugely successful business had regained their sanity. The cost saving is estimated at around 250 million US dollars per year.

Existing Dependency Management Practices in Kanban

My consciousness refocused on the road ahead: I pedaled past the entrance to the Voice of America Park leading to the Dungeness National Wildlife Refuge and the famous New Dungeness Lighthouse, five miles out in the Straits of San Juan de Fuca at the end of the sand spit. I jumped out of the saddle as the bike wobbled its way up the hill and turned again to the north, rolling down toward the waterfront.

On the Friday morning of class in Barcelona, I modified the agenda and inserted a new classroom exercise: "Identify all the ways you've learned this week that can be used to better manage dependencies." I had done this exercise in my head and I reckoned that there should be at least fifteen practices:[57]

- Checkboxes on tickets indicating specialist work needed
- Date fields on tickets indicating scheduled integration points
- Decorators on tickets to indicate peer dependencies, or items that need to be delivered together, representing a collective bundle of value
- Rows or swimlanes on kanban boards for work of a type defined by its source—the requesting kanban system
- Capacity allocation of kanban across rows, or work item types
- The design of kanban boards that show sequential dependencies flowing left to right from column to column
- Split and merge board designs that show integration dependencies

56. https://www.history.com/news/here-are-6-things-albert-einstein-never-said

57. There are now at least 20 practices recognized in the Kanban Method and Enterprise Services Planning for managing dependencies. These have been collected in an infographic poster available for free download from KMM. Plus. https://kmm.plus/en/book/kmm/dependency-management/

- Two-tiered kanban board designs for parent-child dependencies
- Mapping shared services to columns on a service delivery kanban board; that is, creating ghosts or copies of tickets that exist on one column of a parent board and perhaps flow through several columns of a child board belonging to a shared service
- Parking lots on boards for dependent requests waiting for service in another system
- Marking blocked items with blocker tickets
- Blocker clustering—harvesting and analyzing blocker tickets to better understand the risks associated with dependencies
- Risk Review
- Operations Review
- Delivery Planning

Fifteen practices for dependency management in Kanban without having to think much about it. Fantastic! Case closed! Kanban already scales because of its service-oriented organizational architecture, and dependency management is built in. Unfortunately, the good folks of eDreams Odigeo were unimpressed. They needed to be able to point to one or more specific practices that would turn Kanban into Enterprise-Scale Kanban.

I was deflated. The Mediterranean wind dropped out of my sails and I'd returned to Seattle wondering what it would take before the Agile world was willing to accept that Kanban was an effective method to enable large-scale business agility.

First Epiphany: Reservation Systems

I'd reached the bluffs, shifting my weight, the frame beneath me tilted to the right, and the wheels veered around eastward onto Marine Drive. Sitting high above the water, I could see clearly over the sand spit, across the straits to the city of Victoria and Vancouver Island, Canada. Ahead of me, sitting proudly snow-capped in the distance, the majestic Mount Baker, on the mainland. I peddled on through the hollowed-out little village of New Dungeness. Once a thriving little port, changes to the regulations on crabbing had closed the pier decades earlier, and newer planning restrictions along the coastline meant that slowly it was being returned to nature. Most of the formerly commercial buildings on the main street had been converted to homes. I passed the old schoolhouse and the one remaining business, a farm store selling local produce. I glanced at my watch: twelve minutes since I left home, four miles on my trip computer. I was heading south now on the Sequim-Dungeness road past the lavender farms.

And then it hit me! These people sold airline tickets for a living—they understood reservation systems. We'd seen reservation systems used with kanban boards for years. Perhaps the earliest example was the "Top 10" at Posit Science, but a calendar-style reservation system had first been documented in Finland[58] a couple of years later. And I realized that I'd seen one at eDreams Odigeo. I couldn't remember which department or who the manager was, but I did remember which building at the World Trade Center in Barcelona, and that it was on the top floor. They had a reservation system divided into calendar weeks (similar to Figure 16.1) and they placed tickets into them, effectively booking a spot to start the work on that week. With this barest of descriptions, the team at eDreams later tracked it down to "Bianca" and a finance department—not part of the product group at all, not core to the large-scale Enterprise Services Planning initiative Peter and Ivan were leading.

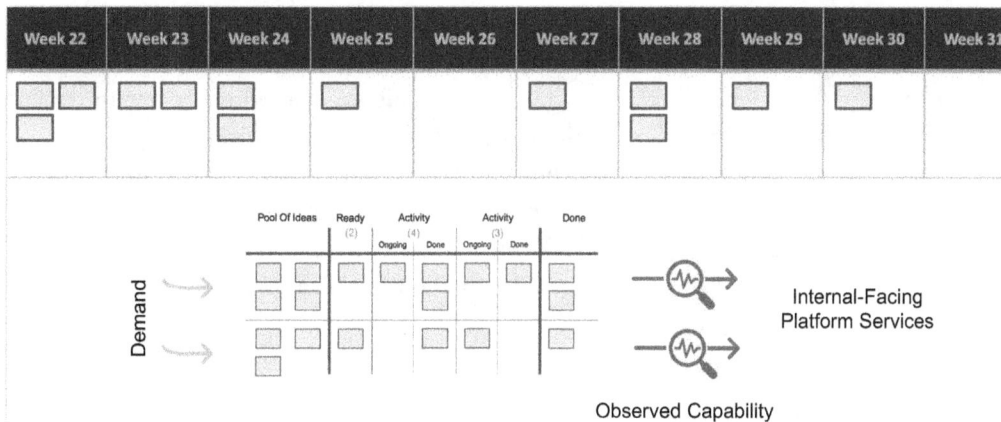

Figure 16.1 Reservation system kanban board

Dynamic Reservation Systems

However, this wasn't enough in itself. The airline industry had long had a solution for managing complex dependencies—reservation systems weren't static; they were dynamic. Not only did airlines offer different classes of service, such as business class or economy class for the seats they sold on their flights; they also historically offered different classes of reservation.

In the glory days of air travel, before there were budget airlines, it was still possible to travel on a modest budget through the purchase of a "stand-by" ticket. Stand-by tickets meant that the traveler wasn't guaranteed a seat on any given flight. They literally had to stand by while the flight was boarding, and if there were spare, unsold seats, then they'd be allowed to board. This was only possible with hand luggage—no check-in bags, as there wouldn't be time to load them into the hold before departure. While this class of reservation had largely disappeared in the era of budget air travel, it was still used for managing complex dependencies. Major hub airports that often suffered outages due to bad weather, such as Chicago's O'Hare (ORD), would issue stand-by boarding passes to

58. Basic reservation system board, first reported by Sami Honkonen in 2011. https://www.slideshare.net/AGILEMinds/sami-honkonen-scheduling-work-in-kanban

displaced passengers who'd missed connections due to late arrival of their incoming flight. The high probability was that passengers for the next onward flight would in turn arrive late, and hence, spaces would free up. This then allows the stand-by passengers to get on board. Their checked bags wouldn't travel with them, but there are separate solutions to cope with that. When I worked for Motorola in the early 2000s, their corporate travel policy insisted that international flights connect through Chicago. Consequently, I had on several occasions enjoyed personal experience with being rebooked, standing by, and having my delayed baggage arrive in Seattle the next day.

It seemed to me that a dynamic reservation system—an additional board for queuing tickets, divided by calendar week (or other time slots), with capacity based on the average delivery rate of the kanban system, and offering different classes of reservation—was the answer to large-scale dependency management in Kanban. And where better to try out this idea than a travel business and in their airline ticket product unit.

There were five miles yet to ride south into the wind until the town of Sequim and my favorite coffee stand—a convenient place to stop. I put my head down, pedaled harder, and left the idea on repeat inside my head. When I arrived at the coffee stand, I took a seat on a bench, leaning my bike against it, and I pulled out my iPhone, opened up the Notes application, and began typing vigorously.

Classes of Reservation

Airlines use more than two classes of reservation. Traveling by air inside Spain, I'd encountered another, the Shuttle ticket, offered by Iberia between Madrid (MAD) and Barcelona (BCN). I'd also heard that a collaboration between British Airways and American Airlines was offering such tickets between London Heathrow (LHR) and New York John F. Kennedy (JFK). A shuttle ticket is completely flexible and effectively trumps a first-class or business-class ticket. Shuttle ticket holders don't need a reservation for a specific flight. They just show up at the airport and ask to get on the next flight, as if they were queuing for a bus.

Imagine a businessperson living and working in Barcelona, on the Mediterranean coast, with an important business meeting in Madrid on a Friday morning. The meeting will involve tricky negotiations. If it all goes well, everything could be completed before lunch, but if agreement cannot be reached it might roll over into lunch and drag on into the afternoon. To hedge this risk, a business-class ticket reservation might have an 8:00 a.m. departure out of Barcelona and a 7:00 p.m. return flight in the evening. If the meeting ends early, it might still be possible to return to Barajas airport and ask nicely to get on an earlier flight. But it is Friday, and the flights might be heavily booked. What to do? Well, pay a little extra for a Shuttle ticket. If everything goes well and the meeting is wrapped up soon after 12:00, it is easy to jump in a taxi and be at the airport twenty minutes later. Present the shuttle ticket at check-in and board the next flight. Arrive back in Barcelona with enough time to drive to the golf course on the Costa Brava and get a full round of eighteen holes in before dusk.

So, at least three classes of reservation are common: standard reservations that guarantee you a seat on a specific flight; stand-by reservations that don't guarantee you a seat unless there is unsold capacity; and shuttle tickets that guarantee you'll be on the next available flight, even if they have to bump someone else to make space available. It seemed to me that we could replicate equivalents of these classes of reservation to create a sophisticated dynamic reservation system for large-scale Kanban implementations, as shown in Table 16.1.

Table 16.1 Classes of Booking

Class of Booking	Description
Guaranteed	An item is guaranteed to start on this date.
Reserved	If capacity is available, this item will be started on this date.
Standby	If additional capacity is available, this item will be considered for selection against other items in the Ready buffer upstream of commitment. It will be given strong preference. If it isn't successful, its class of booking may be elevated to Reserved at the next or a subsequent opportunity.

Return on Investment Isn't Cost of Delay

The following summer, 2016, again I was back home—the off-season from training, conferences, and consulting work around the world. In summer, my regular daily constitutional workout was a twenty-mile clockwise circuit of New Dungeness and Sequim, that I liked to call the "Tour de 98382" (after the Zip code for the municipality of Sequim and surrounding unincorporated county). Mostly flat, it was usually more challenging because of the incessant crosswinds; no matter the time of day or what the weather, the question wasn't whether it was windy or not, only in which direction the wind was blowing. It was wise to keep something in the tank, energy reserves, in case the last five miles would need to be ground out, nose to the handlebars into a howling gale.

What was on my mind was Cost of Delay. For some years since the publication of Donald Reinertsen's *Principles of Product Development Flow* and the appearance of the Scaled Agile Framework (SAFe), there had been considerable focus in the community on the Weighted Shortest Job First (WSJF) algorithm for "calculating" the cost of delay and using it to prioritize—to sequence, schedule, and select—work. Reinertsen's version of this equation

$$\frac{\text{Total Lifetime Profits}}{\text{Duration}}$$

had been altered by the Scaled Agile people into something almost unrecognizable. Nevertheless, both versions seemed wrong to me: They simply didn't match the cost of delay function sketches I'd drawn in 2009 and first adopted at Posit Science. Reinertsen's own observation during his visit to Corbis in 2007—that our classes of service were driven by cost of delay—seemed, therefore, to be at odds with the idea that WSJF was the correct way to measure cost of delay.

Additionally, I was uncomfortable with the language, the algebra and the geometry. Cost of delay implies that cost, perhaps opportunity cost, should be the numerator and delay the denominator. Instead, we had total profits or value as the numerator and duration as the denominator. While delay and duration are both denominated in units of time, they are not the same. The algebra didn't match, and if you drew it as a function, the labels on the x and y axes also didn't match. Under what circumstances did duration equal delay? Under what circumstances would lead time represent delay? For lead time to be equivalent to delay, an item in progress needs to block the start of another item. For this to be true, the WIP limit needs to be one.

WSJF also just felt wrong. People were arguing that lead time wasn't duration. The implication was that only effort, value-added working time, contributed to duration. It seemed like duration was, in fact, just a proxy for cost—with total lifetime profits a proxy for value. If this were true, then what we actually had was

$$\frac{\text{Value}}{\text{Cost}}$$

and this is the equation for Return on Investment (ROI). As we observed at Microsoft XIT in the very first Kanban implementation, ROI is not cost of delay. If you select work based on cost of delay, it will be done in a different sequence from work prioritized by return on investment. ROI doesn't reflect the urgency of an item, only its long-term benefit compared to its cost. Possible loss of benefit due to delay is not considered—delay simply isn't a variable in the equation.

This conflict had been troubling me for several years, and I had failed to find an explanation.

Second Epiphany: Delay Equals Replenishment Cadence

And then it hit me, just as I rolled past the old schoolhouse in Dungeness: Delay in a kanban system is equivalent to the cadence of replenishment!

At a replenishment meeting, we choose what to start based on available free kanban. By choosing what to start from a set of options in our ready buffer, we, in turn, choose what to leave until later. If we choose not to start something at this week's replenishment meeting, then we must wait until next week before we get another opportunity to select it. At each replenishment meeting, the delay under consideration is the delay until the next meeting—typically a week.

We don't control when items are finished. Our control point is selection, pulling an item into our kanban system—choosing to start the item. Lead times follow a probability distribution curve. So, we start something, and it will be completed within some time window expressed by probability. So the question we should be asking is, "What is the probable cost of delay in not starting an item?" If we don't choose to start an item today, at this replenishment meeting, what opportunity cost or impact might we suffer in the future if we wait to start the item later?

Once again, I buried my chin onto the handlebars and pumped my pedals furiously down the Sequim–Dungeness road until I could stop and record this epiphany as a note on my phone.

Discovering the Mathematical Evidence for Empirically Derived Cost of Delay Curves

To calculate cost of delay mathematically, we needed to convolute the lead time distribution curve with the value acquisition lifecycle curve for the item in question. Non-trivial! This was the world of advanced quantitative analysis. Ugly.

I became obsessed with this. I spent several days producing a spreadsheet with eleven different examples. I was working on it at home and in local cocktail bars, cafes, and restaurants. What emerged was an analysis of the probable cost of delay in starting based on different lifecycle value acquisition curves, as shown in Figure 16.2. These curves resembled the sketches from 2009, and it became clear that it was possible to group sets of curves into four categories.

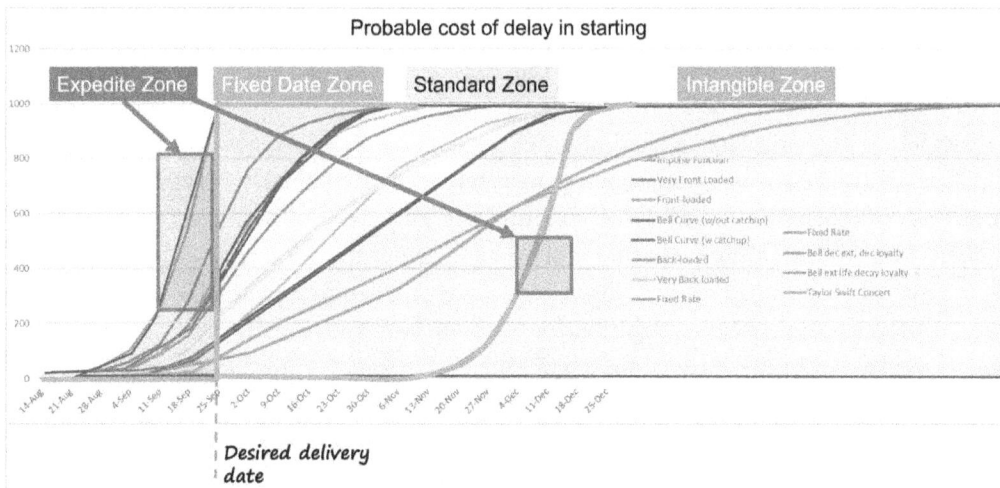

Figure 16.2 Four class of service PcoDS function zones

We now had a full mathematical explanation validating the curves first used with Posit Science in 2009, and an explanation for why the four classes of service, and our understanding of how they related to cost of delay, had proven so robust over approximately a decade. The advanced mathematics matched with the intuition. What had emerged at Corbis in

2007 and had been refined while working on *Kanban* in 2009 provided a very simple yet powerful risk-management technique—just four classes of service and four cost of delay curves provided a suitable classification system to enable sophisticated risk management based on urgency.

Third Epiphany: Classes of Dependency Management

However, it took a third epiphany to synthesize the first two together to produce the full solution for large-scale implementation. The important question is "How does cost of delay in a customer request affect dependency management?" We already had classes of service for how an item should flow through a kanban system and classes of reservation for how that item should be treated while queued and scheduled to start; to complete the solution, we needed classes of dependency management, also based on cost of delay, to determine how an item should flow across kanban systems and how dependent requests cascade through a network of kanban systems. While four such classes of dependency management, policy based on the four cost of delay function shapes, might have been sufficient, in the end I designed six. I decided to consider the impact of fixed constraints—dates that cannot be changed. This produced two variants for standard class and fixed-date cost of delay. The standard class is broken into two, roughly mapping to low versus higher maturity, and the level of trust varies between the customer and the delivery organization. Deadlines are often used in low-maturity organizations as targets and stressors to motivate behavior. It was important that my model accommodate this dysfunctional reality. The fixed-date class is also broken into two, separating out fixed constraints—those hard dates such as Christmas, or regulatory deadlines—from merely very steeply rising functions where the impact is severe over a short period of time.

This gives us six sets of rules, or a policy, regarding dependency management: rules regarding whether we need to do upfront analysis to detect dependencies and cascading requests and rules regarding whether and how to use our dynamic reservation systems.

I now had what the eDreams Odigeo people were demanding, a tangible set of practices we can point to as the scaling solution for Kanban. Enterprise-scale Kanban requires an ability to use cost of delay, dynamic reservation systems with three classes of reservation, capacity allocation based on average delivery rate of the kanban system, and six classes of dependency management based on cost of delay and whether or not an additional fixed constraint, a deadline, is involved.

If we can tag an incoming request with the correct class of service based on cost of delay, and we should know whether it comes with a fixed constraint for delivery, we already know enough to let it and any cascading requests flow through our network of interdependent services, each node acting autonomously using simple rules (policies) for the class of service, the class of reservation, and the class of dependency management (see Table 16.2). There is no need for centralized control.

Table 16.2 Six Classes of Dependency Management

Class of Dependency Management	Calling Service Ticket	Called Service Ticket	Calling Service Reservation	Called Service Reservation	Nature of Dependency Management
1. Don't Care	Intangible	Intangible	Optional Standby	None	No dependency management; dynamic, just-in-time dependency discovery
2. Trusted Availability	Standard w/ SLE	Standard	Optional Standby	None	Dynamic, just-in-time dependency discovery; capacity allocation on called service to guarantee service when needed
3. Tail-Risk Mitigation	Standard w/ Deadline	Fixed Date	Optional Reserved	Standby	Standby class of reservation (just in case); dynamic, just-in-time dependency discovery; use filtered lead time distribution—assume dependency exists to determine start time and calling service ticket's class of service.
4. Fixed Date	Fixed Date	Fixed Date with high-priority start	Reserved	Reserved	Up-front dependency detection, with reserved class booking on called service; definition of ready requires up-front analysis and a reserved class booking.
5. Guaranteed On-Time	Fixed Date w/ zero tolerance for delay	Fixed Date w/ guaranteed start	Guaranteed	Guaranteed	Up-front dependency detection, with guaranteed class of booking on called service; definition of ready requires up-front analysis and a guaranteed called service reservation.
6. Expedite	Expedite	Expedite	None	None	No dependency management; dynamic dependency discovery; expedite dependencies when discovered.

The Assumption of Thin Tails

It all seems so elegant, so simple, so understandable. What could possibly go wrong? The reality is that most organizations aren't yet ready to implement these otherwise quite simple practices. There are quite a few assumptions built into everything that I've described in this chapter. At the core, the key assumption is that service delivery is predictable and trustworthy, that lead time distributions are thin-tailed[59] (that is to say that exceptionally

---

59. "Thin-tailed" refers to a distribution curve or function that is super-exponential in nature, and would aggregate with a large number of data points to a broadly Gaussian distribution. Gaussian implies that the head and tail of the curve are asymptotic to the x-axis, while the popular understanding is that they are bell curves. Gaussian-distributed data will regress to the mean (the arithmetic average) with a modest number of data points. Nassim Taleb refers to this class of distributions as "mediocristan"—in other words, boring and low risk.

long lead times are rarely or never seen), and that the use of Little's Law[60] is possible because the concepts of an average lead time and an average delivery rate are meaningful concepts. The implication is that our network of interdependent kanban systems must be operating mostly at Maturity Level 3. Maturity Level 3, where we have reliable and predictable service delivery, implies that our lead time distributions must be thin-tailed. It is almost impossible to deliver consistently against a customer expectation without a thin-tailed lead time curve.

Hence, to scale effectively, we need to mature our organization. To do that, we need to work on the culture—to lead with values. To be successful at scale we need appropriate leadership at all levels. We need leadership at every service node in our network—leadership in every kanban system. You don't scale by installing a framework. You scale by developing and enabling leadership.

---

60. Little's Law is an equation in queuing theory that relates the average rate of arrival to the average work-in-progress and the average lead time. It can be used to estimate the WIP for a capacity allocation based on an agreement to deliver work at a given average rate. However, it relies on the ability to calculate a meaningful average from a modest set of data points. This can only ever be true when the lead time distribution is thin-tailed.

Takeaways

- Corbis and Petrobras are two organizations that were able to scale Kanban with as many as 450 people using interdependent kanban systems.

- To scale Kanban, do more of it!

- Large-scale frameworks generally have not worked well, often because of a lack of leadership.

- Kanban already has at least fifteen practices that help manage dependencies.

- A dynamic reservation system with different classes of reservation can be used for large-scale Kanban implementations.

- Four classes of service and four cost of delay curves provided a suitable classification system to enable sophisticated risk management based on urgency.

- If an incoming request is assigned the correct class of service based on cost of delay, and whether it has a fixed constraint for delivery is known, it and any cascading requests can flow through a network of interdependent services. Each node acts autonomously using simple rules (policies) for the class of service, the class of reservation, and the class of dependency management.

- For an organization to scale effectively, it needs to have a level of maturity that enables leadership at all levels.

17

Out of Crisis, Leadership

To Learn How to Scale, Ask an Entrepreneur

It was still dark in Bilbao when I woke on the first Monday of October, 2021. My phone had registered three calls from my younger daughter, the one we first met in Chapter 1 at age three months; she was now sixteen. At this age I only ever heard from her when she needed money or there was an emergency. I called her back.

"Mama has been taken poorly. She's in the ICU[61] in a hospital in Oklahoma City."

"Wait. What happened?"

"She was playing in a tennis tournament—Nationals. She seems to have collapsed from exhaustion over the weekend. She's in ICU. We're on the way to the airport right now. We have a red-eye flight to Dallas connecting to OKC in the morning."

It was well before midnight on Sunday evening in Seattle.

"Call me tonight, my time, after you get to the hospital tomorrow."

I'd been preparing for this day for fifteen years, but nothing really prepares you.

I made a few calls and arranged an urgent appointment with a notary[62] for lunchtime that day to create a power of attorney. After three years living in Spain, building a credit history and a trusted relationship with my bank, and as much time looking for properties, I had recently

---

61. Intensive care unit

62. Americans reading this should understand that in Europe, notaries are lawyers who specialize in administrative law and contracts. Notaries perform land title conveyancing and legal paperwork for bank loans, mortgages, employment contracts, powers of attorney, and similar activities.

agreed to buy a fifty-year-old mid-century farmhouse twenty minutes out of Bilbao. The contract was due to close the following week.

Just a week earlier, I had signed lease papers on an apartment in Austria close to our office and the location of our annual Kanban Leadership Retreat. Suddenly, a lot of real-life drama was happening all at once.

My travel agent got me on the first available flight out of Bilbao, and I set off back to the United States for the first time since the Covid-19 pandemic lockdown started in early March of 2020. The trip was beset with problems. My flight out of Bilbao couldn't leave because of fog. We all took a bus to Santander in the neighboring province of Cantabria. I missed my connection in Madrid and was rebooked a day later. That flight was later cancelled due to problems with the aircraft. I was rebooked on a flight to Miami. It left almost five hours late. I missed my connection to Oklahoma City and had to spend the night in Miami, rebooked on an early flight through Dallas. It was lunchtime on Thursday when I finally arrived at the hospital in Oklahoma City. Both of my daughters were there. The older one, who had left behind her medical school studies in New Orleans, had taken control. One of the residents, rightly impressed, whispered to me, "She's been running the show all week." The news from the doctors wasn't encouraging.

The following week we said our goodbyes to my wife of twenty-two years in a private family ceremony at a funeral home in Oklahoma City. It was Covid times. Large funerals were illegal. It would be nine months before we could arrange a suitable memorial service for all of her teammates, tennis club friends, former nursing colleagues and classmates, neighbors of twenty years, and long-time family friends to pay their respects.

Sometimes you just can't control the amount of real life that happens all at once. You can't choose the quantity of personal crises in progress. When someone dies unexpectedly, there is a lot of paperwork to clean up. Grief doesn't make it any easier.

I returned to Seattle with a distraught sixteen-year-old. She was angry with the world. Her high school was very understanding. I sent a message to the leadership team at my firm: "I'm going to be away from work for an unknown period of time. You have the con."

"Roger that. We have the con."

I began to address the legal paperwork. The first job was making sure that the lights, quite literally, stayed on—that all of the household bills were being paid. To manage my stress, I started taking long walks every morning and, while I was at home, I left the TV running with safe, comforting content—soccer, Spanish La Liga, anything with Athletic Club or Real Sociedad, and English Premier League, Liverpool, Manchester United, or Arsenal. To be honest, it didn't matter which teams were playing; it was all good.

The news came back from Bilbao that the contractors had moved into my new home. The house was in much worse condition than was thought.[63] The electricity was illegal

---

63. Americans reading this will be puzzled that these problems were not discovered during a home inspection prior to closing the exchange of title deeds. Such a practice is not common in Spain or more generally in Europe. Although

and unsafe; the plumbing was old, leaking, and smelly. The hot water system was inadequate—a home with five bedrooms and five bathrooms had enough hot water for only two showers. The single-pane, uninsulated, hardwood framed windows (state of the art in 1974) would all need to be replaced, too. I'd agreed to buy the place "as is," and the owners had literally walked away, handing over the keys after forty-eight years, taking only a few cherished pieces of furniture. The news was that the house would eventually need to be gutted, stripped back to the concrete shell and rebuilt entirely.

I'd known it was a fixer-upper, but I had no idea just how much deferred maintenance was now urgent.

I was only the second owner. The sellers, a sweet old couple in their late seventies, had commissioned the house to be built in the early 1970s when they were newly married. The woman had inherited the land from her grandmother. They hired a promising young architect. Later, he would become professor of architecture at the University of the Basque Country (UPV) and design their new campus just outside Bilbao. He had an illustrious career and became mildly famous at a national level. As a young man, he'd clearly been experimenting with this design—spiral staircases on the exterior, typical of Scottish Baronial style, and the Arts and Crafts era was represented by Gaudi-esque stained glass windows that must have been hand-crafted in Barcelona, with a mid-century modern, mono runner, open staircase on the south terrace. This was straight out of a Sean Connery–era James Bond movie. It was easy to imagine Goldfinger in his quilted silk dressing gown and slippers carrying a fluffy Persian cat enjoying the morning sun as he promenaded down the steps toward the swimming pool. "Ah, Mr. Bond, we've been expecting you!" Apparently, the staircase, the choice and color of the stone pathways, and other exterior landscaping features had been Japanese-inspired. The house was worth restoring. Just not now. It was one personal crisis too many. I was at the limit.

A plan was made to make the house livable in the short term. Safe-ish. Functional, mostly. Don't blow dry your hair while the tumble-dryer is running in the kitchen. That sort of thing.

Home & Garden Television

I'd been in ongoing discussions about the house with our architects in Bilbao who had designed the interior reformations of both offices in the city: the David J Anderson School of Management training center on Gran Via and the Mauvius Group Europe office two blocks away. Plans were being made for a grand reformation of my new home.

---

it is possible, sellers are likely to be insulted by the request and unlikely to grant access. If you want a property in Spain, you can't risk losing the deal by asking for a home inspection. I had mitigated some risks by asking that my architects be allowed to tour the house to consider interior decoration plans. Although I asked them to look out for problems with infrastructure, they were unable to make a detailed inspection.

I started to watch HGTV.[64] I left it on in the background all day from 9:00 a.m. until 9:00 p.m. Thinking about remodeling my home in Spain was a wonderful distraction: daydreaming in paradise, free from estate lawyers, call center associates at banks, insurance companies, legal paperwork, and a heartbroken teenager.

It was shows on HGTV that gave me my final epiphany about scaling. If you want to learn how to scale, you should ask an entrepreneur!

Focus on Quality

Tarek El Moussa is a property investor in Southern California—Orange County, mostly. Tarek specializes in buying mid-century, atomic ranch-style homes built in the 1950s or 1960s that are in poor condition, often unlivable, then renovating them with sleek, modern interiors. He "flips" them to new owners—usually making a profit. He started on his own, in his twenties with almost no money, living in his mom's garage so that he could put all his funds into his business. Through a lot of hard work and entrepreneurial risk-taking, he's built up a thriving property investment and construction business.

For more than ten years, he's been a presenter on HGTV, first together with his first wife, Christina, on *Flip or Flop*, which ran for ten seasons and, more recently, *Flipping 101*, now in its third season. The premise of *Flipping 101* is that Tarek works with younger, novice property investors. He gives them advice and helps them to be successful. His focus, with his apprentices, right from the start, is always scaling. If they are to be successful, then they need to learn how to scale.

Tarek's first rule of scaling your business is that you must stop making mistakes: You must focus on quality, and first-time right. Quality problems and necessary rework undermine trust in your brand and damage your reputation. Fixing mistakes and quality problems costs time and, with property investing, there is a tangible cost of delay. If the investor has borrowed money to fund the project, then more time means more interest paid on the loan, which, in turn, eats into any profit they might hope to make later. All avoidable wasted time carries an opportunity cost. Fixing mistakes also increases costs and can blow out the renovation budget. Poor quality and the subsequent delays caused by rework mean completion is unpredictable. This adds risk and makes it hard to know when to list the house for sale, to arrange for staging with nice furniture and decoration, and to schedule open-house viewings to attract buyers and real estate agents. Lack of predictability, therefore, leads to poor economic performance.

Tarek's advice: Hire or develop your own competent people who can work unsupervised. Good people cost you more. This saves you money in the long run. Focus on quality and first-time right.

---

64. HGTV is a Warner Brothers Discovery cable TV channel: Home & Garden Television. Founded in 1992, it was the vision of an executive at Scripps Networks. Many of its shows still carry copyright notices for Scripps Networks.

Increasing Resilience

Our family dog was emigrating to live with me in Spain. He mocked me, "You humans complain about Covid vaccination and negative tests and extra paperwork and bureaucracy before you fly. Try being a dog. It's triple the effort for us and it has always been this way." He was right. And it wasn't just vaccinations; it was the export license paperwork issued by the US Department of Agriculture. Tricky stuff—you can't apply for it until ten days before travel, but their processing SLA is five to ten days, and the paperwork has to be sent by mail in both directions. I made some phone calls. They were very helpful. The advice: "FedEx the package to us overnight. Include inside a return FedEx envelope addressed to yourself, pre-paid. Make sure all of the paperwork is in order, with all the stamps from the vet. Include a check for the processing fee. We'll keep an eye out for it. We understand the time challenges—everyone doing this has the same challenges." I was dealing with a totally unfit-for-purpose service. The people inside this system, powerless to affect it, had instead figured out the best workarounds. Luckily, I had called them first. With their expert advice to expedite everything, I had the paperwork back three days later. Phew!

Next would be the inspection at the airport. I'd bought a flight crate recommended for this breed of spaniel. Except, my kids warned me, "He's a little big for his breed, about two pounds overweight and taller." Measuring the crate again, and reading the guidelines issued, this time by the airlines, it was going to be marginal—down to the centimeter whether or not they'd let him on the plane. I couldn't take the risk. So, I made a mad dash on a Sunday afternoon, touring pet shops in Seattle looking for USDA-approved flight crates in the correct size. Found one! Lucky. We were still on track. The dog would fly with me to San Francisco. Overnight there and then take a flight to London, where he was booked for an overnight stay at HARC (Heathrow Animal Reception Centre)—the pet hotel at LHR. This additional stay in London meant yet another layer of bureaucracy and paperwork. The UK being an island archipelago off mainland Europe that has remained free of rabies, it has always had its own strict rules for traveling animals. The dog scoffed at my Basque Country European Covid vaccination passport and my negative PCR test, "What are you complaining about?"

Two days later, together with my daughter, who would turn seventeen over the holidays, we were reunited in Bilbao. Ever resilient, the dog was adapting to his new home and new life.

It was fortunate I'd worked myself out of a job and had been able to leave my business in capable hands. Tidying up our family affairs in the United States was proving to be a full-time job.

Work Yourself Out of a Job

Tarek El Moussa's second piece of advice might be more easily paraphrased as "You need to work yourself out of a job!" If you are in the bathroom, tiling the shower because doing it yourself saves you money, then while you are doing that you cannot be out looking for the next deal, the next property to buy, fix up, and flip. If you are doing the work yourself, your business will be stop-go, stop-go. You'll miss a lot of opportunity. You won't have smooth flow. Your cash flow will be turbulent.

What does it mean to "work yourself out of a job"?

In the simplest sense, it means that you've trained your replacement—that there is a succession plan. It's too easy to stop there, and it is too easy to assume that working yourself out of a job leads to unemployment—the presumably younger, cheaper deputy or apprentice can take your place at a lower cost. This is certainly a risk in lower-maturity organizations—organizations that are doomed to fail at scale. Working yourself out of a job means freeing up your time so as to take on greater scope, greater responsibility, and more challenging or more value-adding work. The reward for working yourself out of a job in a higher-maturity organization should be a new job with greater challenges.

In modern professional services jobs in intangible goods industries, most of us "think for a living," and much of what we do is make decisions. Every sentence, every paragraph, every chapter in this book involved many decisions—the value is in the decision making, not the typing. Voice recognition technology can type the words for me, but even the most advanced AI engines can't write this book. So, the challenge of working yourself out of a job is to ask yourself, "Which of the decisions I have to make could be automated or delegated to someone else? What would need to be in place such that I could trust the automation or the empowerment of others to work effectively?"

You work yourself out of a job through codification of what you do. Leadership by insight brings clarity to things that seem complex or opaque. Simple codification systems, such as our four classes of service based on cost of delay, form the basis for delegation and empowerment. Composing those into a decision framework helps make the process of decision making repeatable, predictable, and trustworthy. You work yourself out of a job by defining processes and procedures, by introducing feedback mechanisms—checks and balances to govern and steer in your absence.

You work yourself out of a job by developing other leaders, by empowering them: If they lack confidence, give them some—let them practice and rehearse in a safe environment. Instill values such as altruism and service. Teach your nascent leaders that if they want to be trusted, respected, admired, and copied, it can't be all about them; rather, it must be in the service of others. Communicate your values—make them explicit. Measure and reward those who follow your values and respect your organizational culture. While outputs and outcomes are important, equally important are the means to produce them.

Follow the maturity model to guide you—to guide what you do to work yourself out of a job—and to guide how you develop others to do that job, to make decisions that you will no longer need to make on your own.

Creating Robustness

My younger daughter and Teodora Bozheva's daughter are just three months apart in age. Their family lives about sixteen kilometres (ten miles) from us in the beach town of Sopela. The kids hadn't seen each other since before the pandemic. Now, just before Christmas, they arranged to meet in the neighboring town of Algorta, near Pizzeria Toto. Teodora's family knows it well. Now a chain with four locations, the original restaurant is located just fifty metres from their apartment. They had a long-standing family tradition to order take-out pizza on Friday evenings. Teodora had watched as the founder grew the business, developing a loyal customer base who enthused about the quality and the great service at Toto in Sopela. Sopela residents were so proud to have such a good local place that they were happy to recommend it to anyone.

Encouraged by his success, the owner decided to expand, opening a second location in Algorta, just three kilometres (two miles) away, then another in Bilbao city, and then yet another in the capital city of the Basque Country, Vitoria-Gasteiz, eighty kilometres (fifty miles) away in the neighboring province of Alaves. However, expansion came at a price. When the Algorta location opened, the quality and service, to which his loyal customers had become accustomed, declined. When the owner wasn't present in Sopela, mistakes were made, quality was erratic, service often slow. Teodora might turn up to collect a take-out order, and it wasn't ready when promised, ingredients were missing, or the wrong order had been fulfilled.

At a scale of just one owner-operated location, the quality and service produced outcomes at Maturity Levels 3 and 4. Now, that had slipped back. Things were still good on the nights the owner was present, but otherwise, Teodora and her family learned to avoid it. They would order pizza only on nights when the owner was working in the Sopela branch. As an organization, scaling had caused a regression to Maturity Level 2. Scaling up was actually putting the core business at risk.

Scaling wasn't just a matter of finding and opening new premises, staffing them, providing them with the menus and recipes, and figuring out logistics such as ordering ingredients and supplies, such as boxes; to adequately scale, the owner had to work himself out of a job. The owner couldn't be in two or three or four places all at once. To scale effectively, the owner's role as the head chef and manager had to be delegated to someone else. There needed to be deputies in each branch, capable of leading just like the owner, and capable of making all the same decisions at the branch level that the owner would normally make on his own. To his credit, he worked through this. He developed trustworthy people to play his role when he wasn't present. Quality and service improved again, back to the same level it was when there was only a single location. He had successfully worked himself out of a job. He had delegated the focus on quality to other people. Scaling up and opening more locations was now a matter of capital investment and time to develop adequate leaders in each new location. The Pizzeria Toto chain was robust.

My younger daughter elected to return to Seattle and finish high school in the United States rather than switch to the excellent American School of Bilbao. Changing schools in her junior year of high school, and adapting to Spanish culture and language, was asking too much. When the holidays were over, we returned to Seattle.

Awakening

"What's your name?"

"How old are you, David?"

"Where are you from?"

"I live here. I have a house."

"Yes. I live with my daughter."

It was a strange dream. Muddled, confused. There was a pink Jeep, or maybe it was a faded red early model Toyota Landcruiser? I was being interviewed by a paramedic, speaking to my daughter on the phone, lying on my back, riding in some sort of vehicle in traffic. Why was I talking to my children on the phone?

"Hi, David, I'm Doctor Chalmers. You're in the ER at Harbor View. How do you feel?"

"What happened?"

"You were hit by a car crossing the street. The paramedics who brought you in said it was a hit and run. You were found wandering in the road, blood pouring from your head."

"What time is it?"

"It's around 7:45 p.m."

Eight hours earlier I had been finishing my morning walk, crossing the main road just four short blocks from our family home, around 11:45 a.m. In Washington State, pedestrians have the right of way at intersections; every intersection is essentially a crosswalk. I remembered reaching the median, seeing two cars excessively speeding in a 25-mph zone, and letting them pass. Five more cars were coming up the street but the first of them had more than enough time to see me, slow down, and concede the right of way.

The next eight hours are missing from my memory. Apparently, I was semi-conscious, at least for a while. I was able to talk to a police officer and some paramedics. My jeans were scuffed with pink paint from the vehicle that hit me. Months later we got the police report. It seems that two minutes later, in the next wave of cars from the traffic light, a woman who was driving up the main road, trying her best to avoid someone she thought was a drug addict or alcoholic in the middle of road, hit me again. She called 911. The paramedics in the fire truck were on the scene two minutes later. The police, six minutes after that.

Europeans reading this will be incredulous: A car hit me while I was crossing the street and didn't stop, and at least four following cars drove on by. In Europe, every one of them (not just the hit-and-run driver) would have been committing a criminal offense. In the United States, no one cares, no one wants to get involved, no one wants their day or their lives disrupted.

I was lucky to be alive.

There had been a spate of such accidents around Seattle in the months since the pandemic lockdown ended. An influx of people from other states, unaware of Washington State traffic laws, brought a lot of new people to the city. A billboard campaign with the slogan "Slow the FLOCK down" was educating drivers on their responsibilities. The use of the F-word wasn't an accident.

The right side of my face was smashed—fractured in three places. I had no vision on that side, my face swollen and bruised. I was a mess. However, they'd scanned me head to toe all afternoon with an arsenal of high-tech equipment. They could see very little physically wrong with me at all—an ankle injury and another to an elbow, strangely on different sides of my body. The good news was that I didn't have cancer! Small mercies! I discovered a month later that as many as one in three people who have cancer are diagnosed when they inadvertently visit an emergency room as a patient.[65]

I was scheduled for a series of outpatient clinic visits. My daughter came to collect me an hour later. Earlier paramedics had told her, "Your dad is going to be all right." She had a track meet. She was running hurdles. She wheeled me out of the hospital and drove me home.

Now, I really didn't need an excuse to binge-watch HGTV all day. Lucky that I'd worked myself out of a job.

Two weeks later I was given an all clear—my vision was unaffected, my brain function seemed unaffected, and the smaller physical injuries to my legs and arms were healing nicely. My head would take at least a year to fully heal. I was told to continue with the painkillers. I flew home to Bilbao sitting in first class with a shiny black eye. Oh, the life of a rockstar!

The dog didn't care. He was pleased to see me!

Identify Your Leaders and Enable Them

Ben Napier is a master craftsman and artisan carpenter who owns the Scotsman Company in Laurel, Mississippi. He and his wife, Erin, an interior designer, co-host another show on HGTV called *Home Town*. The premise is simple: Ben and Erin help local people in the small town of Laurel, about two hours outside of New Orleans, buy up older, historic properties and renovate them. In doing so, they are reviving the heart of their small town, breathing new life into it. It's a mission and a passion—they are saving Laurel, one rundown old house at a time.

Home Town has become one of the most popular shows on HGTV. People love the mission, they love the romanticism of restoring smalltown America, and they love the

---

65. https://www.theguardian.com/society/2022/apr/07/more-than-third-uk-cancer-patients-diagnosed-in-emergency

on-screen chemistry of Ben and Erin and their friends, relatives, and neighbors who play supporting roles on the show. After five successful seasons, people around the country were asking, "If you can do this for Laurel, can you come and do it for us and our small town?" Responding to this demand, HGTV looked to expand the *Home Town* franchise with a spin-off show called *Home Town Kickstart*. The premise was simple: Small towns around the nation would be invited to apply to participate, and six would be chosen. To help Ben and Erin scale, five other pairs of hosts would be drafted from other HGTV shows to come and help. And a whole season of episodes would be filmed in six locations.

The secret would be to codify the formula and use it to lead by example. To lead by example on two levels: The TV show couldn't hope to rejuvenate a whole town, nor to stay for years while that happened; instead, it would "kickstart" the process and hope that, inspired and filled with new confidence, the local people would carry on where the show would leave off and, in turn, other towns around the country would be inspired by the show and would be able to copy the template to kickstart their own revival. Over 3,000 small towns submitted applications; the response to the idea was overwhelming, and humbling. Six were chosen.

Asked, "How do you scale?" Erin Napier replied, "You identify your leaders and you enable them."

Home Town had started as a TV show about renovating older homes and turned into a national movement. It had transformed Ben and Erin from a carpenter and an interior decorator into leaders of a national social movement to revive smalltown America and rebuild communities. If they were to scale, it wasn't simply a matter of HGTV drafting ten more hosts to help make a TV series; if they were to scale, Ben and Erin had to replicate themselves in each and every small town that wanted to follow their lead. They needed to create leaders of a movement and enable those leaders.

The kickstart template was simple: They would pick three properties to be restored—a commercial business in the town center, a public or community space, and the home of a community leader, someone who lived in an older property in the heart of the town. The community leaders might be owners of a childcare center, or volunteers at the Boys and Girls Club, or long-serving members of the emergency services such as firefighters or paramedics—the key criterion was that they were respected leaders in the community. The same should be true for the owner of the business selected—perhaps they'd already been active in efforts to revive the fortunes of the town or the business district.

The goal was to recognize people who shared the original show's values, who were already showing leadership, to reward them through the show and the renovation of their property, and to signal that altruistic, service-oriented behavior would be recognized and appreciated. *Home Town Kickstart* leads by example, it leads by signaling, it leads by inspiration, and it leads through the insight of its formula and the clarity of its approach. It shows what can be achieved on modest budgets, and it is therefore pragmatic and its guidance actionable. It ticks all the boxes for leadership at Maturity Level 4.

Ben and Erin had to work themselves out of jobs that they never had—they had to clone themselves. Their approach was to reward, amplify, enable, and inspire.

Reward good leadership with more resources, more time, greater scope, more money, more space, and more people.

Amplify leadership by encouraging more of it. Give good leaders greater responsibility and accountability. Encourage them to step up to the next level. Set expectations of leaders and the role they must play in their communities and organizations.

Enable leadership by setting people up for success. Provide the resources, training, equipment, time, and space to be successful. Think in systems. Create an organization that is an adaptive system that can learn and evolve.

Inspire others to follow your lead. Lead by example. Signal your values. Encourage aligned behavior. In a situation like *Home Town Kickstart* you have no control to begin with, so you don't need to learn to give it up. For those who lead in organizations, you need to learn to let go, to give up control; don't seek to centralize decision making and control through conformance to a framework; instead, substitute leadership and develop organizational maturity.

Closure

Our dog was due for a fresh round of vaccinations, this time at his new vet in Bilbao. He became the first member of the family to receive a European passport.[66,67] Rather cheekily, it declares his nationality as Basque, not Spanish!

We held a very moving memorial service for my late wife at a church in Seattle in the summer. The church was filled with tennis club teammates, former nursing school colleagues, friends, and neighbors. There were piano and violin recitals, eulogies, and prayers. With closure, it was time to move on. At the Kanban Leadership Retreat in Mayrhofen in the Austrian Alps later that same month, I announced to the crowd, "I've been away for quite a while. Now I am back!" I asked them what I could do for them, for the Kanban community globally. To write this new book was the most popular request.

Summer turned to fall. Another year had passed. Renovation work was due to start on my home near Bilbao. Consequently, as a family, we would celebrate Christmas and New Year's at our apartment in the Alps. My younger daughter turned eighteen. Kanban had come of age. I sat down at my desk in Ramsau-im-Zillertal and started to write.

---

66. I, together with my two daughters, lost our European citizenship when the UK left the European Union in January 2020. Only after ten years of permanent residency in Spain can I regain European citizenship.

67. Technically, the dog's passport is a vaccination passport; it permits him the freedom to travel throughout the European Union with the reassurance that his vaccinations are up-to-date.

Takeaways

- If you want to learn how to scale your business, ask an entrepreneur.
- First, focus on quality and first-time right. Mistakes and the rework to fix them are costly in both time and money.
- Hire or develop your own competent people who can work unsupervised. Good people cost more, but it saves you money in the long run.
- Increase resilience. Make sure you have people who can take over in your absence.
- Work yourself out of a job. Empower others to make decisions by asking yourself which decisions could be automated or delegated to someone else.
- Codify what you do by defining processes and procedures and by introducing feedback mechanisms. Composing those into a decision framework helps make the process of decision making repeatable, predictable, and trustworthy.
- Create robustness. Develop trustworthy managers who can do what you do, who can play your role when you are absent.
- Identify your leaders and reward, amplify, enable, and inspire them:
  - Reward good leadership with more resources, more time, greater scope, more money, more space, and more people.
  - Amplify leadership by encouraging more of it. Give good leaders greater responsibility and accountability.
  - Enable leadership by setting people up for success. Provide the resources, training, equipment, time, and space to be successful.
  - Inspire others to follow your lead. Lead by example. Signal your values. Encourage aligned behavior. Don't seek to centralize decision making and control through conformance to a framework; instead, substitute leadership and develop organizational maturity.

Appendix A

The Original Kanban Values

Collaboration

Collaboration implies that individuals work together as a team to achieve a common goal. In fact, the definitions of collaboration and team are effectively mutually dependent: to be a team requires collaboration and to collaborate effectively requires a team. Generally, collaboration is seen as a deeper form of cooperation—a more worthy form of cooperation. Cooperation implies that humans work on their own but in a manner that is compatible with the work of others and may enable a shared outcome or a common goal. A value stream in which each function in a chain is performed separately can be viewed as a cooperative chain; there isn't collaboration—one function does not assist another—they merely do their own part and pass the work on for the next function to do its part. Strangely, our observation is that collaboration appears at the team level before effective cooperation appears between teams to deliver a product or service. There could be several reasons for this: the scale involving more people makes it more complicated to achieve cooperation at a wider level than collaboration at a team level; the greater leadership required at a higher level to drive collaboration at a larger scale and effectively form a much larger team; or the metrics and incentives used focus too heavily on the individual or small, easily identified and contained groups of individuals, namely a team. We don't see the emergence of cooperation across teams until Maturity Level 2. The degree of difficulty is higher, and it takes greater leadership and more developed managerial skills.

An organization must encourage and value collaboration to foster resilient and robust teams capable of producing a variety of work with consistent quality. To do this, it must encourage sharing and altruistic behavior from individuals to other team members. Collaboration is what truly separates Maturity Level 1 from Maturity Level 0. When a small group has an identity but they consistently work alone as individuals, even if the work is of a similar nature, they are not truly a team. The Maturity Level 1 sub-level Transition captures this concept. We have seen it in case studies and believe it is a necessary transitional step. A small group of individuals with a shared identity are most likely being managed by focusing on people and resource efficiency or utilization rather than embracing the Kanban service delivery principle of "manage the work and let the workers self-organize around it." In Kanban, we want you to measure flow efficiency and customer-valued items such as work-in-progress, lead time, and delivery rate. In a service-oriented organization, it's important to care more about the where and when of the customer-requested work and less about the where and when of the workers.

We must encourage managers and team leaders to see themselves as serving the delivery of products or services to the customer. Often, we find that department managers and team leads believe their role is to best match tasks with available workers, optimizing for efficiency based on the skills and experience of the individual. As a truly service-oriented approach, the Kanban Method discourages this. Instead, we need managers to manage work and to encourage a broad range of skills to be developed and shared by most or all team members. We require that individuals collaborate by sharing their skills and developing those skills in others.

In general, a business needs to shift away from an inward, individual focus and encourage altruistic behavior. Initially, this is altruism toward fellow team members, and as it progresses to higher, deeper levels of maturity, this altruism must grow in scope and scale.

Collaboration builds trust. The act of collaborating with someone—getting to know them closely, understanding their skills and competencies, and seeing them act altruistically to help you—releases oxytocin and strengthens trust between team members. Collaboration is key to enabling trust, and greater trust encourages greater collaboration—a virtuous cycle, where one reinforces the other and so forth.

Evidence for collaboration can exist in both the positive sense—demonstrating collaborative behavior—and in the negative sense—demonstrating failure to make the shift to service-oriented and altruistic behavior. Positive evidence might include personal goals and incentives to share knowledge and pass on skills to other team members. Negative evidence would include individual utilization and resource-efficiency metrics or stack-ranking staff in annual reviews. If perverse incentives exist to hoard information or selfishly protect skills, the organization clearly fails to embrace collaboration as a value.

Transparency

Valuing transparency means valuing information availability over information hiding. At a team level, transparency means that everyone on the team knows what others are working on. This transparency may extend to the manager and to people external to the team, potentially including customers. The control of information and its flow is a source of power in organizations and social groups, so valuing transparency explicitly undermines this source of power. Consequently, transparency can meet with resistance if individuals, usually managers, find that transparency has undermined their source of power and therefore undermined their self-esteem and their sense of self. We have seen anecdotes of, for example, the vice president of a project-management organization (PMO) at a Southern California–based internet company ripping a portfolio kanban board from a wall early one morning and trashing it. Why would a VP of a PMO not want such a board on a wall? Why would he feel motivated to destroy it? Because transparency eliminates his ability to control information and to control the narrative. He cannot lie to his superiors about progress on projects if the information is freely available.

Hence, valuing transparency embraces the idea that the organization must face up to its reality, however ugly that picture may be. Transparency is about pragmatism and action orientation rather than wishful thinking and deferring action in the hope that problems magically fix themselves or simply go away altogether. Transparency and action orientation go hand in hand.

Transparency increases social capital. You no longer need to trust that someone is working on something if the information is freely available. You no longer need to trust that someone is capable of making good decisions if the decision framework they use, and information about their actual decisions, are transparently available. Transparency removes uncertainty from the environment and improves the trustworthiness of that environment. Social capital measures the trustworthiness of a social group or a social entity such as a business.

The ability to value transparency requires leadership development coupled with the development of management skills and competence. No one need fear transparency when they have the skills, competence, and confidence to "do something about it!"

What we aren't saying here is that all information should be available to everyone. Such a rule could overwhelm people with data and render them paralyzed if they are swamped and unable to interpret what they are seeing. Equally, some information should be hidden for regulatory and compliance reasons or hidden in order to maintain confidence and security. Recognize also that some information may be seen as humiliating and affect the dignity of individuals or teams and consequently their ability to function effectively. Leaders need to choose carefully when ritual (and potentially public) humiliation may be necessary, either to rebuild trust or as the correct motivator for change. So, our directive that your organization embrace transparency as a core value isn't a blanket demand to make all information available to everyone; rather, it is a request to share as much information as possible to enable an ever more trustworthy organization capable of taking action faster and more effectively.

Evidence of valuing transparency is easy to find and easy to measure—information is either available or it is hidden. Policies are either explicit or they aren't. Values are either explicit or they aren't. Decision frameworks and information about how decisions are made—the reasoning behind them and the trade-offs they require—are either explicit or they aren't. People are either recognized and rewarded for being transparent—such as honestly reporting progress on a task or the existence of an impediment or blocker, or admitting that they lack the skills or experience to complete a piece of work—or they aren't.

Flow

Flow may also seem like a strange thing to value as an organization. However, when an organization embraces the Kanban service delivery principle to "manage the work and let the people self-organize around it," then the pursuit of an efficient flow of work becomes natural. When an organization recognizes that lead time and timely and/or predictable delivery are almost always customer fitness criteria, then it recognizes that it improves the optionality in its processes by improving flow. High flow efficiency enables it to manage risk better and produce superior economic results.

Delay is often the largest contributor to customer dissatisfaction. Impediments to flow result in failure to be fit-for-purpose. Flow is key to improving the management of knowledge work and professional services. If work is delayed, waiting for any reason, then it isn't flowing. Valuing flow means valuing removing delay.

Beyond the basic removal of delay, the organization also values smoothness. A smooth, steady arrival of work is respectful to the people doing the work, and a major contributor to providing relief from overburdening. Smoothness produces more predictable outcomes and is therefore attractive to customers. Smoothness also reduces the need for contingent staffing and slack resources, improving economic results without affecting customer satisfaction.

The Toyota Way identified three main types of problems in workflows: *muri*, or overburdening; *mura*, unevenness; and *muda*, non–value adding activity, or waste. Valuing flow directly addresses *mura* through the pursuit of smoothness and acknowledges its contribution to *muri*, relieving overburdening through an even flow that can be managed effectively with a simple WIP limit.

Evidence that an enterprise values flow can be seen through the adoption of many Kanban practices described in the Kanban Maturity Model, such as the use of WIP limits, visualization of blockers and WIP aging, blocker clustering and Risk Review, dependency management, and the use of policies for "definition of ready" and local "definitions of done," showing that work is available to pull to the next step. Greater collaboration between teams, going beyond mere cooperation to include providing assistance when needed, is also an indicator that flow is valued.

Respect

Respect here does not mean "courtesy" or "politeness," although these are both important aspects of a culture and the social norms in an organization. In this usage, respect means recognition of capability, circumstances, or context. In Kanban, we respect people, systems, customers, regulators, sponsors, owners, taxpayers, and other stakeholders and benefactors.

We respect people by providing them with an organization and a system in which to work that sets them up for success. They should have the training, resources, skills, equipment, time, and space in which to do great work. They should be trusted and empowered through the use of explicit policies. They should understand why they are there, how they can contribute, and what a desirable outcome looks like. They should be respected such that they have autonomy, can achieve mastery of their work, and have a deep sense of purpose and the value they provide. In doing so, individuals should feel fulfilled. This is what we mean by "respect."

We respect circumstances, context, and capability by understanding it, seeing it as a result of transparency onto work and workflow, analyzing it, and modeling it such that outcomes can be predicted based on a realistic comprehension of how things currently work. There is no wishful thinking in Kanban! If you find yourself sighing and saying, "If only . . . then our strategy would have worked," fill in the blank—if only our people worked harder, we had better people, we had more time, we had more money, we were better at execution, we were better at delivery, and so on, and so on—then you are failing to respect the current operating reality of your circumstances and capability.

Respect is about recognizing your current circumstances and capability for what they are and making plans accordingly. If your current capabilities don't match your needs, expectations, or desires, you need to invest in improving them before you set stretch goals. Respect means that you live in a pragmatic world, rooted in a solid understanding of reality. There is no wishful thinking in Kanban!

Understanding (Internal)

In the context of the Kanban Method and the Kanban Maturity Model, understanding means that we seek to understand the nature of our environment. We seek to understand the world around us and what drives it.

A Maturity Level 2, and progressing to Maturity Level 3, we want organizations to understand how, what, why, and who through study, observation, collection of evidence, use of models, and experimentation. At Maturity Level 2, our focus is on understanding our internal environment and the forces that shape it—what we do, how we do it, and the variability, risk, and uncertainty that relate to the work and our ability to deliver it within expectations.

We want people to gain an understanding of the work that they are asked to do and how to perform it with consistency and deliver it with quality; the services that they provide, their workflows, and the collaboration involved in providing those services; and the impact their policies have on their capability and performance. Basic understanding focuses on the pragmatism of accepting their own environment and their current capabilities for what they are. There is no wishful thinking in Kanban.

Agreement

Valuing agreement means that we wish to move forward with consensus and shared understanding. In a Kanban implementation where we want to achieve "pull," we agree on system capacity and we respect that capacity, and we agree on what to pull next and when to pull. Policies are made by agreement. We strive for shared understanding as much as possible. As a general rule, we do not allow or encourage bullying behavior, but we recognize that exceptions are necessary, and we push when we must.

Although we value agreement, we recognize that there are times when full consensus and broad agreement are unrealistic. There is no wishful thinking in Kanban. Hence, there might be times when delaying for consensus is not in our best interest, and therefore we will trade our value of agreement for strong, decisive leadership.

Balance

Balance plays a key role in respect and avoiding overburdening people, teams, value streams, service delivery workflows, and entire business units. Balance shows that we value sustainability both at the personal level and at the organizational level. If we are to have consistent customer service to maintain fitness-for-purpose, we must have balance.

At Maturity Level 3, balance implies that we strive to avoid overburdening individuals and service delivery workflows (systems). We want to balance demand against capability to deliver, and we want to limit work-in-progress to the capacity of individuals and the workflow within which they work. WIP limits are used to avoid overburdening people and workflows, while capacity allocation, demand-shaping, and triage are used to keep demand in balance with capability to deliver.

Customer Service

Valuing customer service shows that we recognize that a core purpose of our organization and the services we provide is to serve our customers adequately and meet their expectations of us. We measure our success, our self-esteem, and our capability relative to our ability to meet customer expectations. When we can meet customer expectations consistently, then we can say that each of our services is fit-for-purpose. To be fit-for-purpose is our guiding principle, our true north, our ongoing ambition.

Leadership at All Levels

At Maturity Level 3, we need to extend our view of leadership. At Maturity Level 1, we valued taking initiative. At Maturity Level 2, this deepened to valuing acts of leadership and acknowledging that leadership entails personal risk. Maturity Level 3 is better enabled with an understanding that leadership only from the top causes delay, and that leaders at the top are not best placed to know what is needed or to see the need for action at the bottom. For an organization to move with agility, leadership is needed at all levels. Acts of leadership should be encouraged and expected at all levels, and more senior leaders must seek to provide the confidence, safety, and failure tolerance required to encourage risk taking. Leadership at all levels doesn't happen magically; it happens because more senior leaders hack the culture to enable it. Mature leaders are not threatened by leadership from below; rather, they are empowered by it. Leadership at all levels frees senior leaders to focus on strategic concerns and organizational culture while mid- and lower-level people focus on operational and tactical concerns. It should become a cultural norm for anyone, regardless of their rank or station in the organization, to "do something about it!"

Appendix B

Deming's 14 Points:
Unpacked & Reinterpreted for the 21st Century

W. Edwards Deming's system of management contained what he labeled his "14 Points for Management." Deming said of these that "My 14 Points for Management follow naturally as application of the System of Profound Knowledge for transformation from the present style of management to one of optimization."

What we can see from this is that Deming is pursuing organizational Maturity Level 5, and his system of management is intended to create the decision-making capability and the culture to enable a Maturity Level 5 organization to emerge as a natural consequence of following this advice. Deming's advice influenced and inspired those who created the Capability Maturity Model (CMM), which evolved to become the CMMI. Deming also influenced Toyota, though there is evidence that Toyota was already using kanban and *kaizen* before Deming's visit to Japan in the 1950s. Deming's influence on the KMM is quite evident, and we can readily show a mapping of his 14 points to elements within the KMM and its model architecture, with outcomes, practices, and codification of the required organizational culture.

Create constancy of purpose.

Deming was looking for the ambition to create a robust, sustainable, economically profitable organization that delivers good products and excellent service, creates wealth and good quality employment, and is continually improving in all aspects of this ambition.

KMM achieves these goals in several ways:

- We use the Fit for Purpose framework to understand customers' needs and to drive the evolution of ever better products and services.
- Maturity Level 3 defines the outcomes of acceptable product and service quality.
- Maturity Level 4 defines the outcome of a robust, sustainable, economically viable organization.
- Maturity Level 5 defines an organization that relentlessly pursues improvement in every aspect of its business.
- The values defined in the KMM create a great place to work and a culture capable of sustaining Maturity Level 5.

Take on leadership for change.

Deming actually called this "Adopt the new philosophy." This is the idea that the role of leadership is to create organizations capable of and wired for evolutionary change—wired for continuous improvement. To Deming, if a business isn't moving forward, it is going backward. We've captured this with the value of Competition at Maturity Level 4 in the culture pillar of the KMM.

Cease dependence on inspection to achieve quality.

The title of this point seems arcane in the twenty-first century; however, the point is well made that first-time right and avoiding rework are vital capabilities for modern business agility. The KMM begins to capture this concept as practices at Maturity Level 2 in pursuit of flow. The use of policies to tighten the definition of "pullable" through the kanban system, coupled to the use of metrics such as the lead time histogram feedback mechanisms such as Service Delivery Review, encourages a focus on smooth flow and thin-tailed, predictable, trustworthy service delivery. Explicitly calling out rework—tickets that move backward on a kanban board, or failure demand—tickets that have been created to correct an escaped defect, helps to visualize the impact of poor quality. KMM, with the Management Practices in its architecture, requires managers to focus on the system through policies, feedback mechanisms, and improvement actions to build a trustworthy system that produces good quality consistently.

End the practice of awarding contracts on price alone.

Deming was not a fan of cost cutting for its own sake. Reducing cost is rightly an aspect of a high-performing organization, and the KMM captures this in Maturity Levels 4 and 5. First, learn to do the right thing well, get the Why and the What right, then focus on improving the How to drive down costs without sacrificing quality and customer satisfaction.

When evaluating vendors and awarding business for supplier contracts, the Fit for Purpose Framework can be used as a means to evaluate and select vendors and then to monitor their performance. Cost is unlikely to be the only fitness criterion—we value lead time, functional and nonfunctional quality, consistency, and trustworthiness much more than price.

Improve constantly and forever the system of production and service.

The KMM Management Practices—make policies explicit; implement feedback mechanisms; and improve collaboratively, evolve experimentally—define the means for constantly improving the system of production. Coupling those with the practices of the Fit for Purpose Framework enables the pursuit of effective and satisfactory service delivery. The levels of organizational maturity in the model, together with the Evolutionary Change Model, enable the pursuit of an ever-improving system of production and service, and the definition of Maturity Level 5 acknowledges that an organization has realized Deming's ambition.

Institute training on the job.

Deming believed in apprenticeship and direct skills transfer. The KMM and the Kanban Method don't mandate this directly but provide an environment that encourages it. Visualization, Explicit Policies, and a strong bias in favor of collaboration, as well as open discussion and consensus decision making at Kanban Cadences meetings such as replenishment or service delivery review, create many opportunities for learning and development of less experienced staff.

Institute leadership.

KMM values leadership by explicitly defining taking initiative, acts of leadership, leadership at all levels, and leadership development as values at Maturity Levels 1 through 4. KMM 1.3 adds Leadership as an explicit fourth pillar of the model and provides a codification of leadership and a model for intentional development of the character and maturity of those who lead. KMM provides the means to deliver on Deming's hope and institutionalize leadership development as a core element of achieving and maintaining a deep level of organizational maturity.

Drive out fear.

The Kanban Maturity Model explicitly adopts the teachings of Ray Immelman, who put more nuance on the concept of driving out fear—first make individuals feel safe and secure, then make them feel valued, recognized, respected, and dignified. With its focus on the system, the Kanban Method together with KMM puts the spotlight on the system of production as the source of failure and asks managers to lead changes to the system—new policies, improvement actions, better resources, training, improved capability, alignment of strategy and capability—a setup for success. Together, these system changes drive out fear and create confidence in individuals and collectively in the workforce.

Break down barriers.

Maturity Level 2 and the establishment of flow across a service delivery workflow toward the common goal of delivering a customer-valued item is specifically intended to break down barriers. The Kanban Method explicitly encourages the cooperation and collaboration that Deming was seeking.

KMM also identifies common barriers to improving organizational maturity and cultural barriers to practice adoption. It provides specific guidance for countermeasures to remove barriers and speed adoption of practices, deepen organizational maturity, and improve outcomes.

Eliminate slogans, exhortations, and targets.

In Deming's world of 1950s manufacturing industry, slogans exhorting workers to achieve certain goals were viewed as demoralizing and likely to destroy employee engagement. The underlying reason was that employees were not empowered. Product quality was often and most likely (Deming suggested around 95 percent likely) caused by the system of production, and not by an individual worker's actions. Hence, workers actually had no control over quality or production targets; only managers did.

The Kanban Method and KMM change these underlying assumptions. If leaders pursue the cultural changes required in the KMM, workers are empowered: They are capable of making changes, they can take initiative, and they can show acts of leadership. However, slogans and exhortations, such as decision filters aimed at driving culture change, should be heartfelt and delivered with integrity. The measure of a slogan and whether it has a positive or negative effect is whether leadership and the organization show the integrity to do as they say and follow through on the meaning of a decision filter.

Targets should always be meaningful, achievable, and set with a specific purpose. The Fit for Purpose Framework defines targets specifically for improvement objectives. However, customer fitness criteria, the criteria by which a customer decides whether they like your product or service, are thresholds to be achieved and exceeded, while operational health indicators will have a healthy range, and the target will always be to maintain them within that healthy range.

Slogans, exhortations, and targets have their place to help drive excellence and the relentless pursuit of perfection, but they have a positive impact when deployed in the right culture, and with careful attention to the purpose and meaning of any target.

Eliminate management by objectives: Substitute leadership.

Deming published several versions of this at different times in his career, for example,

- Eliminate work standards or quotas on the factory floor.
- Eliminate management by objectives.
- Eliminate management by numbers and numerical goals.

It is important for us again to consider his context—mid-twentieth century, post–World War II manufacturing industry—when we consider this point. Management by Objectives as concept, as a proper noun, is attributed to Peter Drucker, and there was a time in Deming's academic career when he shared an office with the younger Drucker. Hence, "eliminate management by objectives" showed Deming's direct disagreement on this point with Drucker.

For us, today, in the twenty-first century, working in professional services businesses, what does this mean and is it still relevant?

The KMM explicitly states that:

- Outcomes follow practices.
- Practices follow culture.
- Culture follows values.
- Therefore, lead with values.
- And consequently, all outcomes stem from leadership.

Deming is saying that setting targets—management by objectives—is a crutch for a lack of leadership, that setting targets and objectives is a poor proxy for real leadership. Targets provide an intervention at the practice level and are intended to cajole rather than inspire. When managers think that their role is merely to set targets and then bang their fist, they fail to pay attention to culture, values, and organizational identity and purpose. When Deming says "substitute leadership," he wants managers to inspire their people to achieve more and better results. Deming views targets and objectives as a means of manipulation, or cajoling workers, and he understands that improvements achieved in this manner will not be sustainable. Management by Objectives in this context is the behavior of the "hero manager," and we recognize this as a behavior inherent at Maturity Level 2. To get beyond Maturity Level 2, we must reward true leadership behaviors—not merely setting targets and cracking the whip.

Remove barriers to pride of workmanship: Substitute leadership.

Deming addressed explicitly the role of factory floor "supervisor." We might interpret this for the twenty-first century as "team lead." He wanted such supervisors to be leaders, to inspire their workers, to lead by example, and to signal the right behaviors that produce the best overall system outcome—satisfied customers; fit-for-purpose products and services; and a robust, economically sustainable business capable of continuous improvement both in what it does and in how it does it.

However, we need to unpack "barrier to pride of workmanship" and examine it more deeply. What is required to take pride in your work?

- A sense of purpose, which gives meaning to the effort involved
- A sense of closure—knowing that your contribution actually makes a difference
- The time and space to do the job properly
- The tools and resources to do the job properly
- A dignified work environment and everything that goes with it, including a fair day's pay for a fair day's work
- Respect, recognition, and status for doing a good job

When we examine the KMM model and its focus on leadership and culture, its values, and the definition of the Kanban Method, then we see that it addresses all of these requirements for pride of workmanship starting from Maturity Level 2. At Level 2, work has meaning and purpose; workers and the system of production (the workflow) are relieved of overburdening; the feedback mechanisms, instrumentation, and reporting begin to emerge to ensure that the time, space, tools, and resources are available to do the job properly; and the culture is developing to ensure a dignified workplace that provides respect, recognition, and equitable status for the contribution made. While we see progress on this goal starting at Maturity Level 2, to deliver completely on point 12, an organization needs to mature to ML4.

Institute a vigorous program of education and self-improvement.

Deming recognized that work is done by workers and that those workers need education and a credo that drives them to continuous learning throughout their professional lives.

The KMM value of Understanding is primarily focused on understanding and modeling the natural philosophy of the working environment—the system of production, to use Deming's term—and the risk environment inside which that system of production operates.

The literature of the Kanban Method and KMM provides the means of education to help workers understand the environment in which they operate and to make better decisions. Just one example of this is the importantance of lead time as a customer selection criterion, a vital metric to drive improved customer service, build trust, and create confidence. Prior to the appearance of the Kanban Method, lead time was not a metric used much or at all in the IT industry. Today, not only is it common, but we understand its nature—we understand the elements that influence the shape of the curve, and we understand how fat-tailed lead times destroy trust and drive low-maturity behavior.

Although Kanban and KMM do not explicitly prescribe education and individual self-improvement, the method and the model go a long way to educate the global workforce of professional services, or knowledge workers, and provide them with an understanding of the risks in their environment. Such education removes anxiety and fear, and it enables confidence and good quality decision making.

The transformation is everybody's job.

Deming, like Toyota, realized that continuous improvement (*kaizen*) wasn't the job of management, or senior leadership, or some process-improvement or coaching group (Deming would have called them "industrial engineers" or "time and motion men"); instead, improvement is everyone's business. The Kanban Method has this concept at its very core, and the KMM provides the organizational context and cultural elements to enable it to happen.

Writing in my blog "No More Quality Initiatives"[68] on April 27, 2005, I explained that improvement is everyone's business. This was a response to a challenge I'd been given by members of the Customer Advisory Council (CAC) for Microsoft's Visual Studio Team System product, "Please don't give us another transformation initiative." The requestor worked for a large IT consulting firm based in Texas. He reported that both clients and their own employees had "transition initiative fatigue" and simply didn't want to be exhausted by yet another change initiative demanding adoption of a new process. What was needed was an evolutionary, incremental approach that started where they were and fixed problems one at a time.

This reinforced my belief that business agility would be enabled by a system of management, by training managers to change their behavior, and through a focus on organizational culture. 2005 was the period when the very first Kanban implementation was taking place in the IT department at Microsoft. This was the time when ideas converged to produce what we now recognize as the Kanban Method and the KMM. At least in part, the Kanban Method was created to deliver on Deming's vision for the modern workplace. The KMM exists to democratize the skills needed to wire an organization for evolutionary change so as to catalyze the process of evolutionary change and the pursuit of excellence by continuously improving the production system and the means to sustain it, which creates meaningful employment and delighted customers.

---

68. Later re-edited and published in David J Anderson, *Lessons in Agile Management: On the Road to Kanban* (Seattle: Blue Hole Press, 2012), 381.

Index

About the Author

David J Anderson is an innovator in management thinking for 21st-century businesses. Author and pioneer of the Kanban Method, he has more than thirty years' experience working in the high-technology industry. David has previously worked at IBM, Sprint, Motorola, and Microsoft, where he developed the Kanban Method to greatly improve business outcomes on an enterprise scale.

Originator of the Kanban Method and co-creator of the Kanban Maturity Model, the Fit-for-Purpose Framework, and Enterprise Services Planning, David is a global leader in management training and leadership development for professional services and intangible goods industries.

He is the author of seven leading books for modern business; the most renowned, *Kanban: Successful Evolutionary Change for Your Technology Business,* was published in 2010 and is in the top five best-selling Agile books of all time.

David also founded Kanban University, which includes over 400 accredited trainers and consultants. In addition, he produced multiple global Kanban conferences and is the Chairman of the David J Anderson School of Management, which provides training in 21st-century business practices for enterprise agility, business resilience, and organizational maturity.

The group of companies founded by David is held within Mauvius Group Inc. This group of companies is focused on improving the quality of management, leadership, and decision making for 21st-century businesses.

www.ingramcontent.com/pod-product-compliance
Lightning Source LLC
Chambersburg PA
CBHW080523220326
41599CB00032B/6185